THE RECENT EVOLUTION OF FINANCIAL SYSTEMS

Also by Jack Revell

BANKING AND ELECTRONIC FUND TRANSFERS

CHANGES IN WEST EUROPEAN PUBLIC BANKS AND THEIR
 IMPLICATIONS FOR SPAIN

COMPETITION AND REGULATION OF BANKS (*with Edward P. M.
 Gardener and Christopher Barclay*)

COSTS AND MARGINS IN BANKING: An International Survey

DEREGULATION AND BANK EFFICIENCY: The Case of the Italian
 Credit Co-operative Banks (*editor*)

SECURITISATION: History, Forms and Risks (*with Edward P. M.
 Gardener*)

SOLVENCY AND REGULATION OF BANKS

THE BRITISH FINANCIAL SYSTEM

THE CHANGING FACE OF EUROPEAN BANKS AND SECURITIES
 MARKETS (*editor*)

THE FUTURE OF SAVINGS BANKS: A Study of Spain and the Rest
 of Europe

THE WEALTH OF THE NATION: The National Balance Sheet of the
 United Kingdom

The Recent Evolution of Financial Systems

Edited by

Jack Revell
Professor Emeritus, University of Wales
Consultant Director, Institute of European Finance, Bangor

332.109
R 295

First published in Great Britain 1997 by
MACMILLAN PRESS LTD
Houndmills, Basingstoke, Hampshire RG21 6XS
and London
Companies and representatives
throughout the world

A catalogue record for this book is available
from the British Library.

ISBN 0–333–66868–5

First published in the United States of America 1997 by
ST. MARTIN'S PRESS, INC.,
Scholarly and Reference Division,
175 Fifth Avenue,
New York, N.Y. 10010

ISBN 0–312–16347–9

Library of Congress Cataloging-in-Publication Data
The recent evolution of financial systems / edited by Jack Revell.
p.   cm.
Includes bibliographical references and index.
ISBN 0–312–16347–9 (cloth)
1. Banks and banking—Europe—Case studies.   2. Asset-backed
financing.   I. Revell, Jack.
HG2974.R4   1996
332.1'094—dc20   96–24400
                                                      CIP

This book is printed on paper suitable for recycling and made from fully managed and
sustained forest sources.

10   9   8   7   6   5   4   3   2   1
06   05   04   03   02   01   00   99   98   97

Printed and bound in Great Britain by
Antony Rowe Ltd, Chippenham, Wiltshire

CONTENTS

LIST OF TABLES

LIST OF FIGURES

PREFACE

This is the second volume of papers from meetings of the European Association of University Teachers in Banking and Finance (familiarly known as the Wolpertinger Club), the first volume having been published in 1994 under the title of *The Changing Face of European Banks and Securities Markets*. The nature of these papers differs in two ways from those presented in the first volume. In the first place they are all drawn from one meeting, that held in Alicante (Spain) in September 1995, and in the second place there is a definite theme running through the papers, which is reflected in the title of the book. The meeting was concerned above all with the evolution of financial systems, starting from a bank-orientated phase and then into a market-orientated phase; the main interest was in the third phase, the securitised phase, in which the trend towards the strengthening of financial markets displayed in the second phase was greatly intensified. This phase is nowhere complete, but within Europe developments in the United Kingdom and the Netherlands are nearest to producing a securitised financial system. Since the analysis of the three phases in the evolution of financial systems was first undertaken by Professor Rybczynski, it is appropriate that the first chapter represents his latest thoughts on the subject.

The meeting started with invited papers on the recent evolution of financial systems, and these papers were discussed in a special session containing a number of planned contributions from discussants. This part of the proceedings forms Part I of the volume. The remaining papers were not invited, but Part II of the volume contains those papers that followed up the theme by considering the response of banks to the securitised phase in the evolution of financial systems, either in different parts of banking business or in individual banking systems.

There have been many comments in recent years that the existence of banks is threatened by the growing importance of markets, but plenty of evidence was presented that they are still very much alive and kicking. Banks have adapted to the new conditions by acquiring many of the market institutions like securities houses, investment banks and fund managers, but even traditional banking business is far from dead as the banks have changed, almost out of recognition, over the past thirty years from the type of institutions that were the staple diet of banking textbooks at the beginning of the period.

As was the case with the first volume, this was a co-operative effort between the contributors, the Institute of European Finance in Bangor and myself, as editor, and the co-operation worked very smoothly. This time the authors were asked to provide a final version of their papers on disk in order to save retyping on the word processor; they complied readily and promptly with my requests at a particularly busy part of the academic year. Ted Gardener, as Director of the Institute of European Finance, placed its facilities at my disposal. Christine Owen orchestrated the work in the Institute, and Linda Jeavons and Pam Grant coped efficiently with the production of camera-ready copy from the edited papers. Maureen Simmons once again prepared an excellent index in a very short time. I thank them all for their efforts. I also thank the authors of the many excellent papers given at the meeting that were not close enough to our theme to be included in this volume; their papers will be published in the Research Paper series of the Institute of European Finance.

Finally I should like to thank the publishers for their very quick acceptance of my proposal and for their help and co-operation throughout the editing of the volume. My tasks as editor were to select the contributions to be included in this volume, to ensure consistency in presentation and finally to accept full responsibility for any errors and omissions that survive after the many checks that were carried out. This last responsibility I accept most readily.

JACK REVELL

NOTES ON THE CONTRIBUTORS

Jean-Paul Abraham is Professor Emeritus of Financial Economics at the Facultés Notre-Dame de la Paix, Namur (Belgium) and at the Katholieke Universiteit Leuven (Belgium). He is a Member of the Board and a former Executive Director of Paribas Bank Belgium. He chairs the Société Universitaire Européenne de Recherches Financières (SUERF) and is also a Honourary Director of the Commission of the European Communities.

Yener Altunbas is research analyst in the Foreign Exchange Department of Etibank, Turkey, and his main areas of research focus on efficiency in banking markets.

Martin Andersson is senior economist in the Payment Systems Department of the Sveriges Riksbank. He is also connected to the University of Gothenburg, where he took his PhD. His main field of research has been on payment systems and financial stability.

Göran Bergendahl has been Professor of Business Administration at the University of Gothenburg since 1971. His research has covered various disciplines, such as farm economics, energy economics, transportation economics, international financial management and bank management. He has written six books and more than 100 scientific articles.

Francesco Cesarini is full Professor of Banking in the Faculty of Banking, Finance and Insurance at the Catholic University of Milan. He is the author of several publications on monetary and banking issues, and on problems relating to stock exchange and corporate financial instruments; he was co-author of the Green Book commissioned by the Italian Treasury on *Il Sistema Creditizio e Finanziario Italiano*. Alongside academic and research activity he serves as chairman of Banca Popolare di Milano and as deputy chairman of the Stock Exchange Council.

Lynne Evans is Senior Lecturer in Economics at the University of Durham. Her main research focus is in the area of monetary markets and financial economics. She is currently secretary of the ESRC's Money, Macro and Financial Group.

Edward P.M. Gardener is a banking and financial sector specialist. His main research interests are in banking strategies, regulation and the financial management of banks. He is currently a Professor and Chairman of the School of Accounting, Banking and Economics (SABE) at the University of Wales, Bangor; he is also Co-Director (with Dr Molyneux) of the Institute of European Finance. He holds many other positions including Distinguished Visiting Professorial Fellow in Banking and Finance at Queen Mary and Westfield College (UCL); Colloborateur Scientifique at the University of Namur; and the Bank of Valleta Chair of International Banking and Finance at the University of Malta. He has conducted research and consultancy for a wide variety of research organisations and banks. One of his current (1995/96) major projects is working with a group of Cambridge economists for EC DG XV on the impact of Internal Market Integration on banking strategies.

Elisabetta Gualandri studied at the University of Modena and at the University College of North Wales, Bangor, where she took an MA in Financial Economics. She is now Associate Professor of Financial Intermediaries at the University of Modena, Dipartimento di Economia Aziendale. Her main fields of research interest include supervision of financial institutions, comparative financial systems and asset and liabilities management. She is the author of many publications.

Andrea Landi is Associate Professor of Banking and Economics at the University of Modena, Dipartimento di Economia Aziendale. His main fields of interest include competition in bank markets, efficiency and productivity of credit institutions and theory of financial intermediation. He is author of 'Dimensioni, costi e profitti delle banche italiane' as well as of many articles. He contributed to *The Changing Face of European Banks and Securities Markets* (1994).

Sándor Ligeti was educated at the Karl Marx (now Budapest) University of Economic Sciences and was awarded his PhD by the Hungarian Academy of Sciences. He has been Associate Professor of Banking in the Department of Finance at the Budapest University of Economic Sciences since 1964, and he has also been Associate Professor of Banking at Miskolc University since 1992. He has been adviser to the National Bank of Hungary and to Budapest. He has travelled extensively on study visits to the US, Russia and Western Europe, and has published many articles, books and textbooks.

Ted Lindblom is Associate Professor at the University of Gothenburg, where he was Director of Postgraduate Studies in Business Administration between 1991 and 1994. His main research interests concern pricing strategies and management control. In the banking field he has authored and co-authored several articles and books. He was one of the contributors to *The Changing Face of European Banks and Securities Markets*.

Giuseppe Lusignani studied at the University of Modena and at New York University; he received his Doctoral degree in Financial Markets and Institutions from the University of Bergamo (1989). He is Assistant Professor of Banking and Finance at the University of Bologna and a member of the Scientific Committee of Prometeia (Association for Econometric Research). His main research interests are the economics of banking, risk management in financial institutions and the evolution of financial markets. He has published articles on financial markets efficiency and risk management in financial intermediaries.

Joaquín Maudos was born in Valencia in 1965. He took his BA (1989) and his PhD in Economics (1995) at the Universidad de Valencia. Assistant Professor (1990), Universidad de Valencia. His specialised fields are banking and finance. He has published over fifteen articles in specialised journals.

Joël Métais is Professor of Economics at the University of Paris-Dauphine. From 1985 to 1988 he was attached to the French Ministry of Economy and Finance as a consultant on financial and banking sector matters. Since then, he has also been involved in many working groups set up by the Banque de France, the Ministry of Finance and the Planning Agency. He has published widely, and his main publications include *Les Mutations du Système Financier Français* (co-author) and many contributions on French and international financial topics in various books and reviews, French and foreign. His main research interests are in international capital markets, the industrial economics of the financial sector, the structural changes and the increase of risks in the French banking system and their recent macroeconomic consequences.

Philip Molyneux is Co-Director of the Institute of European Finance and has written widely on areas relating to structure performance and efficiency in European banking markets.

Elisabetta Montanaro is Professor of Banking in the University of Siena. From 1982 she has been Director of the Postgraduate School of Banking

of the same University. She is a member of the Board of Directors of
Istituto Nazionale di Credito Agrario (Gruppo Monte dei Paschi di Siena).
Her publications include seven books and many articles and papers on
banking issues. Her main research interests are banking strategies, credit
risk management and supervision.

José Manuel Pastor was born in Valencia in 1967. He took his BA
(1990) and his PhD (1996) in Economics at the Universidad de Valencia.
Assistant Professor (1990), Universidad de Valencia. His specialised
fields are banking and finance. He has published over ten articles in
specialised journals.

Javier Quesada was born in Valencia in 1950. He took his BA (1972)
at the Universidad de Valencia and his PhD (1980) in Economics at the
University of Cincinnati (Ohio).   Lecturer in Economic Analysis,
Universidad de Valencia. Associate Professor (1983), Universidad de
Valencia and Associate Professor, Instituto Valenciano de Investigaciones
Económicas (IVIE). His specialised fields are Monetary Economics,
Banking and Finance. He has published four books in collaboration with
others and over forty articles in specialised journals.

Jack Revell is Professor Emeritus of the University of Wales, having been
Professor of Economics at the University College of North Wales from
1969 to 1983. He was Director of the Institute of European Finance there
from 1973 to 1985 and is now Consultant Director. He has undertaken
consultancies for various organisations, including the United Nations, the
Statistical Office of the European Communities, the OECD, HM Treasury
and the Spanish savings bank research foundation. Among his publications
are *Solvency and Regulation of Banks, Costs and Margins in Banking* and
Mergers and the Role of Large Banks.

Tad Rybczynski is an Honorary Visiting Professor at the City University
and the City University Business School. He is also a director of a unit
trust company and advisory director to a private company with a large
interest in finance, shipping and real estate. During his career he has held
a large number of professional positions, including economic adviser to
Lazard Brothers and Co. Ltd, Chairman of the Society of Business
Economists and a member of the UK Monopolies and Mergers Committee.
He has published extensively on a wide range of banking, finance,
monetary and international economic issues.

Leo Schuster, Professor, born 1937 in Furth/Bavaria; studied economics at the Universities of Erlangen/Nurenberg, Munich and Vienna; started his university career as an assistant and university teacher at the University of Erlangen/Nurenberg; 1971 full Professor for Banking and Finance at the University of St Gallen and became the Director of the Banking Institute; since April 1990 full Professor at the Department of Business Administration Ingolstadt at the Catholic University of Eichstatt; 1991-1993 Dean of this faculty.

Professor Schuster gained practical experience at the Commerzbank and as a consultant of the United Nations in New York; today he is a member of the board of directors of an international Zurich-based bank and of an insurance company in Nurenberg as well as member of some scientific commissions; consultant to banking institutions in Switzerland and Germany; joint editor of several journals at home and abroad; author of about a dozen books and about 150 articles on banking and financial topics.

Simon Sijbrands was born in 1961 in Amsterdam. He studied economics at the Faculty of Economic Sciences and Econometrics at the Free University in Amsterdam and in 1988 he started working as an internal management consultant for a middle-sized company. He joined the Amsterdam Academy in 1991 to give lectures on strategic management. (The Amsterdam Academy offers higher education for the financial services industry.) At present he is combining his scientific work at the Academy with a job as a strategic management consultant. He is the chief editor of the book *Financial Services Firms and Strategic Renewal*, which was published in 1993, and he is an author and co-author of several articles in national and international management journals. He is currently doing research on the future of the cross-border corporate payments industry and the alternative strategic positioning modes of banks in that respect.

SYNOPSES OF CONTRIBUTIONS

PART I THE LATEST PHASE IN THE EVOLUTION OF FINANCIAL SYSTEMS

Chapter 1 A New Look at the Evolution of the Financial System
T.M. Rybczynski

The evolution of the financial system which until the early nineties had been studied by very few serious academic economists, having been, and still remaining, outside the mainstream neo-classical modelling, has come to the top of research work since the collapse of planned economies and the beginning of their transformation into market economies. This essay, which uses an historical, institutional and analytical approach, advances the view that any financial system passes through three stages. They are: a bank-orientated phase; a market orientated phase; and a securitised phase. During the bank-orientated phase banks are the dominant institutions undertaking the basic functions any financial system must perform, running the payments and clearing system, providing liquidity, transferring savings from surplus to deficit units, monitoring and disciplining users of externally raised funds and pricing and redistributing risk. The market-orientated phase is characterised by the growing importance of financial markets, above all the capital market, which, together with the intermediaries operating them, increasingly take over the last of the five functions mentioned above. In the securitised phase financial markets and the intermediaries linked to them, i.e. all savings-collecting and savings-allocating institutions other than those offering traditional banking services as well as financial market intermediaries, are responsible for the performance of the last three functions mentioned previously.

There are three basic factors responsible for this pattern of development. They are technological advance, the institutional and regulatory framework and a rise in per capita income and wealth. Technological advances reduce the cost of collecting, processing and using information and communications; they are also responsible for globalisation. Changes in the regulatory and institutional framework impose constraints on the type of activities various kinds of financial institutions are allowed to offer and the geographical area where they can operate. An increase in per capita income and wealth leads to changes in the preferences of individual savers and institutions entrusted to hold such savings for various types of financial assets designed with a view to optimising the mix of risk-liquidity-return characteristics. Secondly they result in changes in the ownership (direct and in the fiduciary capacity) of real and financial wealth and changes in corporate governance.

Broadly speaking, one can say that the bank-orientated phase is associated with 'proprietorial capitalism' where proprietors are managers, and there is no conflict of interest between them. The market-orientated phase tends to be linked to 'managerial capitalism', where there is a growing separation between owners and managers, when their interests begin to differ.

Finally, the securitised phase tends to be linked to 'financial or institutional capitalism', in which the bulk of property rights are vested in the hands of financing institutions acting in a fiduciary capacity and in which the relative importance of traditionally defined banking services falls very sharply.

| **Chapter 2** | **The Banking Industry in the Nineties: Do Emerging Trends Challenge the Theory?** *Joël Métais* |

Financial innovation and deregulation, disintermediation, a fast-growing derivatives industry, new players and patterns of competition have reshaped the banking and financial services industry during the past twenty years. Poor profitability and a sudden surge of bank failures have also taken their part in the ongoing process of restructuring of this industry. Simultaneously a new theory of financial intermediation has emerged, which has greatly benefited from developments in the microeconomics of uncertainty, with such notions as asymmetrical information, incompleteness of contracts, moral hazard and adverse selection as its 'keywords'. The industrial economics of the banking sector has also received renewed interest. These advances of the theory are especially enlightening for our understanding of a fast moving reality, which often seems rather puzzling to bankers and economists, who sometimes complain that banking may have entered the stage of a declining industry. It seems indeed more appropriate to underline that banking today is much more shaped by the available technologies and comparative advantages in the various areas of financial intermediation than by regulations. Former banks may in some instances die but banking will stay alive for a long time!

Chapter 3   **The Future of 'Traditional Banking'**
                       Edward P.M. Gardener

This chapter explores the meaning and operation and significance of 'traditional banking' compared with 'modern banking'. Traditional banking is defined initially from both a microeconomic and a bank strategic perspective. It is argued that external and internal changes in banking have substantially altered the strategic environment and strategies of banks in all of their main business areas. This has produced many important strategic challenges for banks. Against this background the 'bank of the future' is discussed.

Chapter 4   **Comments of Discussants**

Bank credit and the stage process
Jean-Paul Abraham

Although market-orientated relations pervade the Western financial systems, this evolution cannot be systematised as an irreversible step in a quasi-automatic and generalised transition from a B(anking) System to a M(arket) System. In this context the permanent role of bank credit as a financing instrument of enterprises and households is emphasised. Market finance is neither a substitute nor a complement to bank credit when small- and medium-sized enterprises are concerned. And even in large companies bank loans do not disappear but shift towards more sophisticated formulae, towards tailor-made financial solutions.

Will the securitised phase last?
Jack Revell

In trying to answer this question it is essential to start with a fundamental analysis of the forces that have led to the transition from the market-orientated financial system to the securitised phase, and these forces are to be found both within the financial system and outside it. It is the thesis of this short contribution that large customers of financial institutions, the global industrial and commercial corporations, were largely responsible for dragging financial institutions in the same direction as they were travelling. It follows from this line of argument that threats to the persistence of the securitised phase can come from economic and political movements that pose a danger to these global corporations, such as the resurgence of nationalism and revolts of the growing 'underclass'.

Local banks and global players in the Italian financial market
Francesco Cesarini

The contribution briefly outlines the major trends emerging in the Italian financial market after the application of EU Directives and suggests that a new division of labour between small/local banks and large/national banks should be actively sought so that the transition from traditional banking to the market-orientated phase can take place smoothly by adequately combining the solid local roots and placing power of the former with the attitude of the latter to play a more comprehensive role in markets for securitised financial instruments.

Comments concerning distribution systems
Göran Bergendahl

The distribution system of a bank will include all services at bank branches. For example, such a system will cover both the collection of funds in terms of deposits and the distribution of funds in terms of credits. A bank distribution system may be subdivided into systems for selling, delivery, payments and control. Joël Métais and Tad Rybczynski have shown what a change the process of securitisation has given to the distribution system in terms of products and markets. Ted Gardener has visualised the effect that change has had on the customers. Most of them are no longer satisfied with one bank but use different banks for different services. The outcome has been that nowadays traditional banking is often replaced by universal banking on the one hand and narrow banking on the other. In both cases a larger emphasis has to be put on selling and on a decentralised control of risk and return. As a consequence, the future banks will have to focus on distribution systems.

Large banks in the EU: what size?
Javier Quesada

Mergers and acquisitions among EU banks during the past decade appear to have had two main characteristics: (1) both domestic and cross-border transactions seem to have been predominantly defensive in character; (2) at least one of the banks concerned has generally been small or of medium size. In order to establish whether an optimal size could be deduced for the larger banks in the EU a very simple statistical exercise on a sample of thirty banks consisting of the five largest in Germany, the UK, France, Italy, Spain and Portugal was performed. It was impossible to find any common points between the banks in the six countries in terms of the relation between size and return on assets (ROA) or return on equity (ROE). Further empirical analysis of efficiency and/or profitability is needed before an optimal size can be established.

PART II   THE RESPONSE OF BANKING SYSTEMS TO SECURITISATION

Chapter 5   **Bank Lending and the Securitisation Process: A Comparative Analysis**
Andrea Landi and Giuseppe Lusignani

This contribution analyses the relationship between bank loan cycles and the development of securities markets in some of the most important financial systems (US, UK, Japan, France, Germany and Italy). The work is divided into two distinct parts. In the first we investigate the evolution of bank loans in relation to the main financial and business cycle indicators. We stress the strong variability of bank loans and focus on the supply factors which can explain this phenomenon. The second part of the paper analyses the changes in the financial structure of the private sector (non-financial firms) as a result of conjunctural and structural factors. In particular our analysis stresses the role played by securities markets and the striking shift from earlier recessions in the corporate financial patterns. Finally, in regard to financial system models and bank behaviour, we offer some indications which derive from the evolving relationship among non-financial firms, banks and markets.

Chapter 6   **Efficient Risk Management in Financial Systems: Universal Bank or Securitisation?**
Elisabetta Montanaro

There have been two contrasting tendencies in financial systems from the early eighties onwards: the securitisation process, which brought about the disintermediation of banks; and universal banks, which resulted from the decline in the functional and institutional specialisation which characterised banks with respect to other financial intermediaries. The contradiction between securisation and the tendency of the bank to become, or rather to return to being, universal is obvious if we consider that securitisation empirically negates the existence of those economies of scale and scope upon which the competitive advantage of the universal bank is based. Seen in these terms, securitisation and the universal bank become an apparently irresolvable dilemma for the microeconomic analysis of the financial industry.

Chapter 7   **Trends in German Banking**
                        Leo Schuster

German banking is traditionally characterised by a strong savings and loan culture. Because of the influence of the Anglo-Saxon securities culture there is recently a certain shift towards more private investments into securities; furthermore, increasing company financing through the different forms of securities and derivatives can be observed. In order to gain the necessary expertise in this type of business German banks have taken over British and American brokers and investment banks. Moreover, they are beginning to establish their investment banking headquarters in London. This change will also alter the hitherto strong relations between companies and their housebanks; the former will prefer transactions banking instead of the traditional relationship-orientated banking in future. The latter will have to develop new marketing approaches in response. Besides securitisation and the linked cultural change some other trends are influencing German banking: the increasing use of information technologies at all levels, reregulation within the EU and the forthcoming single European currency. One of the major problems will be how banks are going to deal with their extensive branch system. Germany has a very dense network of branches, which is very costly and will be replaced to a certain extent by new means of service delivery. The result will not only be the closing down of branches but also the redundancy of bank employees. It is hard to believe, but banking is changing from a 'people business' to a technology driven by business.

Chapter 8   **Universal Banks, Ownership and Efficiency: A Stochastic Frontier Analysis of the German Banking Market**
                        Yener Altunbas, Lynne Evans and Philip Molyneux

This paper uses the stochastic cost frontier approach to evaluate technical inefficiencies for specific bank types and organisational forms in the German market. We find that private, public and mutually-owned banks have mean inefficiencies around the 25 per cent level. Specialist institutions of mixed ownership appear to be significantly more inefficient around the 45 per cent level. This result broadly supports the view that in terms of cost efficiencies universal banks appear to have some advantage over specialist banks.

Chapter 9   **The Restructuring of Banking Groups in Italy: Major Issues**
Elisabetta Gualandri

This contribution analyses the reasons for the process of profound restructuring that Italian banking groups have undergone during the last few years, with the aim of identifying its main critical areas from the management point of view. In the eighties Italian banking groups grew in a manner which was often almost chaotic, with no clear governing strategies. Legislation obliged banks to establish groups of subsidiaries if they were to diversify their activities but, in spite of this, the sector had no real group culture. In the early nineties the Banca d'Italia allocated parent banks specific duties of strategic co-ordination and control and thus provided a stimulus for group rationalisation. A further incentive in this direction was provided by the implementation of the second EEC Directive, which introduced the model of the universal bank to Italy and thus allowed banks to internalise operations formerly handled by subsidiaries. Last but not least, there has recently been a flurry of mergers and takeovers between banks, intended to strengthen the Italian banking system, which has triggered further integration and rationalisation within groups. These processes are encountering problems, sometimes serious, in three main areas of bank management: strategic control and planning; personnel management; and information technology. These are illustrated in the second part of the contribution.

Chapter 10   **Recent Developments in Retail Banking in Scandinavia: Narrow v. Universal Banking**
Ted Lindblom and Martin Andersson

As in most Western countries regulations have protected banks from competitive pressure in Scandinavia. However, the barriers to entry are now decreasing. This is especially true in Denmark and in Sweden, where non-banks have been permitted to start banking activities through subsidiaries. These new banks are able to use cost-effective equipment based on the latest technology, while established banks have already invested a significant amount of capital in labour-intensive distribution systems based on yesterday's technology. In Sweden it is obvious that the new banks have contributed to narrowing interest-rate margins and a vitalisation of the bank pricing strategies regarding payment services. They are applying a different strategy from the one implemented by traditional banks. While established banks regard universal banking as the appropriate business concept, the new banks are specialising in a narrower range of banking products and services. This chapter concentrates on the competition between 'narrow banks' and traditional universal banks. The main focus will be on the Swedish situation, but analogies with the other Scandinavian countries are also made.

Chapter 11   **Universal Banking in Central and Eastern Europe**
Sándor Ligeti

The term universal bank has at least two meanings: on the one hand, a multiproduct firm, on the other, a bank which carries out both commercial bank activities and investment bank activities as well. There are different opinions about the pros and cons of universal banking.

In Central and Eastern Europe, two-tier banking systems were introduced in the late eighties and early nineties. According to the banking laws the new commercial banks were entitled to carry out several financial activities, including investment bank activities as well, except in Hungary where commercial banks cannot underwrite or trade securities.

Many economists argued that these countries chose the wrong model because share ownership does not solve the problems of corporate governance. The stock market does not have a considerable role, there is no fear of hostile takeovers. Many economists suggest that universal banks would be important in corporate governance in transition economies; others state that in the transition economies banks are not in a dominating position and do not have enough capital to own a considerable part of the non-financial companies' shares. The common problem is that the state-owned or the formerly state-owned companies do not have enough capital. During privatisation the leverage of the firms increased; sometimes the banks became forced owners through a debt-equity swap. In Hungary most of the economists suggest that universal banking should be introduced, and many of them think that both the banks and the non-financial firms must be privatised. The lack of domestic capital raises the question of allowing foreign investors into the banking and non-financial sector.

There are different opinions about the advantages and disadvantages of universal banking. These views do not differ considerably from the discussions in the Western countries between the German model and other types of universal banking and the American model. The experiences of different Central and Eastern European countries show that there are not great differences between the performance of the banking systems organised   as universal banks or separate investment and commercial banks.

Chapter 12	**Technical Progress in Spanish Banking: 1985-1994**
	Joaquín Maudos, José Manuel Pastor and Javier Quesada

Over the last decade the Spanish banking sector has undergone a radical structural change. The old bank *status quo* has broken down because of both the impact of technical change and a strong deregulation process, that has given way to a much freer and competitive economic environment. Similarly, the rapid and intensive diffusion of new technologies on information has modified the banking industry in an important way. The effect of these three phenomena (technical change, deregulation and increased competition) on production costs for the Spanish savings banks are the objectives of this study. We review three alternative econometric methods of approaching the impact of technical change. Since we have available an incomplete data panel and with the aim of checking on the possibility that each firm has a particular level of efficiency - captured by the fixed effect - we estimate the function using both techniques, pooling data and panel data. We address the question of whether technical progress affects banks in a different way according to size and, finally, with the purpose of isolating our estimates of technical change from the evolution of financial costs and, therefore, of the role of competition and deregulation, we estimate a cost function using only operating costs. In this way we obtain a stricter measure of the impact of technical change.

Chapter 13	**The Internationalisation of Dutch Banks: New Beginning and Future Developments**
	Simon Sijbrands

In this article an analysis is made of the internationalisation of Dutch banks in the period 1983-92. It is stated that because of dramatic changes in the industry structure and a new categorisation in financial services (broadly described as IT-driven and HR-driven financial services) banks are standing at the start of a new internationalisation cycle. The author expects that banks will internationalise their business, not only by more cross-border co-operation, but also only by the use of information technology on its own. The development and distribution of a broad assortment of financial services (bancassurance or Allfinanz) happens only in the retail market and will probably not take place in the wholesale market, but natural synergies exist between life insurance and investment banking. Co-operation modes, like a strategic alliance, can be a very effective instrument to gain access to these distribution channels, but profitable exploitation occurs only when partners get round a number of pitfalls. The competitive battle will be on distribution channels, but having control over these channels does not automatically mean gaining a competitive advantage. Especially on the channels which are driven by information technology competition will be fierce. Suppliers of network software and free accessible software on the Internet will probably change international banking dramatically. Banks have to make clear strategic decisions to stay in business.

PART I

The latest phase in the evolution of financial systems

CHAPTER 1
A NEW LOOK AT THE EVOLUTION
OF THE FINANCIAL SYSTEM

T.M. Rybczynski

INTRODUCTION

It is now nearly seven years since I wrote a paper dealing with the evolution of the financial system. At that time this subject to a large extent was on the margins of mainstream economics. This was so despite the fact that important basic breakthroughs have been made and a number of fundamental building blocks appeared in the preceding 30 years as well as in the inter-war years and before. It would be remiss of me not to mention here such names as Schumpeter, Wicksell, Gurley and Shaw, Goldsmith, Cameron, Gerschenkon and Patrick, whose studies analytical, historical and empirical have served as point of departure for students of finance in the last ten years or so.

During the last ten years or so, and above all since 1989, the subject of the financial system, its place and role in the economy and its evolution has moved to the centre of the economic studies. It is no exaggeration to say that the old saying that 'Ownership of the means of production is the commanding heights of an economy' has been replaced by the view that it is finance which because of its functions to which I will refer later is the centre of economy, directly and indirectly affecting changes of its structure, direction and pace of development.

The increase in interest in the financial system and an enormous rise in the resources devoted to it is attributable to a considerable extent to a collapse of the Communist economies and the need to replace the command economy with a market-based economy. The urgent need on the part of the policy-makers to help resolve the problems of how to create market economies from scratch has led to the fundamental rethinking of the place and role of the financial system. A steadily and rapidly increasing flow of studies to help policy-makers in their daily tasks, involving a re-examination of the theoretical issues as well as designed to provide answers to immediate policy questions, has enriched our knowledge and expanded our understanding of the subject of finance.

3

In the paper written in 1988 I endeavoured to provide a highly stylised picture of the evolution of the financial system explaining the basic forces responsible for its transformation and linking it to the development of the real economy, that is to say to the changes in its structure and stage of development. My original and also the present paper can be said in retrospect to fall into one of the three main groups of studies and research which appear to have emerged in the last ten years or so. These *three groups* comprise first, studies concerned with *banking and its structure* and above all the basic features and the reasons for the existence of commercial banking on the one side and investment banking on the other. The *second group* has been concerned with *financial innovations* and their place in the financial area and economy at large. Finally the *third* group has covered the *financial system*. Work in this field has covered different aspects extending from allocative functions and the cost of capital for non-financial corporations to re-structuring, sharing of risk and corporate governance. However, to my knowledge, there have been no serious recent comprehensive works dealing with the dynamics of the financial system, that is to say with its evolution. This paper repeats the same exercise introducing new elements which we have learnt about and discovered in the last ten years. While I shall be drawing on a number of studies I will not acknowledge all of them here individually although I must register my indebtedness to them collectively.

The approach

The approach I use is biased towards what can be described as an *institutional and historical approach* emphasising property rights and corporate governance. It is worth recalling that after many years of virtual disregard in the Anglo-Saxon world this approach is now recognised as offering a promising path towards understanding the process of development and as helpful in resolving important policy problems. Its acceptance and the value attaching to it is now reflected in the award of the Nobel prize in economics in 1993 to Douglas North for the work done in this area over many years and the recognition that the conventional approaches were of limited, if any, value in the building of the new financial system in ex-Communist countries of Central and Eastern Europe and the former Soviet Union. Furthermore, the neo-classical model, apart from being in essence an equilibrium and stationary model, for practical purposes disregards money and finance, concentrating entirely on the real economy, and takes no account of the dynamics of the changes in the financial system. Attempts to offer a broad picture of the development of evolution of any system tend to generate a lot of criticism and debate. This is as true of the process of economic developments, as exemplified by works of classical economists and subsequently created growth-based theoretical and historical approaches, as of the evolution of the financial system. Nevertheless, exercises of this type do make a contribution to enriching the understanding of the factors at work and helping in turn both practitioners and policy-makers in approaching the problems they meet in their work.

My examination of the dynamics of the financial system takes as its starting point the basic functions the system performs, the types of organisation which carry them out, the way they do them and the exercise and distribution of property rights, i.e. corporate governance. The evolution of the financial system looked at from what may be described as a functional-cum-institutional point of view tries to see who or rather which types of organisation undertake the basic function, why they do it and the way the evolution of the financial system leads to changes in the relative importance of the main institutions, financial instruments and the financial markets and the emergence of new ones.

FUNCTIONS OF THE FINANCIAL SYSTEM AND CORPORATE GOVERNANCE

There are five basic functions which every financial system operating in a market-based economy performs. These are first, running the payments system; second, providing liquidity; third, collecting and allocating new savings, i.e. transferring excess of income over expenditure from surplus units to deficit units; fourth, monitoring and disciplining users of externally raised savings; and fifth, pricing and redistributing risk. The last three functions are at the heart of the financial system and are concerned with the assumption, measurement, pricing and management of risk. The first two functions have to do with the institutional framework enabling the second group function to be performed. As far as the exercise and the distribution of property rights (i.e. corporate governance) is concerned their development comprises three different phases. They are proprietorial capitalism, when owners act also as managers; managerial capitalism, when owners delegate the right to use assets and decide on the distribution of cash flows to hired managers; and institutional capitalism, when owners delegate the powers to monitor the performance of hired managers, to discipline them and to receive cash flows distributed as dividends to savings-collecting financial institutions.

THREE PHASES OF THE EVOLUTION OF THE FINANCIAL SYSTEM

In this framework the evolution of the financial system can be said to involve movements through three main phases: the bank-orientated phase, the market-orientated phase with two sub-periods, an early or weak market-orientated phase and a mature or strongly market-orientated phase, and a securitised phase. The bank-orientated phase and the whole of the first sub-period of the market-orientated phase, i.e. early or weakly orientated market phase and a part or so of the second sub-period of a market-orientated phase, i.e. mature or strongly orientated phase, tend to be associated with proprietorial capitalism. The later part of a second sub-period of the mature stage of the market-orientated phase tends to be linked to managerial capitalism.   The securitised phase tends to be associated with institutional capitalism.

The market-orientated phase, especially in the mature sub-period, tends to be linked to the emergence of the investment banking activity and, depending on the regulatory framework and other factors, the division of banks between commercial (or deposit) banks and investment banks.

As far as the five basic functions performed by the financial system mentioned before are concerned, the running of the payments system and the provision of liquidity remain in the ultimate analysis in every phase of the evolution in the hands of commercial (deposit) banks. What changes is the type of institution performing the three remaining functions - collection and allocation of new savings, monitoring and disciplining of users of externally raised saving, the assumption, measurement, pricing and management of risk - the financial instruments used and the type and scope of the financial markets facilitating the functioning of various financial organisations.

Bank-orientated phase

The main feature of a bank-orientated phase of the evolution of the financial system is that, apart from the running of the payments system and providing liquidity, the first of the three remaining basic functions which any financial system must perform namely that of collecting and allocating new savings is predominantly in the hands of banks. This of course also implies that the bulk of *external* funds obtained by non-financial firms is obtained from banks mostly in the form of (non-tradeable) bank loans. In this phase of evolution other savings-collecting institutions play a very modest role.

Being the main suppliers of external funds for non-financial firms during this phase banks perform also the *second* of the remaining fundamental function that financial systems carry out, that of monitoring the financial (and real) performance of their clients and disciplining them when necessary - because of unsatisfactory performance - and also initiating re-structuring of individual firms (and industries). Banks occupy the dominant position during this phase because they have access to information available to them to evaluate risks of prospective fund users, to price the relevant risks and diversify them. Needless to say this occurs only when bank operations are based on the principle of fractional banking and when other sources of external funds, i.e. other savings collecting institutions, are of very modest importance.

During this phase there come into existence money and credit markets which operate on a modest scale almost entirely among banks, but there are no other financial markets of any significance. This phase of the evolution of the financial system is associated with proprietorial capitalism, that is the phase when private units are owned and managed by proprietors and there is no conflict of interest between them.

Market-orientated phase

In the first sub-period of a market-orientated phase, i.e. the weakly market-orientated phase, (deposit) banks continue to be the main type of organisation performing the three basic functions and remain the dominant suppliers of external funds to non-financial companies and other units. Other savings-collecting institutions such as insurance companies begin to appear and gradually gain in importance. The absolute and relative size of the money and credit market begins to rise, but they are still used predominantly for interbank business. The capital market also begins to emerge, but its significance is very limited, its main users being various types of governmental bodies. There are no other financial markets during this sub-period. This sub-period is still linked to proprietorial capitalism when individual firms are owned and managed by proprietors and when banks are the main institutions monitoring and disciplining users of external funds.

The mature, or strongly market-orientated, sub-period of the market-orientated phase of the evolution of the financial system nature is characterised by the growing importance of non-bank savings collecting institutions (i.e. building societies and later closed-end investment trusts and later still open-ended investment trusts and finance companies and insurance companies), which by engaging in financial innovations involving the production of new financial instruments compete with banks in the function of collecting and allocating new savings and become involved in carrying out the function of monitoring and disciplining users of funds.

During this sub-period the proportion of external funds raised by non-financial companies from sources other than banks, and especially through the medium of capital markets, begins to increase, reflecting the fact that non-bank financial institutions place some of the savings they collect in the securities listed on stock exchanges. Also banks, if allowed to do so, place some of their savings in listed securities. As a result the monitoring and the disciplining function is performed during this sub-period not only by banks but also by other savings-collecting institutions by reference to and using the capital market. Broadly speaking the disciplining of the users of external funds by reference to the stock exchange involves in principle the selling of the relevant shares rather than direct action. This tends to be taken by banks, and by enterprising individuals through individual purchases as well as collecting proxies, to cause managers to take some remedial action.

The expansion in the type and number of savings collecting institutions and new financial instruments is accompanied by the growth of financial markets. Money and credit markets expand in size and the number of participants, which now include all types of financial institutions and non-financial firms. Capital markets increase in size and relative importance as a mechanism for obtaining additional funds by non-financial companies and also financial ones as well as various governmental bodies. The growth of markets is a reflection of an increase in specialisation as shown by a rise in different types of financial products and the resulting need for exchange of them by way of markets.

This sub-period tends to be associated with the growth of managerial capitalism, that is increasing separation between owners and managers. Owners gradually reduce the degree of control and managers assume the power to determine the use of assets and the distribution of cash flow among their remuneration, in kind and in cash, immediate and deferred and retentions and dividends. In other words corporate governance arrangements change.

In short, the relative importance of traditional banks in collecting and allocating of sources decreases - except that banks now all engage in investment banking and taking participations - while that of other financial institutions and capital markets increases.

Securitised phase

The *third phase* of the evolution of the financial system, which I now describe as a securitisation phase, is characterised first by the fact that the first and second of the main functions of the financial system other than the running of the payment system and the provision of liquidity, that of collecting and allocating new savings and monitoring the performance and disciplining, is done predominantly by the investment banking segment and the financial markets. Financial markets enable non-financial firms and other organisations to raise cheaper external funds in the form of marketable securities and other financial instruments traded in financial markets. The share of banks in collecting new savings in the form of various deposits and allocating them to prospective users, in the form of bank loans or other forms, declines. The obverse side of this change is that the bulk of external funds raised by non-financial firms and also other organisations is obtained through the medium of tradeable financial instruments, the funds being provided by non-bank savings-collecting institutions and, to a certain degree, by banks of the universal type and households or other non-financial firms. Financial markets redistribute liquidity and funds among various financial institutions and play the central role in this phase. They help to monitor the performance of various economic units and discipline them. They are in this phase the main factor in the restructuring of the economy linked to the growth of the market for corporate control in various forms such as management buy-out.

Alongside the expansion of money, credit and capital markets there emerges not only the market for corporate control but also the market for pricing and trading of various financial risks using new financial instruments such as futures, options, swaps etc. usually called the market for derivatives. The securitised phase of the evolution of the financial system is linked to the transformation of managerial capitalism into institutional (or financial) capitalism. Its main feature is separation of owners from managers and the emergence and rapid growth of savings-collecting institutions as the main holders of financial wealth in the form of ordinary shares and debt obligation, with the duty to monitor and discipline the performance of the users of externally raised savings. Thus the function of monitoring and disciplining users of external funds falls predominantly on savings-collecting institutions other than commercial banks undertaking traditional business and which do so by actively using capital markets.

FACTORS RESPONSIBLE FOR THE EVOLUTION

What are the propelling factors responsible for the transformation of the financial system from bank-orientated through weakly and the strongly market-orientated phase to the securitised system and for the change of the arrangement for the exercise of property rights from proprietorial to managerial and then institutional or (financial) capitalism? These developments can be said to be due, firstly, to increases in income and wealth (caused by advances in technology and the accumulation of human and physical capital) leading in turn to social, cultural and political changes; secondly, to advances in technology directly affecting the economics of financial operation; and finally, to changes in the regulatory framework.

How do these factors bear on the evolution of the financial system as outlined above? An increase in income and wealth in general results in the dispersion of wealth, a rise in financial wealth as compared with real wealth and an expansion in the types and variety of financial instruments with different combinations of liquidity, risk and rewards, which in turn enables holders of wealth to seek to create portfolios with a mix satisfying their specific demands. It is this general rise in income and wealth that is the main factor behind the arrangement relating to the distribution and exercise of property rights, or corporate governance.

As regards the financial system, advances in technology reduce the cost of various services and facilitate the production of new services and the segmentation and improvement of existing services by decreasing the cost of collecting and processing information, the cost of calculating and the cost of communications. They are linked to the economies of scale and scope and in some ways can be compared to the benefits the transport industry generated by a fall in transport costs over the past 150 years or so.

The regulatory framework - as set out by law makers - defines which functions can be performed by various institutions and specifies the constraints to which they are subjected to provide a certain degree of protection to savers and investors. The regulatory framework tends to be adjusted to take account of the impact of technological changes, but this happens in a backward manner - as is the case with all legal changes. The distribution and exercise of property rights is closely linked to a rise in income and changes in the regulatory framework - the two forces being interdependent.

In a bank-orientated phase the costs of performing the basic functions of the financial system tend to be relatively high. They are high because the cost of obtaining and processing information, the cost of calculating and the cost of communications tend to be high. In this phase all the basic functions tend to be performed by banks because they have access to information and the degree of specialisation is very limited. The relative size of financial assets in relation to real assets in this phase is small and the type of financial assets is limited, reflecting concentration of ownership and a very modest degree of dispersion of wealth.

The transition to a market-orientated phase reflects first of all the impact of technological advance in that the cost of obtaining external funds through the financial market declines. Also the cost of obtaining and processing information about the prospective users of funds to evaluate risk and making it available to ultimate savers and other savings-collecting institutions becomes lower; second, new savings-collecting (and savings-allocating) institutions become more important and offer new services by producing new financial instruments with different characteristics. New financial instruments offer new combinations of risk/rewards/liquidity and extend and enlarge the methods of monitoring and disciplining the users of past savings. A reduction in the cost of collecting savings, obtaining information and consequently assessing the risk involved leads in turn to the emergence of new savings-collecting organisations and the entry, if allowed by the regulatory framework, of new institutions into the areas where new financial instruments can be used and to the emergence and growth of new financial markets. Financial innovation, due to technological advance, enables new services and products to be created for the performance of the basic functions. The appearance of new products in turn tends to increase specialisation and leads to a rise in the scope of existing and the emergence of new markets.

In the early stage of a market-orientated phase the money and credit markets are in essence interbank markets. In the mature phase their participants tend to include other savings-collecting institutions, and non-financial firms. Also in this phase the relative importance of capital markets increases rapidly. The dispersion of wealth, a rise in the ratio of financial to real wealth and an increase in the proportion of securities in financial wealth in the mature stage of this phase leads to a growth in the relative importance of capital markets as a source of funds for non-financial and also financial firms. However, the place and role of the capital markets, especially during the mature stage of this phase, tends to be influenced by the character of the regulatory framework and its approach towards commercial and deposit banking. The formal separation between investment and deposit banking, as in the US in the early 1930s, and restrictions on branches in limiting their size together with constraints on loans to individual clients before the Great Crash, favoured the emergence of separate investment banking activity and the rapid growth of the capital market. Universal banking, as in Germany, has tended to favour commercial banks.

Further reductions in the cost of collection of savings and increases in the availability of and lower cost of processing information needed for the allocation of savings and for monitoring and disciplining users of past savings leads to the securitised phase. This phase is characterised, firstly, by a great variety of financial instruments designed to provide different combinations of liquidity/risk/rewards, reflecting the opportunities for the 'unbundling' of different types of risk, secondly, the appearance and an increase in use of new instruments leads to specialisation. There is a further rise in the scope of money and credit markets, whose operations now cover banks, other financial organisations, non-financial firms and governmental units. There is very rapid expansion of the capital markets, which become the main source of external funds, and the emergence of and rapid increase in the scope and importance of the market for corporate control and the market for pricing and trading of various types of risk, i.e. derivatives. This phase, as mentioned before, is associated with 'institutional capitalism', when the bulk of new savings is collected and allocated by non-bank financial institutions.

'Institutional capitalism' reflects two trends. The first is an increased tendency on the part of individuals and households to hold and accumulate their savings in the form of collective savings instruments issued by investment companies, offering advantages of diversification and various combinations of risk/returns/liquidity. The second is the growth of funded pension schemes in place of pay-as-you-go pension arrangements and also of savings-collecting organisations, other than banks, placing their savings in shares and bonds listed on the stock exchange. This is associated with a rise in income and wealth in general. There is also an increase in the ratio of financial assets to real assets and a rise in the proportion of shares and bonds in the total of financial assets. Finally, there is a dispersion of wealth in general and financial assets in particular. This last development is closely associated with the rise of funded pension funds, involving an increase in the share of financial assets owned indirectly by the bulk of the population. It is at present impossible to offer with any precision an indication of the level of institutional ownership of shares at which institutional capitalism begins to take root. Such rough guesstimates as can be made suggest that when such holdings, other than by universal banks, reach 30 per cent, or so, the corporate governance assumes new form. It is this factor which is the main propelling element behind the rise of the securitised financial system.

The nature of the regulatory framework bears on the type of organisations undertaking financial functions and especially on the relationship between specialised and universal banks and also on the relationship between commercial banks, investment banks and insurance companies. At the risk of over-simplification one can say that during this phase (i.e. securitised) the pressure for the removal of or separation of these activities grows rapidly.

CONCLUSIONS

Looking backwards one can say that in the early stages of the development of the financial system in the now developed countries all banks were, in principle, universal banks in that, except in the US prior to the Great Crash, as a rule they were free to take equity stakes in addition to traditional bank lending and undertake all financial business, including investment banking, except insurance. In the US the transformation of the financial system into a market-orientated system prior to the 1929 crash was characterised by commercial banks engaging increasingly in investment banking by means of affiliates and accompanied by the change of the proprietorial into managerial capitalism, reflecting rapid industrialisation. The failure of the financial system on the continent of Europe to move into the market-orientated system can be attributed to the continuation of proprietorial capitalism and to a certain degree to special constraints on the activities of traditional banks in countries such as France and Italy and a strong inward orientation of the authorities, leading in the second half of the interwar period to the erection of barriers to the flow of capital across national frontiers.

Legal separation of investment and deposit banking in the US, embodied in the Glass-Steagall legislation, did not prevent the US financial system from moving into the securitised phase as the economy moved after World War Two into de-industrialisation phase and as institutional capitalism started gaining strength from the late 1950s. What has been the outstanding feature of the US system is that the move into the securitised phase has been propelled and led by investment banking houses and not deposit banks. The same technological factors which, together with institutional changes, have turned the US system into a securitised one are now leading to changes in regulatory structure designed to enable commercial banks to expand their activities into investment banking and become universal banks, as they in fact had been prior to the 1933 legislation.

The gradual transformation of proprietorial and managerial capitalism in the countries of continental Europe is leading to the emergence of institutional capitalism and the securitisation of their financial systems. It is perhaps the dominance of institutional capitalism in the UK - far more advanced than in the US - and linked with its growth of the financial markets which has enabled the UK to be the model of the dynamics of the financial system now emulated by and leading to changes in the regulatory framework in other countries.

The evolution and the development of the financial system is now looked at in the context of globalisation. In a sense globalisation reflects merely the impact of technology in the international framework. It introduces new elements in that it links national systems into international systems, extending the scope of operations of individual institutions and markets, but also introduces the problems of harmonising regulatory and prudential framework. It is the transformation of the proprietorial system into the managerial system and institutional capitalism, together with the forces of technology, which are causing the financial systems in industrial countries to assume the securitised form and to converge.

LIST OF REFERENCES

Adelman, I. and E. Thurbeck (1989), 'The role of institutions in economic development', *World Development,* **17** (Special issue)

Arestis, P. and A.S. Eichrer (1989), 'The post Keynesian and institutional theory of money and credit', *Journal of Economic Issues,* **22**, 4, 1003-21

Bhattacharya, S and A.V. Thakor (1994), 'Contemporary and banking theory', *Journal of Financial Intermediation,* **3**, October

Cameron, R. (ed.) (1992), *Financing Industrialisation* (Cambridge: Edward Elgar)

Checchi, Daniele (1993), 'Creation of financial markets in (previously) centrally planned economies', *Journal of Banking and Finance,* **17**, pp. 819-847

Chick, V. (1986), 'The evolution of the banking system and the theory of savings, investment and interest', *Economies et Societes Monnaie et Production,* **20**, 8-9, 111-26

Day, R.G. Elliason, and C. Wihlburg (1993), *The Market for Ownership and Control* (Stockholm and Amsterdam: IUI and North Holland)

Dosi, G. (1988), 'Institutions and markets in a dynamic world', *Manchester School*, **56**, 2

Diamond, Douglas (1984), 'Financial intermediation and delegated monitoring', *Review of Economic Studies*, **51**, pp. 393-411

Gerschenkron, A. (1988), *Continuity in History and Other Essays* (Cambridge, MA: Harvard University Press)

Greenbaum, Stuart and Ansan V. Thakor (1995), *Contemporary Financial Intermediation* (Fort Worth, Texas: Dryden Press)

Hanusch, H. (ed.) (1988), *Revolutionary Economics: Application of Schumpeter's Ideas* (Cambridge: Cambridge University Press)

Kolari, James and Aschar Zarkouhi (1987), *Bank Costs, Structure and Performance* (Lexington, MA: Lexington Books)

Kindleberger, C.P. (1958), *Economic Development* (New York, NY: McGraw Hill)

Kindleberger, C.P. (1984), *A Financial History of Western Europe* (London: George Allen and Unwin)

Nelson, R.R. and S.G. Winter (1982), *An Evolutionary Theory of Economic Change* (Cambridge, MA: Harvard University Press)

Nardozzi, G. (1990), 'The structural evolution of financial systems in the 80s; from its determination to its possible outcome', *Banca Nazionale Del Lavoro Quarterly,* **43**, pp. 71-89

Rybczynski, T.M. (1988), 'Financial system and industrial re-structuring, *National Westminster Bank Quarterly Review*, November, pp. 3-13

Walter, Ingo (1993), 'The battle of the systems, control of enterprises and global economy', *Kieler Vortrage*, Institut fur Weltwirtschaft, University of Kiel

CHAPTER 2
THE BANKING INDUSTRY IN THE NINETIES:
DO EMERGING TRENDS CHALLENGE THE THEORY?

Joël Métais

INTRODUCTION

The history of economics provides us with many examples of facts challenging the current state of theoretical understanding, thus inducing significant and rapid progress of the theory; we may have been experiencing such a situation for the past fifteen years in the area of banking. After half a century of a rather 'quiet life', banking and finance indeed entered a tremendous period in most countries and at the international level, which has sometimes been qualified as a true financial revolution. Bankers, economists and policy-makers have been so puzzled by such radical change that some of them have come to question the mere survival of banks in the not so distant future whereas others lament that it has become a declining industry[1].

These events have undoubtedly stimulated a renewed interest in the analysis of the banking sector and of financial intermediation. There was of course in 1960, the seminal work of Gurley and Shaw on the role of financial intermediaries and some early works in industrial economics concerned with the structure and performance of the American commercial banking sector in the sixties and seventies. But the impetus for what appears now as the new theory of banking and financial intermediaries was given around the late seventies and early eighties.

This paper will first deal briefly and selectively with the major developments in banking during the past years at both the micro and industry level. Financial innovation and deregulation, the disintermediation process, the emergence of a true risk-managing industry, the inflow of quite new players and the advent of new patterns of competition in the banking and financial fields, their consequences on the performance of the banking industry, the surge of bank failures and the restructuring of the sector were the common features of this period in major industrial countries. These will also be the main headings of the first part.

During the past fifteen years, the microeconomic theory of financial intermediation experienced very rapid and significant advances. This paper will thus go on, in a second part, with the presentation of the main aspects of what can be named a new paradigm of the economics of financial institutions. This theory starts by raising the question of why banks exist and has much benefited from significant progress recently achieved in the broader fields of both the economics of uncertainty and the theory of industrial organisation. Uncertainty surrounding the future and information are thus its two originating concepts; asymmetric and costly information, incompleteness of contracts, adverse selection and moral hazard come next. Banks and financial intermediaries can then emerge as providers of liquidity insurance and as monitors of risks and their specific role, as compared to that performed by negotiable asset markets, can be re-assessed: the comparative advantages of banks, the existence and extent of economies of scale and/or of scope can also be re-examined while the rationale and forms of public regulation can be restated in new terms. Finally such diverse problems as the restructuring of the financial services industry or the return of credit cycle or credit crunches then receive a renewed and more illuminating interpretation. As a conclusion, we shall support the view that banks are here to stay.   More precisely, the institutions labelled as banks in tomorrow's world will certainly look more uniform across the main industrial countries as they will be shaped more by technology and comparative advantages *vis-à-vis* other financial vehicles and procedures and less by national regulatory and institutional settings.

1.   THE FINANCIAL REVOLUTION OF THE PAST FIFTEEN YEARS: SOME STYLISED FACTS

It has sometimes been argued that during the past fifteen years the financial systems in major industrial countries and some developing countries alike have experienced more radical transformation than during the preceding half-century. Some words summarise these changes: innovation, deregulation, globalisation. Stiffer competition, declining profitability and bank failures are other salient features of the picture.

Innovation, deregulation and globalisation

Financial innovations (product, process and organisational) started to flourish in the US and Canada in the early seventies before spreading to Europe, Japan and a lot of other (sometimes developing) countries. Today, the innovation may have lost momentum and some lessons may be drawn.

There have been rather few true major product innovations. Although their principle had been known for some decades (and maybe centuries) futures and options (or, to be more precise, their massive use) can be considered as such. Swaps and securitised credits undoubtedly are too. But commercial paper and certificates of deposit (which were introduced in many OECD countries during the eighties) only spread outside the US financial system and through the eurocurrency markets according to the product life-cycle hypothesis. The thriving varieties of bonds, notes and shares are no more than minor innovations as well as the growing sophistication of syndication procedures in the eurocredit (with the NIFs, RUFs, MOFs and the likes) and eurobond areas.

Process innovations were numerous but all refer to the huge introduction of telecommunications and computer technologies to cut operating costs and to enlarge the menu of new services and products available. Production functions of financial intermediaries are now much more capital intensive, whereas their fixed investment displays growing indivisibility and irreversibility.

Organisational innovations did not play such an important role except in some countries, like the US, for long entangled in especially stringent regulations like the Glass-Steagall and McFadden Acts.

Deregulation of the financial sector has also been widespread since the late seventies. Once more, the process largely originated in North America and the UK. Other countries were more or less enthusiastic towards deregulation, but even the more reluctant ones, like Japan and Germany, had finally to follow around the end of the eighties. Financial (product) innovations, new technologies and growing international economic openness were the major driving forces of the deregulatory snowball. Depending on the stringency of their previous regulatory framework the deregulatory moves differed somewhat between countries. However it is now clear that they all shared in some common features. Interest rate ceilings (like the US Regulation Q) on bank deposits have been removed in most countries as savers were offered close substitutes with market yields. Required reserve ratios have been lowered and sometimes withdrawn. Credit ceiling policies (like the British 'corset' or the French *encadrement*) were soon abandoned and foreign exchange controls as well. Banks and other deposit-taking institutions (savings banks and other thrifts alike) were allowed to enter some of each others' lines of business whereas the savings banks, as a counterpart, had to give up some tax privileges. More generally constraints on the fields of activity of banks were eased (especially in the areas of mortgage and consumer credit, capital market activities, investment banking or even insurance) while other financial (and even non-financial ones, like retailers) institutions were granted access to some banking activities.

Capital markets did not stand aside from the deregulation process. The 1975 'May Day' in Wall Street was the first move in this direction. The British 'Big Bang' in October 1986 dramatised a process which was soon to spread all over continental Europe (except for Germany, which finally converted to some deregulation only recently) but has still largely left Japan aside. Freely negotiated brokerage fees, dual capacity (i.e. the ability to act as principal and agent as well), market-making and shareholding of banks and other intermediaries in more strongly muscled market operators now feature on the main stock exchanges.

Globalisation entered the language of economists toward the end of the eighties as one of these magic words often used to portray the new financial landscape. In the first instance, it can be defined as the achievement of a single world capital market. Shrinking transaction costs (induced by an ever growing recourse to new technologies) combined with the removal of foreign exchange controls among the industrial countries were supposed to bring the integration between major capital markets of the world up to a degree never reached before. Many statistical indices have been used to give some evidence of this phenomenon: size of international transactions by banks and on the capital markets reported in the BIS statistics, daily turnover on foreign exchange markets, percentage of foreign transactions on domestic markets, share of foreign assets in portfolios of banks and institutional investors (especially pension funds and life insurance companies) etc. They generally support the globalisation hypothesis. But testing the validity of the growing financial integration hypothesis through econometric procedures[2] often showed mixed results. Today, few markets only, like the eurobond market and those for public debt of major industrial countries, may be considered as global.

New players in the financial arena and the new rules of the game

Financial innovations and deregulation were instrumental in the achievement of a new playing field in the financial services industry[3]. Banks soon saw new competitors entering onto their turf. Of course banks too were keen to try to broaden the scope of their activities. As already noted, in many countries, banks and savings institutions (the latter often non-profit orientated institutions, mutually or publicly owned) started to compete in such fields as chequeing accounts, some tax-privileged savings deposits, mortgage and personal lending. To restrict ourselves to very few examples, those of 'building societies' and 'clearing banks' in the UK or of *'banques de dépôts'*, *'caisses d'épargne'* and *'banques mutualistes et coopératives'* in France are very illustrative and have both been well documented. But there were many other areas of concern for banks. As early as the turn of the seventies in the US, money market funds and mutual funds had encroached in the market for their resources. During the second half of the eighties, French banks, too were strongly hit by the same trend. Insurance companies also tried to capture a growing share of households' long-term savings through the supply of more diversified and sophisticated products. But banks promptly reacted by entering the market for life insurance products[4]. France, where the notion of 'bancassurance' soon came into fashion at the turn of the nineties is a typical case in this respect. In the field of personal financial services at large, another major threat came from the inroads of large non-financial competitors. The success stories of the financial services subsidiaries of General Electric, Ford and Sears Roebuck in the US as well that of Marks and Spencer in the UK are now well known.

Since the beginnings of the innovation and deregulation era the border between traditional banking (i.e. supplying deposits and making loans) and capital market activities has been a hotly disputed battlefield. In all major industrial countries, an ever larger array of negotiable assets (fed by a sustained innovation process) has combined with the massive use of new technologies to support the emergence and rapid growth of money and financial markets[5]. In all countries, banks soon experienced what was then qualified as a 'disintermediation' process, i.e. losing significant market share in deposit taking and loan granting, particularly with large companies and the institutional clientele. Institutional investors, investment banks, brokerage houses and all the actors of capital markets seemed to be, at first glance, the main beneficiaries of such a shift in the financing of the economy. However, because of the narrower scope of activities previously allowed to them, commercial banks in the US were more badly hit than most of their European counterparts. Moreover, banks did not generally stand aside looking passively at disintermediation. They tried to retaliate as far as possible by entering the capital and money markets to tap resources and build up portfolios of negotiable securities. Above all, they became massively involved in securities trading for their own account. Earnings derived from the latter were expected to counterbalance the vanishing revenues from ordinary deposit-loan intermediation. In many countries, particularly the US, they battled in this way against regulations which forbade them to undertake investment (merchant) banking activities like leading and underwriting issues, broking assets, etc. International activities through the euromarkets had already provided them with a first escape. But domestic regulations had soon to be alleviated too. Deregulation of the stock exchanges in the UK and many continental European countries were thus part of a more general move, which offered new opportunities to banks in these areas. In the US, since 1990, the Fed has had to allow commercial banks to make some inroads into the securities business. The Glass-Steagall Act although still in force, is expected to be removed by the end of 1996. In Japan, under the pressure of the major 'City banks', the authorities have in 1994 alleviated article 65 of the Securities and Exchange Law of 1948. Banks could then partly hedge against lost business in their former core activities.

A first and preliminary conclusion emerges from these briefly portrayed trends. Banking had been rather clearly defined for decades. Its scope was broader or narrower according to different national regulations and historical inheritance. As a typical feature of this industry, production and distribution of banking products (services) had always been vertically integrated. The picture is now more blurred as regulatory barriers hardly settle the border between banking and other financial services, between banks and their non-financial competitors. Financial innovations and new technologies are reshaping the process of production and distribution of all financial services according to the comparative advantages of various institutions. As a logical outcome banks see new opportunities to diversify or to focus their supply of financial services according to their relative competitiveness. The question of horizontal and vertical integration in the financial services industry must also be re-examined in quite new terms. More fundamentally, innovations such as futures, options and swaps now enable banks to unbundle the major components of the intermediation process and the respective risks attached. For example, the interest (or exchange) rate risks can be so externalised and managed through markets, where other economic agents are more ready or more able to bear them.

Declining profitability, losses, failures and restructuring

Analysis and international comparisons of bank profitability raise some methodological difficulties. However many studies now agree that banks have suffered declining profitability in most industrial countries since the late seventies. The picture may have been more or less disappointing from one country to another: for example British or French banks have on average suffered much more than their German counterparts. However, since 1993, American commercial banks have clearly reversed the trend while 1995 was their third consecutive year of record profits. The British clearing banks also performed especially well in 1994 and 1995, whereas the Japanese experienced their worst performance since the Second World War. Does this mean that the declining trend has been brought to an end or that banking profits might turn more volatile in the future?

Many empirical studies have pointed to the causes of the decline of profitability, and their arguments can also support the hypothesis of higher volatility in the future. Increased competition is their first and most often cited one. Deregulation, innovations, new technologies and internationalisation indeed compounded their effects to erode the monopoly powers and the corresponding franchise of the formerly protected banking industry. Fierce competition depressed banking performance in almost the same ways in most countries. The narrowing of interest margins in the 'core business' (deposit taking and loan granting) was crucial in this respect. Shrinking demand and time deposits had to be replaced by issuing CDs or bonds at market rates so that banks had to pay more for attracting resources. At the same time, loans were yielding less on average as borrowers were able to tap alternative cheaper sources of funds, thus weakening the position of banks in this area too. To compensate for narrowing interest margins banks entered into fee-generating business on a growing scale. This induced a significant shift in the structure of their gross operating results. American commercial banks led the pack in this field so that some of them now reap close to half of their gross revenues from these areas.

This was not enough however to counteract the sweeping rise of provisions for loan losses. In the early eighties banks had experienced heavy losses on Third World eurocurrency loans. The turn of the nineties witnessed unprecedented losses on loans to real estate, medium-size companies and households. In all major industrial countries, these three sectors have benefited the most from the vigorous upsurge in bank loans induced by the liberalisation. This is no mere coincidence. The explanation can be briefly stated. Credit to these sectors had previously been most constrained by the various credit ceilings (which were tantamount to administrative rationing) as banks then preferred to serve their larger industrial customers first. The removal of these ceilings combined with the growing attractiveness of capital markets for banks' prime industrial customers to leave banks with plenty of money to lend to new clients.

Many banks were severely hit by losses. Some, even the larger ones, went bankrupt or nearly so in the US, France, Spain and Japan. The banking systems in Scandinavia collapsed, whereas some others, like the French one in 1993 and 1994[6], globally lost money. Such events revealed no more than overcapacity in the banking industry and ensuing destructive competition. The monetary authorities were often more or less compelled to bail out their banking system through an extremely accommodating policy of very low interest rates, as in the US. But these debacles sometimes proved very costly for the taxpayer not to speak of their many negative externalities on economic growth! As a classical outcome of such crises in any industry, many banking systems have entered a process of restructuring. The latter has gained an impressive momentum in the US where the system seems trying to catch up with the long-standing drawbacks of the McFadden Act[7]. It has also been significant in Scandinavia. It is more discreet and slower, but at work, in Japan and in France.

The supersonic rise of off-balance sheet activities

Bank profits did not only decline, they also seem to be now more volatile. More generally the economic environment has grown riskier during the past decade for banks and their customers alike: exchange rates, interest rates, asset prices all show higher volatility. This is often considered as an (unforeseen?) outcome of financial innovation and deregulation.

Fortunately futures, options and swaps appeared to help some economic agents to hedge these risks and to provide new opportunities to speculate to many others! Banks were prompt to understand that risk management would be the 'new border' of banking. They entered the business to satisfy customers' needs, but around the early nineties they engaged massively in the derivatives industry, acting more often as principals than as agents! The records are already impressive: in the US and Europe the off-balance sheet activities of large banks, now mainly relating to their derivatives involvement, represent around three or four times the size of their balance sheets! But for some US institutions it may reach twenty times! Such a dramatic move received a strong support (we might also say an unexpected and involuntary subsidy!) from new prudential regulations such as the Cooke ratio and its local cousins (like the European solvency directive). Banks must now be more conscious about the cost of capital and allocate their own funds according to much stricter rules. Off-balance sheet activities appear as low consumers of capital in this instance.

Securitisation of bank loans was a second (complementary) route towards the achievement of the same goal. It has been quite successful in the US, where it soon spread from mortgages and credit card receivables to ever new types of credit. European banks still lag behind their American counterparts but show growing involvement too.

Much has already been said and written on the supposedly high risks involved in these new fields of business. For some observers, the rush of banks into the derivatives and other off-balance sheet activities would be no more than a sort of desperate strategy to counteract their declining profitability. Individual cases may support this view[8]. This move, like the rise of securitisation has more radical implications, however. The emergence of a risk management industry of its own during the past decade must be related to the new opportunities provided by financial innovations and new technologies to various economic agents (financial or not) to take a part in the financial intermediation process (broadly defined) according to their risk preferences, wealth constraints, technological capabilities, etc. New approaches to the theory of financial intermediation will help us to elaborate further on this point in the second part of this paper. As such, these evolutions also belong to the more fundamental and widespread process of redesigning of the banking and financial services industry which we tried to picture in the preceding paragraphs.

2.   BANKING THEORY: THE REVOLUTION OF THE EIGHTIES

Until the late seventies banks were hardly a field of interest for economists outside the study of their role in the monetary policy transmission mechanism. However, regulatory and structural peculiarities of the US banking scene had encouraged research work in the industrial economics of banking as early as the sixties. Except for the pioneering works of Gurley and Shaw, Tobin and a few others, the theoretical understanding of their *raison d'être* and the micro-economics of banks and financial intermediaries (FIs) had remained scant.

The turn of the eighties inaugurated an era of amazing progress in these fields: asymmetric information and transaction costs are the two conceptual pillars which were to sustain the building of a quite new theory of financial intermediation. The latter now enables us to tackle such diverse issues as the existence and true nature of banks and FIs, their role *vis-à-vis* the financial markets, the dynamics of the financial services industry, the influence of financial markets and intermediaries on macroeconomic stability and the rationale for regulation and supervision of the financial sector.

Some early attempts in the theory of financial intermediaries

There may be some irony in that the first attempts by Gurley and Shaw

(1960) to provide an analysis of the role of FIs appeared only two years after the benchmark paper of Modigliani and Miller (1958). The latter provided the basis for a world where FIs need not exist, as was to be shown later by Fama (1980). For Gurley and Shaw, FIs mainly transform assets, experience economies of scale in dealing with some transaction costs inherent to financial markets and derive benefits from the diversification of larger portfolios (than those of individual investors). This approach which clearly stated the respective roles of markets and FIs laid the basis for the then 'New View' of banks and of the theory of monetary policy, as expounded by Tobin (1963). It remained unchallenged during more than fifteen years, although it missed many of the major real issues, as was to be shown later. The enlightening work of Benston and Smith (1976) tried to go ahead with the transaction costs concept as a basis for the existence of FIs. Their demonstration may appear today as an ultimate refinement of the Gurley and Shaw school of thought, but it failed however to understand what is beyond transaction costs themselves.

Enter the economics of uncertainty and information

Only one year later Leland and Pyle (1977) were to open the way to what can be labelled the information-based theory of financial intermediation. Today this theory appears as a true revolution. It first addresses the fundamental issue of why FIs exist. It then offers analytical tools to cope with various problems such as those mentioned in the introduction to this paper. Its fundamental concepts, such as asymmetric information and opportunist behaviour, and like moral hazard and adverse selection, had previously been developed in the seminal papers of Akerlof (1970) and Arrow (1974) on insurance. More generally, it owes much to the economics of uncertainty and relies largely on the notion of optimal contracts and all the ensuing ones of enforcement and verifying costs, principal, agent, etc. Since the turn of the eighties it has developed through tens of articles, but a few major themes clearly emerge.

The current theory first elaborates the two main functions of any FI: brokerage services and qualitative asset transformation. This enables it to show how and why FIs co-exist with markets for negotiable assets, why there are so many types of FIs with broader or narrower fields of activity and why banks are special among FIs. It then develops in two main directions. The first one stresses the role of FIs in the monitoring of risky projects. The second one is mainly concerned with the provision of liquidity by banks and the uniqueness of bank deposits among debt contracts.

A simple starting idea is that savers (investors) want to get some prior accurate information on the return and risk of any project they are likely to invest their funds in. A following one is that such information will be incomplete and asymmetric as the entrepreneur will always know best about the returns and risks of his own projects[9]. Such private information is also costly to obtain for the prospective investor. Relying generally on two-periods models, and under diverse sets of other hypotheses (like these about risk neutrality or risk aversion of agents), authors like Diamond (1984) or Ramakrishnan and Thakor (1984) can then show that monitoring of risks and diversification of assets portfolios performed by FIs improve allocative efficiency and economic welfare as compared with the channelling of funds through markets. Bhattacharya and Thakor (1993, 14) summarise the main results of this theoretical framework in these words: 'intermediation is a response to the inability of market mediated mechanisms to efficiently resolve informational problems'. The models consider different types of informational frictions and rationalise different types of FIs (banks, venture capitalists, financial newsletters, investment banks and bond-rating agencies among others). Some further comments can be made here. If one considers that informational frictions are responsible for various transaction costs incurred to overcome them, it is now possible to restate the current theory of FIs in terms of industrial organisation theory along post 'Coasian' terms according to which firms exist to overcome market imperfections and internalise various externalities. Thus, FIs also exist because capital markets are not as perfect and efficient as stated in the ideal world of Modigliani and Miller, Fama and others. As a corollary, every new technology, new organisational device, new financial asset which improves the availability, reliability and spreading among potential investors of information on borrowers may strengthen the role of markets for tradeable debt instruments. In such instances, new information and computer technologies massively applied to orders transmission, quotation, delivery and custody and, combined with the rise of rating agencies, have been instrumental in improving the relative efficiency of capital markets. Such a move does not preclude that FIs can also capture the benefits of similar innovations to improve their own efficiency. As a consequence, the debate about shifting frontiers between FIs and capital markets and the supposedly inescapable decline of the former receives more rational arguments and its conclusion is all but clear cut.

The uniqueness of banks among financial intermediaries has been a hotly debated issue since the beginning. For those who agree with the idea of some bank specificity, the latter derives from the monetary character of banks' demand deposits. Banks then play a crucial role in the enactment of monetary policy and as such need some form of public regulation. This had been the most commonly shared view during the Gurley and Shaw and Tobin era. Their position has been completely re-examined and restated in quite new theoretical terms since the early eighties. Authors like Diamond and Dybvig (1983) thus underline the role of banks as providers of liquidity. More precisely, in a two-period model, such authors show that non-traded bank deposits provide a liquidity insurance against random individual shocks which may hit individual preferences for the timing of consumption and disturb the formerly preferred withdrawal pattern of invested funds. Although it has also been argued by other authors, like Davis (1994), that well organised markets for tradeable debt instruments may provide such liquidity, negative externalities may at times lead to the collapse of these markets and the vanishing of liquidity. More generally, the demand deposit with banks proves superior to a tradeable debt instrument as a means to provide liquidity.

The argument for the uniqueness of banks has thus received stronger support. Theorists were also much interested in exploring its more straightforward consequences, such as bank runs and the need for deposit insurance, lender-of-last-resort facility and the ensuing public regulation and supervision of banking. This is not a mere theoretical debate. Bank runs, like some human diseases, were thought to have been definitely eradicated. But they came back to the forefront in the US with the near-collapse of the S&L industry and the wave of banking failures which culminated in the late eighties. At the same time, fixed-premium, publicly-run deposit insurance schemes which had proved satisfactory came under growing criticisms and pressure for reform (or more radically, removal). The new theory of financial intermediation helps us to pinpoint why, in which circumstances and according to which dynamic process, banks may suffer a run. It provides us with clear and undebatable arguments for public support of distressed banks so as to avoid a spreading banking panic. It also demonstrates that publicly funded deposit insurance schemes (like the American FDIC) remain necessary to ensure the stability of the banking system and how they can be improved so as to lessen the drawbacks of moral hazard on the part of bank managers and/or shareholders.

New trends in the industrial economics of financial intermediaries and of banks

Earlier studies of the banking firm and of the banking sector were mainly concerned with such issues as the existence of economies of scale, the monopolistic power of banks on local banking markets (in the US) and accordingly the discussion of the rationale for some form of public regulation. Very often, however, it was precisely the highly regulated nature of the banking sector that prevented more extensive research in the industrial economics of the banking industry. Until the early eighties, modelling the banking firm remained largely dominated by optimal portfolio management issues.

Evolutions in the banking sector (and the financial services industry) as depicted in the first part of this paper have given strong impetus to the industrial economics studies of this sector.

The debate on economies of scale has been fed by a profusion of econometric studies almost everywhere in the industrial countries. These studies, which improved on previous ones as they benefited from the use of new types of production functions (such as the translog) and of more accurate econometric methods, often broadened their scope so as to examine at the same time the issue of economies of scope. The methodologies of the various models may differ substantially, but as shown by Humphrey (1990), it is now possible to ascertain the impact of different methodologies on the conclusions of the studies. So many surveys already summarise their results that a survey of surveys might be welcome! The conclusions remain qualified although there are more convincing arguments for the existence of (often modest) economies of scale and, to a lesser extent, of scope. Some studies even point to the existence of 'super-scale' economies! The latter indeed may give some rationale for the wave of 'mega-mergers' among giant banks that we are witnessing in the US and Japan, or which are being considered in some other countries. The debate about the existence of some economies of scope is indeed inseparable from the highly controversial discussion about the removal of such regulations as the American Glass-Steagall Act or of the evaluation of the benefits and costs of financial conglomerates which have been so much in fashion in the UK and some European countries since the second half of the eighties.

Although financial innovations and deregulation have been buoyant during the past fifteen years, the theoretical and empirical work on these fields has remained rather disappointing. The analysis of the financial innovation process has been for the last twenty years largely dominated by the model of constraint-induced innovation framed by Silber (1975). Although it has proved fruitful to depict the financial innovation process in many countries and settings, this theoretical framework now falls short in many instances to explain this process after the removal of many regulatory constraints. More generally, the theory of financial innovations is very far from the degree of conceptual and theoretical sophistication achieved by the analysis of industrial innovation. Similar remarks also apply to the study of the deregulation process. Except for some studies which rely on some simple logically appealing arguments, this area has remained rather unexplored. More precisely, economists have been much more concerned with the rationale for bank regulation than with deregulation (which is not exactly its reverse). The former has made significant progress and has been restated in quite new terms, following advances in the theory of financial intermediation itself. Moral hazard and other forms of opportunist behaviour by bankers, and negative externalities attached to the failure of one bank, are among the major arguments of this renewed theory of regulation (Stiglit 1994). But progress in the analysis of deregulation of other industries (such as the airlines, telecoms and some public utilities) has had until now very few positive externalities on our theoretical understanding of deregulation in the financial services industry.

During the past five years or so, there has been much concern and debate about a so-called over-capacity in banking. The latter might well be responsible for evolutions such as shrinking margins and fees in some areas, and booming volumes of activity in others (following 'bubbles' processes rather than motivated by the rise in economic activity at large). It may also be related to the fact that at times in many countries, banking has turned globally into a loss-making industry. It calls for restructuring of banking which is indeed at work in many countries. But our understanding of this situation remains scant, except for some earlier works which underlined oligopolistic strategic moves in a deregulated context (Davis 1992) or explored the validity of the contestable markets hypothesis in some sectors like capital market activities and wholesale banking. More generally, the size of the banking industry, its frontiers with other areas of the financial services industry and non-financial agents at large is of great concern. But its analysis is still in its early steps, although very promising (Wieland 1993).

CONCLUSION

During the past fifteen years, tremendous change in the banking sector and the financial services industry has been very challenging for bankers, their competitors, the regulatory and supervisory authorities and the economic policy-makers. It has often been difficult to appraise accurately the new borders and conditions of banking and financial activities. Bankers themselves and economists have even sometimes been brought to question the survival of banks in the not so distant future. They are certainly wrong, and there is clearly some misunderstanding in the way they lay out the problem. A correct evaluation of these moves is of course critical when one tries to analyse such controversial issues as the secular decline of the banking industry and its long-run survival perspectives. Many methodological difficulties must be overcome before being able to capture in statistical figures the evolution of various kinds of financial and banking activities. Much depends on what definition of a bank you rely upon. Before the advent of innovation and deregulation, each national definition largely reflected the degree of regulatory tightness of the financial sector: commercial banks in the US corresponded to a much narrower concept of banking than the universal banks of Germany. To-day, banking may be shaped much more by the available technologies and the comparative advantages of various (and more numerous) players in the financial field. Recent advances in the theory of financial intermediation and the theory of industrial organisation fortunately provide us with new and strong arguments which give us many reasons to remain optimistic about the future of banking.

NOTES

1. One extreme (and maybe provocative) opinion supporting this view was recently expressed by Bill Gates, following the launching by Microsoft of its software 'Quicken', who compared banks to dinosaurs!
2. More precisely, if markets are fully integrated the law of one price prevails as price (or covered interest) discrepancies are arbitraged out.
3. We do not want to elaborate here on the much more complex issue of the causes and consequences of financial innovations and deregulation, which will be discussed in the second part of the paper.
4. At least as far as existing regulations did not forbid it.
5. To take only one, the French example is quite illustrative: before 1980 the bond and equity market played a very minor role in the financing of the economy which then mostly relied upon commercial banks and some powerful financial public bodies like the Caisse des Dépôts. A fast-rising public debt in the early eighties, the priority to the fight against inflation and a strong

political commitment to improve the efficiency and competitiveness of the French financial system were instrumental in the very rapid growth of the financial market and the creation of a true open money market trading commercial paper, certificates of deposit and negotiable Treasury bills.

6. Precisely, those which are members of the French Bankers' Association. The situation, although not brilliant, was not so bad for their competitors from the mutualist and non-profit-orientated sector.

7. 340 commercial banks merged in 1995. 3600 disappeared between 1980 and 1993. There were also a lot of 'mega-mergers' during the past three years like those between Chemical Bank and Manufacturers Hanover in New York or Bank of America and Security Pacific in California.

8. The failure of Barings, coming soon after the Orange County and many such derivatives affairs in the US, of course give strong arguments to all those who express fears about these risks.

9. At this point, the theory divides according to two hypotheses: the entrepreneurs possess private information about either their ex-ante returns or their ex-post realised returns.

LIST OF REFERENCES

Akerlof, G. (1970), 'The market for lemons', *Quarterly Journal of Economics,* **84**, pp. 488-500

Arrow, K.J. (1974), 'Insurance, risk and resource allocation', Chapter 5 in *Essays in the Theory of Risk Bearing* (Amsterdam: North Holland)

Bhattacharya, S. and A.V. Thakor (1993), 'Contemporary banking theory', *Journal of Financial Intermediation,* 3, 2, 250

Benston, G.J. and C.W. Smith (1976), 'A transaction cost approach to the theory of financial intermediation', *Journal of Finance,* **31**, pp. 215-31

Davis, E.P. (1992), *Debt, Financial Fragility and Systemic Risk* (Oxford: Clarendon Press)

Davis, E.P. (1994), 'Market liquidity risk', *The Competitiveness of Financial Institutions and Centres in Europe,* D.E. Fair and R.J. Raymond (eds) (Dordrecht: Kluwer Academic Press)

Diamond, D.W. (1984), 'Financial intermediation and delegated monitoring', *Review of Economic Studies,* **51**, pp. 393-414

Diamond, D.W. and P.H. Dybvig (1983), 'Bank runs, deposit insurance and liquidity', *Journal of Political Economy,* **91**, pp. 401-19

Edwards, F.R and F.S. Mishkin (1995), 'The decline of traditional banking: implications for financial stability and regulatory policy', *Federal Reserve Bank of New York, Economic Policy Review* (July)

Fama, E.F. (1980), 'Banking and the theory of finance', *Journal of Monetary Economics*, **10**, pp. 10-19

Gurley, J.G. and E.S. Shaw (1960), *Money in a Theory of Finance* (Washington D.C.: The Brookings Institution)

Humphrey, D.B. (1990), 'Why do estimates of bank scale economies differ?', *Federal Reserve Bank of Richmond Economic Review*, October, pp. 38-50

Jaffee, D. and J. Stiglit (1990), 'Credit rationing', Chapter 16, *Handbook of Monetary Economics*, B.M. Friedman and F.H. Hahn (eds) (Amsterdam: North Holland)

Leland, H. and D. Pyle (1977), 'Informational asymmetries, financial structure and financial intermediation', *The Journal of Finance*, **32**, pp. 371-87

Modigliani, F. and M. Miller (1958), 'The cost of capital, corporation finance and the theory of investment', *American Economic Review,* **48**, pp. 261-97

Ramakrishnan, R.T.S. and A.V. Thakor (1984), 'Information reliability and a theory of financial intermediation', *Review of Economic Studies*, **51**, pp. 248-83

Silber, W. (1975), *Financial Innovation* (D.C. Heath, Lexington, Mass: Lexington Books)

Stiglit, J. (1994), 'The role of state in financial markets', *Proceedings of the World Bank Annual Conference on Development Economics* (Washington D.C.)

Tobin, J. (1963), 'Commercial banks as creators of money', *Banking and Monetary Studies*, D. Carson (ed.) (Momewood, Ill.: Richard Irwin)

Wieland, B.W. (1993), 'Economic change and industry structure: the example of banking', *Journal of Institutional and Theoretical Economics*, pp. 670-89

CHAPTER 3
THE FUTURE OF 'TRADITIONAL BANKING'

Edward P.M. Gardener

1. INTRODUCTION

Never has there been such a period of practical revolutionary change in banking and financial markets as has been experienced during the past two decades. Many of these changes, especially those associated with technology and IT, are irreversible. Bankers, students of banking, strategists and policymakers need to re-appraise their views, strategies and theories in this new environment. Some banks are already re-assessing the use of the word 'bank' in their name and marketing literature.

As we approach the next millennium, there is growing interest and speculation about the future of 'traditional banking', which is usually taken to mean the banking function of financial intermediation or indirect (or institution-based) finance[1]. Associated with this 'model' of traditional banking (TB) are key respective characteristics, like the historic dominance of banks in domestic payment systems, the prevalence of supply-leading banking strategies and the widespread (and implicit regulatory) view that banks are somehow 'unique' or 'special'. Interest in the future of TB has been accompanied by an even more fundamental question: 'Is there a future for banks?'.

This paper explores the meaning, present status and future of TB from several, select but fundamental, aspects. We begin with a consideration of what is TB. This is followed by a résumé of the main forces of change and the environment of modern banking. Banking responses to these 'strategic drivers' and the associated strategic challenges are discussed. The final section considers the future for banks and banking.

There are at least three good reasons why it is important to address the fundamental questions explored in this paper. First of all, leading students like Tobin (1967) have long advocated that researchers in banking should periodically re-examine the fundamentals of the institutions they are appraising; this need is re-emphasised if banking theory is to develop (as it has done historically) using the inductive method. Secondly, it is clear that banks and banking are changing significantly in a positive (economics) sense; theoreticians, policymakers and empirical researchers cannot ignore such changes. Empirical research, for example, may be flawed at best and increasingly irrelevant at worst if there is no recognition that its underlying 'laboratory conditions' are altering. Thirdly, banking and finance are especially important sectors of economic activity. Given the relative economic significance of these sectors - see, for example, Gardener and Teppett (1995) - it is important to understand fully the nature and consequences of the changes that are taking place and are likely to occur in the future.

2. TRADITIONAL BANKING: A MICRO PERSPECTIVE

'Traditional banking' (TB) has many dimensions: some of these are tangible (for example, banks have traditionally dominated the payments mechanism) and others are often implied and invariably unprovable through conventional empirical techniques (an example would be the view that banks are somehow 'unique' and the banking franchise must consequently be protected against the systemic potentials of a bank failure).

A detailed and extensive review of banking theory was undertaken by Santomero (1984). In his review of the question why internal financial institutions exist in the financial market, Santomero (1984, 577) identified three approaches. The first of these relates to the role played by banks as asset transformers. The second focuses on the nature of the liabilities issued by banks and their central place in a monetary economy. The third approach emphasises the two-sided (assets and liabilities) nature of banks as critical explanations or rationales for their existence.

Within the first of these explanations, there are two distinct views: asset diversification and asset evaluation. The asset diversification rationale is that the banking firm is able to offer (and earn a profit in doing so) a risk-return combination in its financial assets that dominates the households' constrained set. This function[2] was a major focus of attention in 'traditional' (pre-1970s) views of the rationale for banks[3]. The second asset explanation, however, is now receiving a greater emphasis. In this sense it is reflective of recent strategic and structural changes in banking and financial markets.

Asset evaluation rationales imply that a bank is essentially an evaluator of credit risk for unsophisticated depositors. In this context, banks act as 'filters' that evaluate signals in a financial environment characterised by limited (and often costly) information. This modern approach is associated with the work of researchers like Diamond (1984): see Santomero (1984) and Bhattacharya and Thakor (1993) for reviews of the cognate literature. Within this literature the importance of asymmetric information and the role of banks as 'delegated monitors' have received a great deal of attention. In short, the emphasis has shifted from the financial intermediation function of banks (associated with the asset diversification rationale[2]) to banks as information-based firms and their special information (monitoring) skills in a deregulating financial environment.

The second of the three approaches identified by Santomero (1984) focused on the liability side of the banking balance sheet. A common feature of approaches within this grouping is the determination of positive money holdings, which is modelled as a function of transactions costs, uncertainty and relative rates of return. In this model, the monetary mechanism, together with bank pricing decisions, gives banks the opportunity to attract deposits, which may be reinvested to earn a spread. In the context of the present paper, this second rationale for banks has evolved from traditional, money-orientated views of the banking firm. Nevertheless, it is still relevant today since banks have sought to retain their dominance of payments systems. For example, Santomero (1984, 580) points out '... the ease of transfer between accounts, the development of cash dispensing options nationwide, and the advent of home banking are all central to the evolution of the banking system's monopoly position.' Nevertheless, the modern bank (compared with TB) is facing increasing competition in its traditional dominance of payments systems and the 'monopoly on moneyness' embodied traditionally within banking liabilities. In Europe banks are likely to see their traditional dominance of domestic payments systems significantly eroded during the next decade: see Arthur Andersen (1993).

The two-sided nature of the banking firm, the third of Santomero's (1984) sets of rationales, is grounded in a more specialised literature. In this literature, covariance between the return on deposits and loans is seen as stimulating intermediation by incentivising the risk-averse maximiser to transform deposits into loans. Like some of the other explanations for the existence of banks, this view assumes some kind of deviation from perfect market assumptions.

A more recent review of the modern rationale for banking was provided by Bhattacharya and Thakor (1993), who focused on theoretical developments during the fifteen years up to 1993. They point out that the theory of banking has been 'substantially reconfigured' during these years in the face of a plethora of financial innovations and advances in information economics and option pricing. The focus in this more recent review is on the role of banks and other financial intermediaries (FIs) in providing brokerage and qualitative asset transformation (QAT) services. Figure 3.1 summarises the brokerage and QAT functions of banks. For present purposes, Bhattacharya and Thakor's (1993) main findings are as follows:

- FIs reduce the cost of transacting with services ranging from brokerage to attribute transformation.
- With informational asymmetries, both depository and non-depository FIs gain from an increase in size because of lower incentive costs per agent. That is, the costs of brokerage as well as QAT are lowered indefinitely by diversification. However, in many circumstances, intermediaries will be of finite size.
- Given significant informational asymmetries regarding borrowers, bank loans are special in that they signal quality in a way that other forms of credit do not.
- Banks enhance aggregate investment and also improve its quality.

The Bhattacharya and Thakor (1993) review, then, re-affirms the increasing 'information-orientated' emphasis on the modern banking firm. Informational frictions, or asymmetries, and respective bank expertise in collecting, storing, analysing and generally using information resources have become increasingly emphasised in modern rationales for banking.

3. A STRATEGY PERSPECTIVE

Practical bank strategies and strategic characteristics of banking provide another, important 'model framework' of TB. A noteworthy strategic characteristic of TB has been the major dominance of supply-side strategies. This is symptomatic of the so-called 'production era' in a 'logical-historical-order view' of the evolution of the modern banking firm: see Clarke *et al.* (1988, 10). During this phase the banking emphasis is on producing and selling. Banks have a predominantly inward-looking (supply-orientated) focus; the banking firm effectively determines the 'four Ps' (place, price, people and promotion) rather than the market (demand).

The movement of banks away from this state is the product of many modern forces, most notably deregulation (*de facto*[4] and *de jure*), intensifying competition and technology. In this 'model' of the evolution of the modern banking firm, banks are seen as evolving from the 'production era' through the 'promotion era' to the 'marketing-control

Figure 3.1   Financial intermediary functions

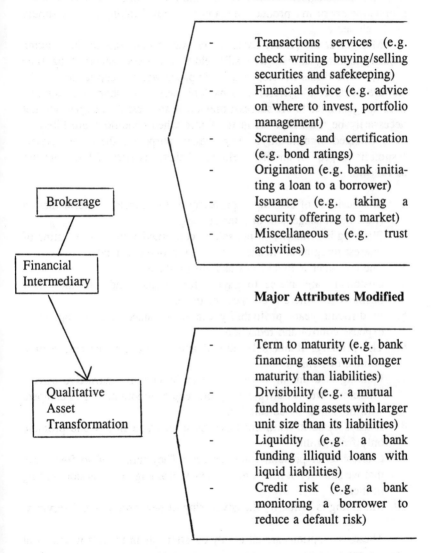

Services Provided

- Transactions services (e.g. check writing buying/selling securities and safekeeping)
- Financial advice (e.g. advice on where to invest, portfolio management)
- Screening and certification (e.g. bond ratings)
- Origination (e.g. bank initiating a loan to a borrower)
- Issuance (e.g. taking a security offering to market)
- Miscellaneous (e.g. trust activities)

Brokerage

Financial Intermediary

Major Attributes Modified

- Term to maturity (e.g. bank financing assets with longer maturity than liabilities)
- Divisibility (e.g. a mutual fund holding assets with larger unit size than its liabilities)
- Liquidity (e.g. a bank funding illiquid loans with liquid liabilities)
- Credit risk (e.g. a bank monitoring a borrower to reduce a default risk)

Qualitative Asset Transformation

Source: Bhattacharya and Thakor (1993, Figure 1, 8)

era': see Clarke *et al.* (1988, 9-11). Within this evolutionary model, the market (demand) increasingly influences and ultimately tends to dominate in banking strategies. TB is located within this model framework in the production era or in a production era view of how banking strategy should be developed[5].

Metzger *et al.* (1984) listed ten classic assumptions of the banking industry that they argued were still held by many US bankers at that time (1984). The thesis developed in their paper was the application of the 'failure of success' syndrome to modern banks. In short, past success does not guarantee future success; previously successful strategies will not necessarily be the best ones in the future when conditions are likely to have changed significantly. For present purposes, these 'ten classic assumptions' provide another useful set of characteristics of TB. They are as follows:

1. The business of banking is primarily that of financial intermediation (i.e., the management of interest margins).
2. Planning is primarily, if not solely, concerned with the forecasting of interest margins as dictated by current economic trends.
3. The customer is loyal to us and our products.
4. Customers are averse to paying for services and will take their business elsewhere if charged for them.
5. In difficult years profitability can be regained through operating expense control and reduction.
6. The primary, if not sole, use of automation is to process a high volume of items faster.
7. Banking is a unique business and an honourable, attractive career. Therefore, we will always get good people without having to compete with industrial-based salaries.
8. It takes years to learn our business so delegate slowly and promote only from within.
9. Clerical/teller personnel are suspect. They turn over so frequently that we should not invest much money, training or career counselling in them.
10. Marketing is primarily the advertising of new products and services.

These assumptions are all highly questionable in today's world. But for present purposes they provide a good perspective of the strategic environment and managerial 'frame of reference' of TB compared with modern banking.

Metzger *et al.* (1984) go on to show why each of these assumptions is wrong and strategically misleading in modern financial markets. We shall just draw out selectively some of their main criticisms in the following summary:

- Banking is now a widening financial services industry (FSI); banks are best seen as financial services firms (FSFs) operating within the wider (and constantly growing/changing) FSI. Market needs drive banking strategies. Managing interest margins is still important (especially in a world where interest rates have become more unpredictable), but it is only one of many key areas that need managing.

- Strategic planning (a competitive tool) is not the same as budgeting (a financial exercise). Strategic planning also encompasses operations, human resources and marketing.

- Customers have learnt that their loyalty is no guarantee of getting the best return from their bank. Customers are now more sophisticated and are prepared to 'shop around'.

- Banks need to increase their fee income in the face of shrinking interest margins. Customers are demanding more customised products for particular needs, but then will only pay for 'clearly perceived value received'.

- A strong US banking view emerged in the 1980s that cost saving, by itself, does not ensure future banking profitability. A cost-saving emphasis can lead to a strategic, or cultural, shift away from customer service within a bank[6]. It is argued that future profitability is best ensured through investing in strategic and market planning, new technological expertise, new services and in better trained staff.

- Besides processing a greater number of items faster, a key function of automation is also to provide bankers with better information in order to make more effective decisions. Better information is becoming even more important for successful bank decision making.

- The modern bank is now an FSF. New kinds of expertise and better training are needed in order to compete effectively. Banks (should) have to compete for better quality staff, who tend to be correspondingly more mobile. Metzger *et al.* (1984, 3) point out: 'The weakest asset the industry has today is management itself, inexperienced and unsophisticated merchandisers'.

- Banking is best viewed as an industry that is neither 'mysterious' nor 'special'. It is important that high quality people are attracted into banking and given the opportunity to implement their ideas and acquire experience through delegation and greater autonomy.

■ Clerical, and particularly teller, staff are the 'point of sale' in banking. They are often the key contact point in building up a good customer relationship. They should be selected and trained with these functions in mind.

■ Advertising is only one of the many facets of marketing.

Metzger *et al.* (1984, 32-34) suggest the following 'replacement assumptions' for modern banking[7]:

■ Interest rates are no longer predictable
■ Marketing must drive the bank
■ Differentiation is the key to success
■ Customers are willing to pay for value received
■ Productivity is a major key to profitability
■ Retail markets are constantly shifting and changing
■ Banking is now the business of financial services merchandising
■ Strategic planning is only as effective as its implementation

In the present context, these eight new assumptions can be used to differentiate TB from the modern bank: the FSF operating within a widening, more competitive and ever-changing FSI.

4. THE FORCES OF CHANGE[8]

The forces of change in European (and global) banking have been subject to a great deal of analysis and speculation during recent years: for example, see Arthur Andersen (1993), Canals (1993), Mullineux (1992), Revell (1994) and Gardener and Molyneux (1993). Throughout the 1980s and early 1990s, banking and financial markets in the EU evolved from being comparatively protected towards more open, or contestable, markets. Historically, protective regulation, together with 'traditional' precedents and conventions (or implicit regulation), helped to segment different groupings of financial institutions and markets. Of course, financial markets have been more open and more rapidly deregulated in some European countries than in others.

The main forces of change identified in a recent survey (Arthur Andersen 1993) are summarised in Figure 3.2. This same survey found that regulatory developments, competition and technology were generally felt to be the three most important broad forces of change in European banking and financial markets.

Figure 3.2 The forces for banking change

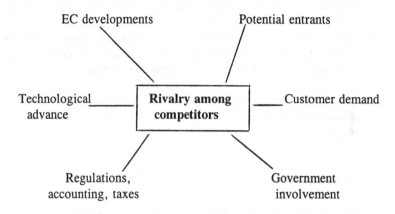

Source: Arthur Andersen (1993, Figure 1.1, 1)

Other similar taxonomies (to Figure 3.2) are also revealing and provide a broader picture of the forces that have changed much of TB in many EU banking markets. Although competition, regulation (including deregulation towards greater competition and re-regulating in risk-containing areas, like capital adequacy) and technology are generally recognised as the three, most fundamental pressures for change in banking, other (usually associated) changes are also important. Some of the most important of these are as follows:

■ 'Integration' (or globalisation), where markets (both domestic and international) that were previously segmented become more integrated through the development of new instruments (like money market funds and swaps) that straddle previously segmented markets
■ 'Securitisation' refers generally to the increasing channelling of credit flows (credit intermediation) through open financial markets rather than through the traditional banking system

- 'Institutionalisation', which refers to 'financial deepening' with the growth of new kinds of FI and new forms of financial intermediation
- 'Innovation' in terms of financial instruments, financial markets, market and institutional practices, and, of course, technology
- 'Universality' applies to the growth of more diversified and wider, deeper ('universal') product mixes being developed by many FSFs as traditional segmented and differentiated markets (and institutions) give way to 'all-purpose banking'
- 'Specialisation' has also emerged as an important strategy with some banks and other FSFs deciding to play to their traditional strengths and proven, tested expertise in the new marketplace

Other and more extensive 'taxonomies of change' exist, but the preceding captures some of the most important 'change drivers' during recent years.

5. BANKING ENVIRONMENT

Banking structures and strategies are now involved in a rather fundamental process of re-alignment and development. Concentration, for example, has increased in many domestic EU banking markets as banks have sought to defend their domestic positions. Of course, many of the changes that are taking place are not only structural; many of them reflect social and macro-economic developments within the EU.

Social changes include the ageing population, better-informed (more sophisticated and demanding) customers and the increasing acceptance amongst many consumers that all financial services should be immediately 'on tap'. This latter view, for example, is stimulating the European financial services industry towards the so-called 'virtual bank model' in retail banking and away from the 'traditional bank model'[9], the TB. In this setting, the traditional bank model is based on the branch. In the virtual model, on the other hand, banks use a variety of different delivery systems (like telephone banking, home banking and ATMs) to facilitate customers' direct access to banking services irrespective of their geographic location. Multichannel delivery systems (including direct mailing) are a distinguishing characteristic of the so-called 'virtual bank model'. The virtual bank is also more willing to form strategic alliances with another bank or company in order to improve its competitive position. It is also more orientated towards co-ordinating inputs from various organisations into a final product rather than just attempting to produce everything 'in house'.

The ageing population has *inter alia* stimulated banks to develop and extend the range of their savings and pension products. It has also been a factor in recent bancassurance, or Allfinanz, moves by banks and insurers in many European countries. As we saw earlier, better-informed and more discriminating customers have resulted in a much greater demand orientation in banking strategies. This has had a marked impact on strategy as banks have become more market-orientated. For instance, banks have given a much higher strategic priority to marketing and related aims like customer focus, customer satisfaction, market share and employee productivity.

Macro-economic changes are also important factors in shaping the banking environment. In the previous section the importance of banking regulation as a force for change was emphasised. During the 1980s more volatile interest rates, exchange rates and inflation were also key features of the banking environment. During the 1990s EMU, the SEM (Single European Market), continued privatisation (reduced state direct involvement) in EU financial sectors, a reduced state role in pensions provision and the opening up of Central and Eastern Europe are likely to be comparatively important.

There are many indicators that the global banking industry has been under considerable pressure within the contemporary environment. Declining bank ROEs, tighter margins, capital adequacy under strain and reduced ratings for some banks are just a sample of these kinds of indicators. More consolidation, increased rationalisation, some failures and banking profits under intensifying pressure have been part of the evolving EU banking scenario for some time. Against this background, the following changes appear to be especially important as banks approach the year 2000:

- Profitability and ROE will become increasingly important, and 'size for size's sake' will be de-emphasised; profitable growth will be the order of the day
- Capital standards will improve as banks become more orientated towards and skilled in managing their overall risks and return
- The banking industry will become more efficient (producing more job losses) as a result of technology investment
- A growing proportion of bank income will come from trading activities

- Securitisation will help to de-emphasise lending, and there will generally be a greater banking orientation towards capital markets
- Bank funding costs will remain high with banks fighting to retain core deposits; fee and commission income will become more emphasised
- Savings products will drive retail banking business; mortgages will be the main source of loan growth, and pension products will be attractive areas of new business

This kind of scenario has emerged from recent survey evidence - for example, see Arthur Andersen (1993) and Gemini/EFMA (1992) - and the views of analysts like Morgan Stanley (1994). Within this challenging but increasingly hostile banking environment more consolidation and restructuring within the banking industry seem a likely scenario for many EU countries.

6. BANK RESPONSE AND MANAGERIAL CHALLENGES

Within this environment, banks have focused strongly on attempts to improve (reduce) their cost/income ratios; rationalisation has been one of the major responses. Faced with the preceding environmental developments, serious asset quality problems (increased risks) and stagnating (and in some cases falling) profits, banks globally have emphasised the importance of cost management. Three relevant findings from a recent study (Salomon Brothers 1993) found *inter alia* the following:

- Few banks have achieved consistent reductions in their cost/income ratios since around the mid-1980s (only in the UK, US and Spain have total bank staffing and branch numbers declined up to 1991, the date of the Salomon Brothers study)
- There is a comparative wide range of cost/income ratios for banks in many countries
- Many banks have followed successfully policies that have reduced their cost/income ratios.

Table 3.1 shows one aspect of the restructuring of the banking industry now under way across the EU. The French, Italian and German banking industries have been slower to rationalise than many other EU countries because of labour constraints. In the UK, Spain and the Nordic countries, however, there has been an improvement in efficiency with the attrition of staff numbers and branches. Table 3.1 (Section b) also implies the potential for greater use of automation in countries like Belgium, Germany and Italy compared with the UK, Switzerland and France.

Table 3.1 Branches and ATMs in Europe

(a) Branches[1] per country

	End-1987	End 1991	End 1992
Belgium	9,984	10,178	10,379
France	25,492	25,589	25,479
Germany	44,207	49,169	49,685
Italy	15,365	19,078	20,789
Netherlands	5,718	5,520	5,168
Sweden	3,498	3,064	2,910
Switzerland	4,005	4,190	4,111
UK	21,961	19,475	19,024

(b) ATMs per million people

	1988	1992
Belgium	85	109
France	206	305
Germany	122	235
Italy	99	245
Netherlands	69	263
Sweden	206	254
Swtizerland	262	387
UK	245	316

Source: Morgan Stanley (1994, Tables 8 and 9, 6 and 7)
Note: 1. Commercial, savings, co-operative and rural banks

Rationalisation, restructuring and consolidation summarise a great deal (and a wide variety) of the responses by banks to the new and developing environment in Europe. The deregulation-induced cycle of enhanced competition, lower margins and profits, and consolidation or specialisation is one crude view of the dynamics of the kind of banking pressures now being experienced. A sustained period of reconstruction now characterises the European banking industry as the present apparent 'excess capacity' is eroded in the EU banking market. Some of the broader strategic options available to banks appear to be growth through acquisition, to be acquired or to become more specialised; failure, or exit, is another option. Most banks will no longer be able to provide 'all things to all men'. Table 3.2 illustrates the considerable differences that exist in overbanking (measured crudely by assets per bank and capital per bank) throughout the EU. It suggests that the scope for rationalisation is greater in some countries (like Italy) compared with others.

Table 3.2 Rationalisation of the European banking industry

Country	No. of banks in top 1000	Assets $bn	Assets per bank $bn	Capital $bn	Capital per bank $m	Capital as % of GDP
Austria	20	248	12.4	11.1	554	6.0
Belgium	10	444	44.4	12.3	1,230	5.6
Denmark	11	155	14.1	7.4	671	5.2
Finland	7	110	15.7	5.4	778	5.0
France	24	2,048	85.3	81.5	3,395	6.2
Germany	85	2,648	31.2	84.6	995	4.8
Ireland	2	53	26.5	2.6	1,315	5.4
Italy	91	1,464	16.1	79.9	877	6.5
Netherlands	13	653	50.2	30.5	2,346	9.5
Norway	6	71	11.8	2.6	426	2.3
Spain	45	690	15.3	42.1	936	7.3
Sweden	9	283	31.4	10.6	1,178	4.3
Switzerland	32	715	22.3	39.5	1,234	16.3
UK	33	1,217	36.9	56.0	1,698	5.4

Source: Morgan Stanley (1994, Table 15, 11)

One of the major strategic developments in Europe is bancassurance, or Allfinanz; the coming together of previously segmented life insurance and retail banking sectors. The essence of this concept is the provision of a full range of financial services by a FSF to its customers. Although the two main areas affected are traditional retail (consumer) banking and life insurance, the concept can be extended to all personal financial services (including general insurance) and to business customers. Banks and insurers have followed several approaches in implementing bancassurance or Allfinanz (see Lafferty 1991).

7. STRATEGIC CHALLENGES

These examples, illustrating the scale and depth of the changes under way in the EU banking industry, have raised many strategic challenges. In the case of bancassurance, for example, there is recent empirical evidence[10] that banks are not so successful at cross-selling products (a key strategic motive behind many bancassurance moves) as they might like to be. There are also problems of 'corporate culture clashes' when banks seek to work closely or develop any kind of working partnership with another type of FSF. These kinds of managerial 'culture clashes' can be exacerbated when cross-country differences are also involved if FSFs in different countries seek to co-operate[11].

A major challenge for many banks (and to TB) has been the need to develop a greater 'market orientation' within their strategies and operations: see for example Gibson and Donnelly (1985), Clarke *et al.* (1988) and *International Journal of Bank Marketing* (1990, 3-15). This has meant that the TB culture (typically characterised by an inward focus within the organisation, a skills orientation and short-term planning horizon) has had to change (see the previous Section 3). The desired market-orientated culture implies a greater outward-looking focus that is more concerned with the market, with external demand. Marketing departments and the marketing ethos, under the pressure of the 'unseen hand', have helped to change banks from inward looking 'producers' into marketing institutions. Making these kinds of changes away from TB has not been easy or costless. Also, in some cases, banks may have attempted to become excessively market-orientated[12].

Two general, strategic priorities have been questioned in the current environment. One is the unqualified acceptance that banking strategies should be wholly demand- (or market-) driven. In many banks it appears that supply-side factors[13] may need to be given a higher priority in shaping successful banking strategies: see, for example, Gardener (1994, 75) and Abraham and Lierman (1991). We saw earlier (in Section 3) that another (and related) cautionary note is sounded by McLean (1994). She argues that banks run the risk in the contemporary environment of being too cost conscious; banks can follow one of two cultural 'models' in the 1990s, the cost-control culture (which prioritises cost containment) and the customer-service culture (which prioritises customer satisfaction). The danger is that a cost-control culture may be at the expense of customer service, and the longer-term consequences of such a strategy have yet to be seen.

After the strong market-orientated drives of the 1980s, many banks (especially in the UK) are reconsidering where their future best lies. The drive to be a universal bank and to follow every shift in market demand are being reappraised. In part this is reflective of the present strategic emphasis by banks on their cost management, meaning cost cutting (see the earlier Section 5), but it is more than this alone. Many banks believe that their most profitable (and safer) future lies in 'playing to their strengths'. This has led to the shedding of some of their existing and previously planned products and services.

Another fundamental challenge to TB has been the inexorable rise of securitisation. Bryan (1994, 42) points out in this general connection: 'Bank intermediation - the use of banks as "middlemen" in allocating capital - is very expensive and, when compared with securities intermediation, is inefficient at absorbing and diversifying risk'. In the past (and under TB) various barriers have constrained all economic units from accessing the securities business system for the majority of banking services. Bryan (1994, 42) points out:

> To overcome these barriers, particularly in US markets, the securities industry applied both hard and soft technologies. Volumes in money-market and bond funds - as well as in commercial paper, mortgage-backed securities, and pooled receivable notes - have exploded, at the expense of deposit-based intermediation. This process is likely to unfold in Europe and elsewhere with about a six-to-ten year lag behind the US.

Banks have three basic choices in this new environment; these choices are not necessarily mutually exclusive.

First of all they can develop their own investment banking capabilities and de-emphasise at least some of their traditional and less profitable financial intermediation skills. Secondly, they can seek to 'play to their strengths'; for example, banks may specialise in areas in which they have established skills that they can develop. A related strategy under this heading is to specialise in particular stages of credit intermediation, like initial credit appraisal and origination. A third option is to attempt to take on more risk without having to pay the necessary premium. However, attempting to 'fool the market' in this way is, at best, a short-run and an increasingly difficult option in today's deregulating financial environment; at worst, this third option is a strategy for decline and possible exit from the industry.

Securitisation is part of a much wider process that emphasises the need to 'add value' within a financial transaction. This process may be called 'marketisation': a rough definition is that it refers to the increasing and inexorable drive towards subjecting all financial transactions to the test of a liberalising market[14]. If banks are not able to 'add value', they need to adapt and reconfigure their portfolio in order to achieve 'value added'. In a real sense this is reflective of the most fundamental 'strategic driver' that differentiates TB from banking of today and tomorrow. This 'driver' is the increasing need for the modern bank to recognise that it is ultimately the consensus of an increasingly more freely functioning financial market supplied with more information than ever before about banking performance and condition that will decide whether a bank is 'successful' and ultimately 'viable'.

This 'marketisation' trend is the inevitable consequence of deregulation and bankers' own lobbying for greater freedoms. The result is that banks will increasingly have to consider 'shareholder wealth maximisation' as a more fundamental and pressing strategic and operational target. The practical relevance of this objective was explored in US banking by Leemputte and Kearney (1990). US banks that restructured during the 1980s without recognising the difference between accounting and 'real', or 'economic', profit did not achieve 'value added', improved share value performance.

A result of these developments is that the modern bank has to pay much closer attention towards achieving 'value added' within its portfolio of activities, existing and planned. Society and business today are increasingly driven by value added rather than more traditional 'values' like loyalty to the organisation and appeals to historic conventions and precedents. In a practical context this means *inter alia* that modern banks must seek to allocate internally their own capital and other resources on an effective risk and return basis. This has lead to the recent rise of more sophisticated risk-adjusted-return-on-capital techniques within banks. More effective (in trading off risk and corresponding return) pricing and the development of more efficient internal risk-management cultures within banks are also prioritised in this new environment. Within this general context, improving a bank's productive efficiency (cost management) is a necessary first step towards shareholder wealth maximisation.

Securitisation and marketisation have brought a new emphasis for banks to manage effectively the risks and corresponding returns within their own portfolios, existing and planned. In one sense this vision returns us to the modern micro-economic rationale for banks and the contemporary emphasis on more freely-functioning financial markets and information economics. There is a kind of 'double-edged sword' within these two contemporary trends. Securitisation means *inter alia* that better rated credits increasingly go to open financial markets; banks are consequently left with the poorer credits (adverse selection). As a result the need for even better credit management skills within banking is re-emphasised. With growing marketisation, however, the market will increasingly 'test' (through 'value added' tests) the ability of banks to respond efficiently to these new challenges.

8. CONCLUSIONS: THE BANK OF THE FUTURE

What is clear from the preceding survey is that TB, meaning essentially banking of the pre-1970s, has changed markedly in modern deregulating financial systems. In many respects it has changed almost beyond recognition. Deregulation and other trends have also produced an 'excess capacity' problem (an opportunity for some banks) in many systems, which is being addressed through restructuring and consolidation. In one sense, this phase is to be expected following an era of essentially protective regulation for banks.

The question that I was asked to explore was the future of traditional banking (TB). One conclusion that I draw is that much of TB has a reducing relevance, and in many cases no relevance at all, within the contemporary and developing financial market. In Section 3, for example, it was emphasised that banks are now FSFs operating within a wider, constantly changing FSI. We explored selectively the most important 'change drivers' that have moved TB towards the modern FSF. We saw in Section 5, for example, that the so-called 'virtual bank model' is replacing the 'traditional bank model' in modern retail banking. In all banking product/market segments intensifying competition and the need for banks to 'add value' are increasingly driving bank strategies. All of these developments have changed the face of TB.

'TB is dead; long live banking' is my next conclusion. Despite the negative views of some students, I do not believe that banking is a doomed industry. Banks are not necessary in the future, but banking will be; successful banks have to recognise this market reality. We have already discussed (for example in Section 7) the challenges that the bank of the future will face and how some of these challenges are likely to be addressed. For example, the bank of the future will be an institution that successfully manages the need to locate and 'add value' through its portfolio of activities, on and off the balance sheet. Although the world is changing, human nature is unlikely to do so. Sanford (1994, 19) points out in this connection: 'A very basic element of that nature is a hunger for security - law and order, job security, retirement security, decent and affordable health care, and financial security'. Banks can continue to be competitive in providing the basic financial functions[15] needed by more financially sophisticated and demanding customers. The most successful banks are likely to recognise increasingly and target their comparative advantages within the characteristic set[16] that delineates the existence of a 'value-producing'[17] product or service. One of the recent lessons in banking is that the bank of the future will need to carry its customers with it. Technology must be increasingly seen, targeted and marketed as a vehicle to improve customer service[18]. The bank of the future will face ever more severe marketing challenges as technology increasingly distances banks from their customers.

The bank of the future will also have to pay close attention to the quality and support of its own 'human capital', its staff, and still one of the most valuable resources within a bank. Although staff levels are likely to reduce further with technology advances, the corresponding importance of effective HRM policies is likely to be enhanced. In the bank of the future, a smaller number of more highly trained staff will inevitably have more internal influence and potential 'power' over all of the bank's resources.

Brown (1995) summarises Morgan Stanley's vision of the 'Bank of the Year 2000'. This bank would have:

- capital adequacy and ratings to attract funds on the finest terms
- the ability to support customers through lending and/or the underwriting and distribution of securities domestically and internationally
- a significant presence in international fund management and domestic savings products, including private banking

■ management focused on profitability through tight credit controls and efficient use of staff resources and technology.

Although these might seem rather obvious, Brown (1995) believes that very few banks in Europe will be able to achieve these objectives. He goes on to suggest: 'Only time will tell if the strategy of investment banking and international fund management is less risky than LDC and property lending and buying into foreign banks without the necessary expertise.' He suggests that the best prospects for growth in banking income within the bank of the future lie in capital markets, fund management, life assurance and private banking.

Banking, then, has a potentially exciting, but inevitably more demanding future. 'TB is dead, long live banking', however, requires one important *caveat*, with which I will conclude my survey. This *caveat* relates to the wider macro and regulatory view of banking. It revolves around the question about whether banks will continue to be regarded as 'unique' or 'special' by governments. Governmental (and the associated regulatory) views, implicit or explicit, on this fundamental question may have a bearing on how some banks can effectively manage their risk and return trade-offs.

If governments continue to regard banks as 'special', they will continue to seek to protect the banking franchise. On the one hand, this means that banks will remain subjected to (probably ever more) supervisory re-regulation in areas like capital adequacy; this increases the potential costs of bank intermediation. On the other hand, it implies that governments and central banks will continue to behave as if contagion, or systemic, risk is an inherent possibility in a bank failure - especially in the case of a big (core) bank or a particularly important one.

It seems unlikely that most governments will shortly abandon these implicit 'too big' or 'too important to fail' policies, even though no central bank would admit to such a policy for obvious reasons. Although the US government and the Bank of England have (and are developing) a more market-orientated approach towards bank collapses (potential and actual), it seems unlikely that either would allow a core or important bank to fail. Most other central banks are much less market-orientated. Coupled with deposit insurance and the lack of an effective market in bank corporate control within Europe, moral hazard remains a 'traditional' banking problem. In this specific respect, one must conclude 'TB is dead; long live TB'.

NOTES

1. As contrasted with Gurley and Shaw (1962) direct finance: that is, market-based intermediation or securitisation.
2. Though transforming large-denomination financial assets ('primary assets' in Gurley and Shaw terminology) into smaller units ('secondary securities').
3. These traditional views were developed by leading students like Gurley and Shaw (1962).
4. *De facto* deregulation can occur when, say, a technological development (like telephone banking) allows new competitors into a market segment previously dominated by a 'traditional' FI.
5. It will become clear later in this paper (Section 6) that this is not to imply that modern banks should ignore supply-side considerations in their strategies: see, for example, Abraham and Lierman (1991).
6. For example, see McLean (1994).
7. Metzger *et al.* (1984) were primarily talking about retail banking, but many of their proposals have an applicability to banking in general.
8. This and the following two sections draw on Gardener (1995).
9. See *Retail Banker International* (1994).
10. See, for example, *The Banker* (July 1993, 68-69).
11. There are, of course, many good examples of successes to date with these kinds of ventures, like the strategic link between the German Dresdner Bank and the French Banque Nationale de Paris.
12. For example, many banks and other institutions in the build-up to London's Big Bang during the 1980s were highly 'market driven': see Gardener (1990). This led to an implicit downgrading of their own internal resources and constraints, and an apparent 'follow the herd' behaviour pattern rapidly developed.
13. Like the bank's own internal staff resources and morale, together with the bank's managerial capability to handle certain kinds of change.
14. The 'market' in this context includes external stakeholders like investors, bank analysts and bank supervisors.
15. Sandford (1994, 20) lists these as financing, risk management, trading and positioning, advising and transaction processing.
16. This 'characteristic set' view covers both the extant attributes of a product or service and the 'downstream' chain of activities that are needed to produce it, put it into a 'value producing' form for the market.

17. 'Value producing', in this sense, has two complementary dimensions. First, the customer has to perceive the product or service as producing 'value' (some kind of needed service) for him/her. The second of the two dimensions is that the product/service must also 'add value' (generate 'real' profit) for the bank itself. These complementary requirements are well-known to modern bank marketeers.
18. See, for example, Wanless (1993).

LIST OF REFERENCES

Abraham, J.P. and F. Lierman (1991), 'European banking strategies in the nineties: a supply side approach', IEF Research Papers in Banking and Finance RP 91/8 (Bangor: Institute of European Finance)

Arthur Andersen and Andersen Consulting (1993), *European Banking and Capital Markets: A Strategic Forecast*, The Economist Intelligence Unit, London

Banker, The (1993), 'The road to ruin', July, pp. 68-69

Bhattacharya, S. and A.V. Thakor (1993), 'Contemporary banking theory', *Journal of Financial Intermediation*, **3**, pp. 2-50

Brown, Keith (1995), 'The Bank of the Year 2000 comes closer', *Morgan Stanley European Banking Strategy*, 4 May, pp. 1-36

Bryan, Lowell L. (1994), 'The forces transforming global financial markets', *Bank Management Magazine*, March/April, pp. 40-45

Canals, Jordi (1993), *Competitive Strategies in European Banking* (Oxford: Clarendon Press)

Clarke, P.D., E.P.M Gardener, P. Feeney and P. Molyneux (1988), 'The genesis of strategic marketing control in British retail banking', *The International Journal of Bank Marketing*, **6**, 2, 5-19

Davis, Evan, Claire Gouzouli, Magnus Spence and Jonathan Star (1993), 'Measuring the performance of banks', *Business Strategy Review*, **4**, 1 (Autumn), 1-14

Diamond, D.W. (1984), 'Financial intermediation and delegated monitoring', *Review of Economic Studies*, **51**, pp. 393-414

Gardener, Edward P.M. (1990), 'A strategic perspective of bank financial conglomerates in London after the crash', *Journal of Management Studies*, **27**, 1 (January), 61-73

Gardener, Edward P.M. (1994), 'Bank marketing organisation and performance' in Jack Revell (ed.), *The Changing Face of European Banks and Securities Markets* (Basingstoke and London: Macmillan)

Gardener, Edward P.M. (1995), 'Banking strategies in the European Union: financial services firms after the Cecchini Report' forthcoming (1995) in *Perspectivas del Sistema Financiero*

Gardener, Edward P.M. and Philip Molyneux (1993), *Changes in Western European Banking: an International Banker's Guide* (London: Routledge)

Gardener, Edward P.M. and Jonathan L. Teppett (1995), 'A select replication of the Cecchini microeconomic methodology on the EFTA financial services sectors: a note and critique', *The Service Industries Journal*, **15**, 1, (January) 74-89

Gemini/EFMA (1992), *European Banking: A View to 2005* (Paris: EFMA, Gemini Consulting)

Gibson, J.L. and J.H. Donnelly Jr (1985), 'Integrating organisational structure and strategy; achieving a market-oriented financial institution', *Journal of Retail Banking*, **7**, 3 (Fall) 13-22

Gurley, J. and E. Shaw (1960), *Money in a Theory of Finance* (Washington DC: Brookings)

International Journal of Bank Marketing (1990), 'The changing face of banking', **8**, 5, 3-15

Lafferty Business Research (1991), *The Allfinanz Revolution: Winning Strategies for the 1990s* (Dublin: Lafferty Publications)

Leemputte, Patrick J. and Mary E. Kearney (1990), 'Where is value created in your retail business?', *Journal of Retail Banking*, **12**, 4 (Winter) 7-18

McLean, Jan (1994), 'Looking after the customer', *The Banker*, May, pp. 64-5

Metzger, R.O., I.I. Mitroff and S.E. Rau (1984), 'Challenging the strategic assumptions of the banking industry', *The Bankers Magazine*, July-August, pp. 29-34

Morgan Stanley (1994), *European Banking Strategy: New Fundamentals for the Bank of the Year 2000*, Morgan Stanley, London

Mullineux, Andy (ed.) (1992), *European Banking* (Oxford: Basil Blackwell)

Retail Banker International (1994), 'Moving towards the virtual bank', 15 April, p. 10

Revell, Jack (ed.) (1994), *The Changing Face of European Banks and Securities Markets* (Basingstoke and London: Macmillan)

Salomon Brothers (1993), *Cost Management In Global Banking: The Lessons of the Low Cost Producers*, Salomon Brothers, New York

Sanford, Charles S. Jr (1994), 'Financial markets in 2020', *Federal Reserve Bank of Kansas City, Economic Review*, **17**, 1, 19-28

Santomero, A.M. (1984), 'Modelling the banking firm', *Journal of Money, Credit and Banking*, **16**, 4, November, 576-602

Tobin, James (1967), Comment on Allan H. Meltzer, 'Major issues in the regulation of financial institutions' in *Journal of Political Economy*, August, pp. 508-9

Wanless, Derek (1993), 'NatWest's vision - where the customer rules', *Banking World*, November, pp. 8-9

CHAPTER 4
COMMENTS OF DISCUSSANTS
Jean-Paul Abraham: Bank credit and the stage process

INTRODUCTION

Presenting the evolution of financial systems as a stage process has become a standard procedure. In Eastern and Central Europe this approach focuses on the transition from monobanking to commercial banking, from the dominance of a state bank, which combines and monopolises central and commercial banking, to the interaction between a public, macro-orientated central bank and mostly private, micro-orientated commercial banks. In the West, as exemplified by Rybczynski's writings, analysts concentrate on the transition from the B(anking) System to the M(arket) System. The former is based on intermediation, relations banking and a global approach to the customer, cross-subsidisation of bank products, stability and non-price competition. The latter, on the contrary, stresses diversification of products and participants, transactions banking, specialisation, securitisation, market-determined pricing of products and services, efficiency and volatility.

The purpose of the present paper is *not* to deny the obvious fact that market-orientated relations pervade the Western financial system. It argues that this evolution cannot be systematised as an irreversible step in a quasi-automatic and general stage process. In this context the permanent role of bank credit as a financing instrument of enterprises and households is emphasised. Examples are drawn from the Belgian experience.

THE DRIVING FORCES BEHIND THE MARKET-ORIENTATED DEVELOPMENT

Financial economists - whether they do or do not adhere to the stage process approach - stress the strategic and mutually reinforcing role of four driving forces in the present market-orientated development: deregulation, globalisation, concentration and securitisation. However, the quantitative impact of these forces on the financial systems and more specifically on the financing mechanisms of enterprises and households, although increasing, seems to remain quite limited. The following table brings together some of the results of the recent inquiry by the BIS on the structure of credit to the non-government sector in member countries.

Table 4.1   Characteristics of debt finance to the private sector (loans and securities, year 1993)

	USA	UK	Germany	France	Belgium	Netherlands	Italy
1. Total debt finance Ratio debt finance/GDP	114	117	125	90	86	115	64
2. Share of loans Ratio loans/Debt finance	80	81	94	85	93	97	95
3. Share of banks in: loans total debt finance	50 40	92(1) 75(1)	89 84	85(2) 72(2)	90 84	73 71	89 85

Source: Claudio E.V. Boro, 'The structure of credit to the non-government sector and the transmission mechanism of monetary policy. A cross country comparison', BIS Working Paper 24, April 1995, various tables

Notes :   1. Including building societies
           2. Including specialised credit institutions

The ratios in sections 2 and 3 of Table 4.1 show that the share of loans in total debt finance (loans and securities) generally exceeded 80 per cent in 1993, even 90 per cent in most countries of continental Europe. Banks provide an overwhelming share of these loans. In this way, they still play a decisive role in the financing process and in the global financial system of most countries. Their role is only substantially reduced in the US. Are European countries simply lagging behind? The evolution in recent years seems to suggest such a conclusion. The share of 'market finance' is increasing in most but not in all countries. Obviously this occurs, at least partly, at the expense of bank credit and the importance of banks in the financial system. As mentioned above, the key question is whether this evolution is (i) automatic, (ii) general and (iii) irreversible.

Some underlying factors, especially those of a technical nature, are permanent and irreversible. Progress in data processing and telecommunication has favoured, and still favours, geographical globalisation of financial transactions and determines a more rapid growth in international globalised markets than in domestic markets. At the same time it increases the critical size required to be considered as a significant industrial or financial 'global player' in internationalised markets.

Nevertheless, one continues to observe the lasting importance of regional industrial and also financial markets, even in the EU. These markets are still based in a significant way on historical customer relations and, in the financial field, on relations banking. European integration and internal deregulation have reduced, but not destroyed, these historical links. The recent failure of many European banks to penetrate the domestic markets of other member countries is a striking example of such a phenomenon. It is my opinion that this resistance to globalisation will remain quite strong, especially in countries whose economic structure is based on small- or medium-sized enterprises. As exemplified by the experience of the small Benelux countries, these regional markets will, in the future, be less demarcated by national borders or national currencies than by geographical proximity, cultural similarities and historical links. Anyway, they will remain regional.

The comparative advantage of banks and bank credit versus other financial intermediaries and other financing instruments is stronger in these regional markets with historical customer relations. If small- or medium-sized enterprises are predominant, as they often are in such markets, the need for *ex ante* screening and *ex post* monitoring of risks is high. Under these circumstances the statement by Borio (1995, 13) fully applies:

The greater the need for *ex ante* screening and *ex post* monitoring on the part of the lender because of the nature of the borrower or the use of funds, the greater is the likelihood that this finance will be provided by a credit intermediary and take the form of a non-marketable loan rather than tradeable security.

It is obvious that in such cases the stage process is blocked not because of accidental or temporary reasons but by *structural* factors. The economic structure of the country or the region favours the B(anking) System and hampers the M(arket) System.

Institutional factors can have the some effect:

- In countries like Germany and Switzerland, where *universal banking* prevails, the development towards more market-orientated relations is 'absorbed' by the banks themselves. Therefore the functioning of the financial system remains, based on a (modified) Banking System.
- In countries like France and Belgium, with extensive public social security systems, the number of *institutional investors* like pension funds which have sufficient size and sufficient funds to engage themselves in mega-investments on globalised markets is limited. This reduces the scope for market finance.
- For large multinational corporations *less* dependence on bank credit does not necessarily mean *more* dependence on market finance. Intra-company systems of netting and loans may reduce the global need of external financial resources.
- Some signs of re-regulation appear as a reaction against the high volatility and the financial scandals in some markets. This may function as a brake on the further increase of globalised market-orientated relations.

Finally *cyclical* factors may interrupt or even reverse the transition to the M(arket) System. Market finance instruments, especially long-term instruments like bonds and shares, are instruments *for good seasons*. They prosper in times of prosperity. But as soon as clouds appear, the markets become less liquid and hence less attractive. When financial thunderstorms burst, market participants leave in panic, looking for shelter in the banking system. The successive Mexican crises are a dramatic example of possible disruptions in capital markets, which make the transition process very irregular and possibly reversible.

All these considerations suggest that the stage process approach, at least in its strong version, is more an elegant analytical device and an utterly simplifying stylisation than an accurate description of what is going on in the Western financial world.

THE CHANGING ROLE OF BANK CREDIT

This does not mean that the development of market finance does not affect bank credit, not only in its growth but also in its functions. The real issue is whether or not market finance is a substitute for or a complement to bank credit. From the previous analysis we can conclude that it is neither substitute nor complement when small- and medium-sized enterprises are concerned. What Davis (1995, 171) stresses for equity can also be applied to long-term instruments of debt finance considered as investments of pension funds and other similar institutions:

> Pension funds and other institutional investors may not invest in small firms, given illiquidity or lack of marketability of their shares, levels of risk which may be difficult to diversify away, difficulty and costs of researching firms without track records and limits on the proportion of a firm's equity that may be held ...

Therefore, banks will remain the principal providers of external funds to this category of enterprises. And their main instrument will remain bank loans because even universal banks appear not to be universal enough to involve themselves in a significant way in risk capital for small- and medium-sized enterprises. The real problem concerns large companies. They may wish to have access to market finance in the form of negotiable securities: bonds, commercial paper, medium-term notes. Their principal motivation is to find funds on the market under more favourable conditions than at the banks. But even now access to the market is restricted to large-size companies with an excellent reputation, preferably confirmed by one of the leading rating agencies. In most countries these criteria are only met by multinational groups and a very limited number of national companies with a large domestic base and preferably with a listing on the local stock exchange. When these criteria are not met, bank credit remains the predominant source of external finance. And even if they are met, the access to market finance applies only to standardised finance, not to tailor-made operations. Institutional investors, the main market participants on the demand side, ask for liquidity of the market. Generally liquidity requires standardisation of terms and conditions and excludes detailed specific provisions. Tailor-made conditions can be negotiated in a more adequate way through loan negotiation between the bank and its corporate customers. In such cases a modified B(anking) System takes shape. Standardised funding will be provided by market finance. Tailor-made funding will come from specialised bank credit. Both fundings will be arranged by the bank, the former as an off-balance sheet operation, the latter as an on-balance sheet one: in economic terms, fee business, financial assistance on the one side, financial intermediation on the other.

A representative example of such package is given by the largest operation on the Belgian market in 1995: the acquisition of the Canadian beer manufacturer Labatt by the Belgian group Interbrew. The acquisition was financed partly by a multi-currency revolving credit underwritten by a syndicate of banks and partly by a programme of commercial paper placed in the market. Additional finance came from the sale of peripheral activities, while the remaining core business is being financed by a long-term bank loan. The whole package was devised mainly by one bank. In this way market finance and bank credit do not exclude, but complement each other. Bank loans do not disappear but shift towards more sophisticated formulas, towards tailor-made financial solutions.

CONCLUSION

In the next few years bank credit will remain the main source of external finance for large categories of debtors in Europe. But the nature of bank loans will be changing gradually towards more sophisticated formulas, at least in the financial operations of large companies. These aspects should be integrated more consistently in the analysis of the evolution of the financial systems. In Europe at least, the transition to an M(arket) System will neither be general, nor automatic, nor irreversible.

LIST OF REFERENCES

Banque Paribas Belgique (1996), 'Le crédit aujourd'hui', special issue of *Notes Economiques*, January

Borio, Claudio E.V. (1995), 'The structure of credit to the non-government sector and the transmission mechanism of monetary policy: a cross-country comparison', BIS Working Paper no. 24, April

Davis, D. Philip (1995), *Pension Funds. Retirement Income Security and Capital Markets. An International Perspective* (Oxford: The Clarendon Press)

Rybczynski, Tad (1993), 'The development of European capital markets: the main trends and their implications', *Revue de la Banque - Bank- en Financiewezen,* January, 23-32, also in Jack Revell (ed.), *The Changing Face of European Banks and Securities Markets,* Chapter 11, (Basingstoke and London: Macmillan; New York, NY: St. Martin's Press)

Jack Revell: Will the securitised phase last?

I chose this topic because I see a danger in deducing from Tad
Rybczynski's masterly analysis of the various phases in the development
of financial systems that we have reached the final goal, the optimum
financial system, and that we shall never go back again to earlier stages
of evolution. In order to answer this question we must examine the
fundamentals and ask what are the main factors in the change from the
market-orientated phase to the securitised phase. Five to ten minutes is a
short time in which to analyse the problem, but I will do my best.

A large part was certainly played in the change by the internal logic
of financial systems, the structures that have been inherited from the past
and largely determine the exact shape of the securitised system in each
country. It is possible to argue, as Nardozzi (1990) has done in his article,
that there is no 'progressive evolution unalterably leading to a superior
stage of financial development'. He saw the changes as arising from the
crisis of a specific national model, 'that of the extreme specialization of
financial intermediaries set up in the US during the '30s'. On this view the
securitised phase is little more than a revolt against the highly regulated
system established in the US, a revolt which is in the course of spreading
throughout the world because of the financial and political dominance of
the US.

There are two factors that make the securitised phase different from
what has gone before: (1) that it is fast becoming global, ironing out the
idiosyncrasies of individual financial systems in countries that need to raise
grants or external market funds, a high proportion of all countries, and (2)
that it has been made possible, as Tad Rybczynski has emphasised, by the
development of information technology.

Let me interpose a methodological point here. I do not see any one
of these factors as having *caused* the securitised phase, in the sense of
having driven the other factors before it. I see the internal logic of
financial systems, globalisation and technology as interacting continuously,
each probably becoming the dominant factor for a short while and then
passing the baton to another factor. We cannot talk of technology as the
cause because that only invites the question why technology has taken that
particular direction, and it is no answer to say that globalisation is the
driving factor because we have to ask why globalisation should be on the
agenda at this particular time.

I think the main causal factor must be sought outside the financial
system in the globalisation of large corporations, largely but not

exclusively American. It was their demand as much as that of banks and other financial institutions that drove information technology in the direction of providing the computer and telecommunications networks that represent the vital infrastructure to globalisation both within finance and outside it. This came about despite de-industrialisation, as the examples of McDonalds and Coca-Cola bear witness, and who would have thought only two or three years ago that the income tax records of all British residents would be held on computers owned and operated by an American computer services company, EDS?

This line of reasoning is a continuation of the argument that I first developed in my book *Mergers and the Role of Large Banks* (Revell 1987), in which you may remember I attributed the rise of large banks between about 1870 and 1920 to the fact that the technology of industry had changed from relatively small companies to the much larger enterprises needed for steelworks and chemical factories; these were much more dependent on outside sources of funds than were the smaller companies that preceded them as the typical industrial enterprise, and the loans they needed were many times larger. This is the recognition of the tremendous importance in any financial system of the 'large customer'.

Large customers occupy a special place in the economics of banking and of financial markets. In banking their main accounts are always managed from head office, and even when banks have partially suspended competition among themselves by means of cartels, they invariably continue to compete fiercely to capture the accounts of large customers. It was the same large customers that were responsible for the wave of innovation from 1982 onwards because of their flight to the capital market: their large accounts and large transactions make the effort of designing special solutions to problems economic. On securities markets retail customers are impelled to convert themselves into surrogate wholesale customers through their use of collective savings institutions like insurance companies and investment funds; the investment business of pension funds is mainly carried out by fund managers.

The same argument can be used to explain the foundation of the eurodollar and eurobond markets in the previous market-orientated phase, when large companies were multinational and banks became international as a result (to use the dominant buzzwords of the time). The most favourable feature of these markets in the eyes of multinational companies was that they were largely beyond the reach of national regulators and fiscal authorities, coupled with the fact that they were based exclusively on American practices, indeed they were the means of transport that brought these practices into international banking throughout the world.

These two features have been carried over into the global system of the securitised phase, bolstered by the dominant free-market ideology (I think it is fair to call it that), which is on the lips of every national government and of every international agency. I would compare its role at the present time to that of the doctrine of free trade in the period of building up British imperialism.

The answer to the question I set myself would seem to be that some regression to a previous stage in financial systems could come about if the strength of the globalised 'transnational corporations' (as we must now call them) were affected by something like the crisis of 1929-33 in the US, and spreading, as that crisis did, throughout the world. Another plausible cause of regression could come from the political side in the form of resurgence of nationalism to a greater extent than we have yet seen. The weakness of the free market doctrine is that it appears to condemn a growing proportion of the population in all countries to greater impoverishment, and many of the new regimes would soon revert to protective barriers against imports, even if they did not completely dismantle those elements of free markets that they had built into their financial systems.

What would not be lost for all time is the widening of choices that came with the securitised phase, the demonstration that the gaps in the spectra of instruments, institutions and markets can profitably be filled in to increase the efficiency of the whole system. This store of knowledge would be available when conditions changed yet again.

LIST OF REFERENCES

Nardozzi, Giangiacomo (1990), 'The structural evolution of financial systems in the '80s: from its determinants to its possible outcomes', *Banca Nazionale del Lavoro Quarterly Review*, 172 (March), 71-89

Revell, Jack (1987), *Mergers and the Role of Large Banks*, IEF Research Monographs in Banking and Finance no. 2 (Bangor: Institute of European Finance)

Francesco Cesarini: Local banks and global players in the Italian financial market[1]

In many industrial countries, and especially in those belonging to the EU, both banks and the securities industry are passing through a phase of important changes which are likely to enhance the competitive climate in the market for financial services. Two main trends are emerging:

- the globalisation of markets, both domestic and international, which become less segmented as a result of progress in information technology and of the growing importance of new financial instruments, such as derivatives, and of new types of professional investors, whose portfolio choices increase the economic and functional links among different markets
- the evolution of financial systems which tend to move their focal point from intermediation in lending to trading in securities. Financial markets which grow bigger and operate in a large number of securities allow business companies wider opportunities to get in touch direct with investors and to sell them easily negotiable financial instruments; consequently the share of lending intermediation business taking place in the traditional forms of bilateral financing is getting lower in respect of the fund flows (both of loan and of risk capital) which are channelled through markets

The present position of the Italian financial system, in my opinion, can be considered to be halfway in both evolutionary processes. On the one hand, the historical dominance of bank loans in the overall financing of business companies is being gradually eroded, and steps have been made towards an increase of securities-based financing also through a more efficient organisation of primary and secondary markets; on the other hand, international investors and securities firms pay some attention to the Italian market, being attracted by the large size of its savings flows and by the importance of the financial dealings that are originated by privatisations. Mention should also be made of the interest aroused, somewhat unexpectedly, by a recent piece of legislation permitting the creation of local secondary markets for securities of small companies, a trend which seems in contrast with the actual disappearance of official local stock exchanges, with the full utilisation of telematic technology in securities trading and with the fact that a sizeable share of large trades in Italian blue chips takes place on SEAQ International.

In this context, which is somewhat uncertain and contradictory, the mutual relationships of local and global financial circuits need to receive specific attention from bankers, scholars and policy-makers.   My contribution to the discussion of this topic is aimed at outlining, at least at an intuitive level, a workable new 'division of labour' between local/small banks on one side, and global/large banks on the other, in the field of the so-called traditional banking and in the intermediation activity in markets for financial instruments.

From a juridical and institutional point of view the evolution of the Italian banking system has followed two directions:

- the enactment of unified banking laws, which took place on 1 January, 1994, has formally eliminated the functional specialisation of banking activities, thus paving the way for banks to provide depositors with a complete set of direct fund-collecting instruments (from demand deposits to long-term bonds) and to offer their business clientele a full range of loans (from short-term to long-term, including leasing and special purpose loans) and also, within certain limits, capital funds in the form of subscription of corporate shares

- EC Directive no. 93/22 on investment services, which is expected to become effective at the beginning of 1996, will produce, in its turn, two important effects: it will allow banks to take part directly in trading in corporate shares on secondary markets, thus broadening the scope of their securities intermediation activities; it will open trading in the Italian securities market to foreign intermediaries, especially large British and German broker-dealer and investment firms

A consequence of Directive no. 93/22 which is frequently overlooked is that it effectively promotes full competition among securities markets of different countries by removing barriers to entry and levelling the playing field to intermediaries; as a consequence, it will become indifferent for an Italian investor to effect his trading through a domestic or a foreign intermediary, the choice being exclusively dependent on the cost and the quality of service. By the same token, if the Italian financial system is able to react adequately to the new competitive environment, Italian intermediaries may be selected by foreign investors for business to be traded on Italian exchanges or in foreign markets.

While the effects of recent legislative changes have not yet significantly influenced their product mix, there is no doubt that the retail market is at present the core business of all Italian banks. Evidence of this fact can be found in the massive dissemination of new branches that they have pursued in recent years in order to make up for the delay caused by previous restrictive regulations and to enhance their proximity to wider groups of customers, whose demand for investment and lending services can be considered more complex and exacting than it used to be in the past. The retail market is also now very important to very large banks because it provides them with a stable and altogether sizeable customer basis on which they can rely for absorbing fixed costs and which they can exploit as an outlet for their ability in creating and innovating financial instruments and services. The strategy of both large and small banks is thus based on the concept of proximity to customers, which will also continue to be important in the future, although it will probably be realised, at least in part, in forms other than direct contacts at bank counters.

The benefits that banks can obtain through proximity to their deposit or investing customers do not need to be recalled here; proximity is indeed not less important in respect of borrowing customers since the process of evaluating, granting and managing loans to business companies must obviously be based on adequate information on the economic and financial characteristics of borrowers and hence on strict and constant relationships with them. In a multibank relationship environment, such as the one up to now prevailing in the Italian financial system, proximity to business clientele is all the more important for those banks which want to take advantage of the recent liberalisation of their product mix, which allows them to extend term loans and leasing finance, and even to buy or subscribe to corporate shares, although within certain limits.

It goes without saying that a comprehensive knowledge of the client company is an indispensable prerequisite if a bank wants to provide financial assistance and, especially in the case of relatively large companies, services connected with their direct recourse to money and capital markets through the issue of commercial paper, investment certificates, bonds and shares. This sort of financial service, in my opinion, is bound to gain importance inasmuch as the expected decline in the practice of multibank relationships will compel banks to organise themselves in order to select borrowers in a more rational and cost-effective way and to offer each of them quantitatively more important and diversified financial support.

Jointly considered, the importance of retail business and the strategy of proximity to customers lead to the consequence that banks, whatever their size, must be able to maintain a certain degree of localism, which can obviously be pursued in different juridical forms and with different organisation structures. In the case of banks of relatively small size and geographical scope, which are often organised in the form of co-operatives, localism is realised in an almost automatic and natural way, thanks to the strict links that they have historically built with their territory and sometimes to the presence of representatives of the local business and political community in the managing board or in the top personnel of the banks themselves. This kind of localism needs, however, to be carefully maintained even when the bank enlarges its size through mergers with other banks operating in nearby geographic areas; as a matter of fact, in my opinion, localism realised in these forms is likely to produce satisfactory results both for the bank and for the territories in which it operates provided that the management of the bank keeps a constant watchful eye on the problems of geographic and sector concentration of risks. Larger banks, on the other hand, must purposely pursue a certain degree of localism, and in their efforts in this direction they may face some considerable difficulties: the key to the solution of such problems may lie in organisation forms which attribute local bank officers an adequate degree of autonomy or which otherwise allow decision-makers adequate information on local business needs and provide local customers with prompt answers to their requests.

With reference to securities intermediation and investment services, the importance of which is also rising rapidly in the funds allocation process in the Italian economy, the role of banks can be examined under four main headings:

- trading in secondary markets, both regulated and over-the-counter, where intermediaries will be called upon more frequently to take up position risks by acting as dealers and sometimes as market makers
- underwriting in primary markets, a function which appears essential if business companies are to increase the volume of their direct market financing
- the provision of retail investment services and products
- asset management

Both trading and underwriting imply that the bank is active in organised markets for securities in an effective and efficient way; as a matter of fact, such activities are out of bounds to most Italian banks because they require large investments in technical and human resources and a considerable attitude and capacity for risk-bearing. The choice of being active in the above-mentioned markets is thus restricted to large banks and is consistent with their choice of attacking aggressively the retail market for investment and intermediation services. It may be recalled that the foreign banks which have taken the lead in this area of business have done so as a reaction to the emergence of the trend towards securitisation, which brought their large borrowers to finance themselves directly on the capital market. By the same token, it is quite likely that some large Italian banks, which lend prevalently to large business companies, will become more interested in trading and underwriting business as a reaction to the stringent EC rules on large loan exposures, which will compel them to move part of their loans from their own balance sheet to investors' portfolio.

An efficient presence in capital markets is by its very nature a global one: it must cover all the main financial instruments and all the main financial centres, on account of the existence of numerous very strict relationships among different markets, which have been made even more important by the growth of institutional investors, professionally engaged in securing the highest possible returns, as well as by the intensive use of information technology, which allows access to markets all over the world without imposing on dealers the burden of physical presence. The proliferation of financial instruments, and particularly of financial derivatives, permits the subdivision and the transferability of risk among intermediaries and the selection of portfolios which are more efficient on a risk/return basis. Prerequisites for an effective presence in such markets are therefore an operational and managerial approach and a business culture altogether different from those which are typically required for retail banking activities. Furthermore an effective presence in global markets requires the adoption of organisation schemes which are apt not only to avoid contamination and confusion between the professional identity and skills of those who operate on markets and those who are engaged in retail activity, but also to co-ordinate them properly so that each activity may take advantage of the efficient performance of the other.

For most Italian banks the choice which appears to be more advantageous from a strategic and economic point of view is to exploit their widespread branching and close proximity to customers also in the securities intermediation business at the retail level without searching for a direct and continuous presence in securities markets. Such a strategy consists, for instance, in exploiting the placing power deriving from retail activity in order to provide business companies with the support they need if they are to follow the securitisation path.

The placing power of a relatively small and local bank appears to be particularly valuable when the securities to be sold to the public are issued by companies which have developed a strict and long-standing customer relationship with the bank itself and it may be put at the disposal of an institution specialised in originating and floating new corporate issues, which consequently has the experience and the skills required for promoting the sale of financial instruments and for tailoring them according to the needs of the parties involved.

With reference to asset management, it can hardly be doubted that it shows very interesting growth prospects since the percentage of investors' wealth presently managed by professionals, although showing considerable increase in recent years, is still quite below the average for major industrial countries. This segment of the securities intermediation business also requires of banks a clear strategy which should properly take into account the market position and the organisation structures of each of them. The largest banks, which can already avail themselves of a significant and efficient activity in financial markets, in which they tendentially act as global players, may try to pursue a larger coverage of market functions and instruments and a more sophisticated level of service so as to attract large private and institutional investors as a separate business segment to be added to the traditional retail services market.

The success of their efforts will obviously depend on their ability to build up a solid reputation and a recognised professional experience, which in their turn are related to the availability of qualified research staff as well as to a steady and significant presence in all major markets, including those dealing in innovative instruments, which may permit them to take full advantage of market information and opportunities and to provide their most sophisticated customers with a complete set of high-level financial services.

Smaller banks, on the other hand, may take advantage of their solid local connections in order to supply standard investment management services (such as mutual funds, fund management services on a collective basis) which are appreciated by small investors and which may be produced externally or by securing the services of a specialised institution. They may, for instance, entrust the investment in foreign securities of their customers' funds to large banks or distribute financial products created by the latter. In other words, in their relationships with financial intermediaries specialised in the securities business, banks may obtain considerable synergies related to the different roles played in the financial intermediation process.

Whatever their choice in these areas, most Italian banks, and especially small ones, need to increase, both qualitatively and quantitatively, the professional skills of their staff in the area of securities intermediation business and thus fill a cultural lag largely due to the overwhelming importance up to now attributable to their traditional loan intermediation activity; as a matter of fact, the inevitable trend towards securitisation of bank liabilities, as well as the more pronounced propensity of their customers to minimise their liquid assets to the amount strictly necessary for transaction purposes, will cause growing competition between traditional bank fund-raising instruments and negotiable financial assets.

The above discussion of the links between local and global activity and functions in Italian financial circuits leads to the conclusion that, although capable of playing in the entire financial market on the same terms, banks must search for and realise a new division of labour, possibly along the following lines:

- retail activity, both for traditional lending and for securities intermediation, forms the core business of all banks and must continue to be deeply rooted in proximity factors, and hence in strict links with local business communities, in forms which each bank must carefully devise and maintain according to its size, traditions and organisation

- wholesale lending activity should preferably be performed only by large banks, which appear to be better equipped to co-ordinate it with securitisation techniques and instruments

- a considerable number of banks can profitably develop the retail distribution of investment and securities intermediation services, without the need to produce the more sophisticated ones direct and thus without the burden of presence on all the principal markets; a basic condition for pursuing such a strategy is that the bank personnel, and especially the sales force, possess an adequate level of financial culture

- only very few large banks can realistically be considered capable of acting as global players in financial markets, including the most specialised ones; for successfully performing such a role it may be preferable that they use staff and structures parallel to, but separate from, those engaged in retail business, on account of the different skills and attitudes required by trading on markets in respect of traditional retail activity

- a division of labour between small/local banks, on one side, and large/national banks, on the other, can be mutually advantageous, especially if the retail placing power of the former is properly combined with the professional skills and the ability of the latter to operate in the main markets for securitised financial instruments

NOTE

1.   I wish to thank Dr. Paolo Gualtieri for the useful discussion of the topics analysed in this paper.

Göran Bergendahl: **Comments concerning distribution systems**

1. WHAT IS A DISTRIBUTION SYSTEM?

Banks have for a long time worked as intermediaries in the financial markets. They collect surplus funds from private and commercial sources. They lend funds to firms and individuals that need credits for operations and investment. They 'store' funds with central banks or other banks in order to have a reserve for unexpected needs. They also act as a vehicle for transfer of funds from one customer to another. All these activities can be identified as activities in a network, where each bank may find itself at a hub with incoming and outgoing transfers.

Incoming and outgoing transfers will often follow the same infrastructure in terms of deliveries of cash or messages concerning non-cash transfers. But even if they follow the same infrastructure it may at a first glance seem natural to identify the treatment of incoming transfers in terms of 'collection systems' and the treatment of outgoing transfers in terms of 'distribution systems'. Such a partition would be reasonable if the collection of funds made use of different procedures from the distribution of funds. However, in reality collection and distribution of funds are performed simultaneously. At one moment a single customer may deliver funds and in another moment collect such funds all through the same procedures. Consequently, it would be misleading to assume that there are quite different procedures when funds are collected and when they are distributed. In fact, similar services are used for the collection and distribution of funds.

A more suitable distinction would be between *services* of production and *services* of distribution. With such a view, services of production for a bank would cover the operation of central management and computer systems, the back-office work and the interaction with the central bank and other financial institutions. All these activities would then form a *production system* for a bank. With such a definition the services of distribution would include all activities at the bank branches, including both the collection and the distribution of funds. Here these service activities will become units of the *distribution system* in a bank.

With such a definition it will become evident that the production system and the distribution system will intersect. But even so, it is often practical to treat them as two separate systems with separate responsibilities. Here we will concentrate on the distribution systems for financial services in a bank. Such a system may be subdivided into the following subsystems, namely those for

- selling services
- delivery of services
- payments for services
- control of services

Banks have for a long time performed these services through networks of branches. In this respect the branches have offered multiple services and multiple products. They have been able to do so because no other organisation than a bank has been allowed to serve customers with interest-bearing deposit accounts.

Joël Métais has shown that the process of securitisation has changed the distribution system completely. Nowadays, both private and commercial customers are offered a large set of new alternatives for deposits and borrowing in the form of securities. Such securities are deposits and loans that are defined in fixed terms, for fixed time periods and are tradeable on a secondary market. This large degree of flexibility concerning terms has made the use of securities very attractive. The effect has been that the banks have lost a substantial part of the market for borrowing and lending.

2.   THE EVOLUTION

During the last ten years there has been a rapid evolution in the market for securities. This has been nicely demonstrated by Tad Rybczynski. A main part of that evolution has been in terms of the financial instruments. First, these instruments have become more specific in terms of pricing. As the market has grown, there has been an increased demand for their resale on a secondary market. Price conditions have been established. Off-balance sheet instruments have been developed in order to protect the prices or values of these instruments. This change has demanded an increased knowledge from the personnel at the bank branches.

Another reason for the evolution comes from the fact that the customers have become more active and more informed. One reason for this fact is the ageing population, which has been stressed by Ted Gardener. A new market segment has emerged in terms of older and more wealthy customers.

The development of the number of securities on the financial markets has increased the risks of changes in value ('interest rate risks' and 'currency risks'), credit losses ('credit risks'), and the need of liquidity when payments are delayed ('payment risks' and 'liquidity risks'). All these risks have called for more regulations and a stricter government control.

At the same time there has been a parallel movement towards less regulation. This process has in many ways been stimulated by the movement in the EU towards free competition. This evolution has resulted in the banks having to change their role on the markets for deposits and credits. Not long ago they borrowed and lent money in their own names. Nowadays, they often work as *commissionaires*. They let the market match customers who would like to invest funds with those who want to borrow funds.

The transfer of loans and deposits from bank accounts to market instruments seems to have increased the market efficiency as the competition has become more intense. That has also had the effect that there is less value added in the intermediation between investors and borrowers. Joël Métais has shown that these changes will lead to shrinking margins and to a substantial overcapacity. Ted Gardener has proved that many banks have adjusted themselves to this evolution by reducing the number of branches. Most of the traditional work in bank branches will no longer be needed.

3.   THE STRATEGIES

The transfer of intermediation from banks to markets has had an immediate effect on the activities in a traditional bank. Markets with limited competition exist no longer, and non-banks and near-banks have entered the arena. Bank management has become more complex. A limited range of bank products has been replaced by a massive growth of new services for deposits, loans and products for hedging. An assumption of homogenous customers has been developed into a view of different segments of customers with heterogenous needs.   The customer requirements have expanded, and nowadays most commercial and private customers make use of more than one single bank.

Traditional banking has been replaced to a large extent by universal banking on one hand and by narrow banking on the other. *Universal banking* implies more products per branch and a more efficient use of the branches. One consequence is that pricing has to become more efficient and more competitive. This implies that most forms of cross-subsidisation have to be reduced. Another consequence is that *selling* must become the key word for any branch. Therefore, the future banker must have quite different qualities from those of the traditional one. He or she has to become more customer-orientated than before. Consequently, more staff training will be needed and new principles for the recruitment of personnel will become necessary.

Narrow banking takes quite an opposite direction. For such a bank the products have to be few but extremely profitable. Certain products have to become standardised in order to be more cost-efficient. Computer systems will take a large role in the activities, and contacts with customers through branches will become small. Other products may become tailor-made to suit more wealthy customers. They will need qualified services in terms of a skilful asset management. Ted Gardener has shown that 'Small is Beautiful' is a relevant concept for the branches of narrow banking. Cost management and price differentiation will become key words for all their products.

For both the strategies, universal banking and narrow banking, *selling* will come into focus. Bank branches may be transformed into self-service centres for standardised products and counselling centres for high-value tailor-made products. At the same time the control of risk and return will get a high priority. This demands a better use of computer systems like asset and liability management (ALM).

Certain banks will leave traditional banking to become universal banks. Others will become narrow banks. And a few will form their distribution systems as a combination of universal bank branches and narrow bank branches. This means that traditional banking is and will become challenged, and it is doubtful whether it will survive. An alternative slogan to Ted Gardener's 'Long Live Traditional Banking' may be the following one:

Traditional Banking is dead.
Long live Universal Banking and Narrow Banking.

Javier Quesada: Large banks in the EU: what size?[1]

Different rankings by size and profitability of the top five banks belonging to six European countries show no evidence of the existence of an ideal common size. Large banks are very profitable in some countries but perform very poorly in others. Different rankings show how individual banks performed during 1994 in relation to other banks in the sample.

By now it is known (Revell) that countries that are members of the EU have been well overbanked for the last decade. Under this condition of very competitive markets - difficult to penetrate - the creation of a unified European financial market made firm size a strategic variable for many banks operating in different countries. For those banks anticipating the creation of a European market and not having the minimum required size needed to expand internationally, mergers and acquisitions of domestic banks were the adequate strategies to follow during the eighties. If one looks into what has happened during the last decade, it seems that what inspired most of their actions was more the fear of seeing foreign competitors penetrating their market than their own intention of expanding abroad. Also the ability to retaliate against almost any foreign competition did require a minimum size of banks to make the menace credible.

For those banks expanding in cross-border operations, mergers but, more likely, acquisitions of medium- or small-sized banks were the most rational strategy to penetrate a new market. In this way, through the purchase of a share of the market, the capacity of the banking sector remained unchanged. But not only expanding banks anticipated the need to increase their size; small banks also protected their regional and local markets through agreements and mergers with other regional or national banks as part of a 'defensive strategy' of adaptation to a changing environment rather than as an aggressive policy based on their own initiative.

Within the EU the size of banks as well as that of banking sectors differs quite substantially by country. Obviously, the relative importance of the role of banks in performing the task of channelling savings into investment depended upon the development of the alternative institutions, the non-bank intermediaries and the money and capital markets. Those countries that are more inclined to the use of financial markets employ a smaller amount of global resources in channelling financial funds than those which reserve banks a more predominant role in this function.

In general, one should expect the absolute size of banks to be, at least weakly, related to the size of the markets in which they operate. With the trend of internationalisation, the extent of markets increased and so did banks operating and expanding into foreign countries. One of the driving forces in international banking that caused an increase in the size of banks was the entry into new markets, like carrying out wholesale banking on a very large scale in loans to governments and multinational corporations. Only large banks, and very often through syndicated loans, could meet the borrowing needs of long- and short-term financing of these special customers.

On the domestic front the traditional argument explaining the need to enlarge the size of banks was associated with the benefits of economies of scale supposedly present in large banks. Many studies found evidence of the presence of economies of scale at small sizes, but frequently they also found no evidence either in favour of or against the existence of scale economies after a given size of banks well below that of the largest banks. According to these results, the reason why banks grew so large should not be so much in the reduction of average costs but in gaining market share and improving their profitability. But, again, size and profitability are two variables not directly correlated.

To illustrate whether there is a right bank size for a European bank we have carried out a very simple exercise. A comparison of the top five banks (by size) belonging to six European countries has been performed. The countries are Germany, the UK, France, Italy, Spain and Portugal. Since we are considering the adequacy of a given size on a European scale, some homogeneity in the sample was required, so only large (more than $200m. in assets) private commercial banks in each country have been chosen. Those are the banks that are already present or could potentially expand in other countries. The year of comparison is 1994. Figure 4.1 shows the relative size of the sample of banks by countries where Germany and France hold the largest share.

When we rank the banks by size we find the largest banks in the largest countries, namely Germany, France and the UK (see Table 4.2). Similarly, we find the smallest banks in the tiniest economies, Portugal, Spain and Italy. The two reasons given above for finding large banks are in play. Not only are the domestic markets largest in the bigger countries but also their banks have a more active role in international markets.

To check whether there is an adequate size for banks in Europe we ranked the sample by profitability using two different measures. Table 4.3 ranks banks by return on assets (ROA). We find the UK and the Portuguese banks the most profitable ones in the sample, and their size, the largest in each country, is quite unlike; between 10 and 25 times their relative size. On the contrary, the less profitable banks are to be found in France and Italy. In this case we see large- (French) and medium-sized (Italian) banks with the lowest ROAs. In sum we find large banks very profitable in the UK, relatively profitable in Germany and not profitable in France. This we consider an indication of a weak relation between size and profitability.

Figure 4.1   **Comparison of aggregate total assets of five largest banks in six European countries (percentages)**

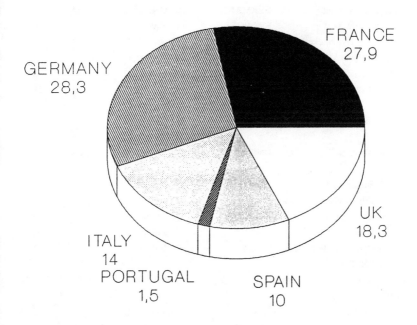

Table 4.2   Sample banks ranked by total assets

	Country	Total assets	ROA (%)	ROE (%)
Deutsche Bank AG	GERMANY	363,978,085.3	0.56	15.65
Crédit Lyonnais	FRANCE	327,893,225.5	-0.57	-21.0
Société Générale	FRANCE	277,542,732.5	0.39	11.15
Banque Nationale de Paris BNP	FRANCE	271,626,902.1	0.21	5.30
Dresdner Bank AG	GERMANY	252,176,685.7	0.44	12.44
Barclays Bank plc	UNITED KINGDOM	249,004,687.5	1.17	28.64
National Westminster Bank Plc	UNITED KINGDOM	245,145,312.5	1.01	24.18
Commerzbank AG	GERMANY	217,637,832.6	0.51	16.95
Bayerische Vereinsbank AG	GERMANY	201,604,729.0	0.35	12.60
Banque Paribas	FRANCE	175,759,287.9	0.25	10.52
Bayerische Hypotheken- und Wechsel-Bank AG	GERMANY	173,600,112.2	0.41	13.00
Gruppo Bancario San Paolo	ITALY	149,650,020.0	0.25	5.88
Midland Bank Plc (Group)	UNITED KINGDOM	123,714,062.5	1.14	29.62
Istituto Bancario San Paolo di Torino SpA	ITALY	117,709,080.0	0.37	8.65
Lloyds Bank plc	UNITED KINGDOM	114,375,000.0	1.78	34.00
Banco Santander SA	SPAIN	113,818,122.0	0.94	17.14
Banco Bilbao Vizcaya (BBV)	SPAIN	98,733,756.0	0.88	15.26
Union Européenne de CIC	FRANCE	97,835,941.4	0.18	6.00
Banca di Roma	ITALY	91,296,480.0	0.06	0.85
Banca Commerciale Italiana SpA (COMIT)	ITALY	90,500,880.0	0.41	7.20
Banca Nazionale del Lavoro (BNL)	ITALY	84,649,380.0	0.07	1.54
Banco Central Hispano	SPAIN	79,466,541.0	0.42	8.03
Royal Bank of Scotland plc	UNITED KINGDOM	70,921,762.2	1.20	27.70
Banco Español de Crédito (BANESTO)	SPAIN	43,077,804.0	-0.31	-8.40

(continued)

	Country	Total assets	ROA (%)	ROE (%)
(continued)				
Banco Exterior de España	SPAIN	41,782,950.0	0.44	8.75
Banco Português do Atlantico (BPA)	PORTUGAL	22,667,660.0	0.80	13.69
Banco Totta & Açores SA	PORTUGAL	17,753,560.0	1.05	19.60
Banco Comercial Português SA	PORTUGAL	13,953,532.0	1.13	12.99
Banco Espirito Santo e Comercial de Lisboa (BESCL)	PORTUGAL	13,694,168.0	1.19	18.30
Banco Pinto & Sotto Mayor	PORTUGAL	9,320,148.0	0.14	3.36

Table 4.3   Sample banks ranked by return on assets (ROA)

	Country	Total assets	ROA (%)	ROE (%)
Lloyds Bank plc	UNITED KINGDOM	114,375,000.0	1.78	34.00
Royal Bank of Scotland plc	UNITED KINGDOM	70,921,762.2	1.20	27.70
Banco Espirito Santo e Comercial de Lisboa (BESCL)	PORTUGAL	13,694,168.0	1.19	18.30
Barclays Bank plc	UNITED KINGDOM	249,004,687.5	1.17	28.64
Midland Bank plc (Group)	UNITED KINGDOM	123,714,062.5	1.14	29.62
Banco Comercial Português SA	PORTUGAL	13,953,532.0	1.13	12.99
Banco Totta & Açores SA	PORTUGAL	17,753,560.0	1.05	19.60
National Westminster Bank plc	UNITED KINGDOM	245,145,312.5	1.01	24.18
Banco Santander SA	SPAIN	113,818,122.0	0.94	17.14

(continued)

	Country	Total assets	ROA (%)	ROE (%)
(continued)				
Banco Bilbao Vizcaya (BBV)	SPAIN	98,733,756.0	0.88	15.26
Banco Português do Atlantico (BPA)	PORTUGAL	22,667,660.0	0.80	13.69
Deutsche Bank AG	GERMANY	363,978,085.3	0.56	15.65
Commerzbank AG	GERMANY	217,637,832.6	0.51	16.95
Banco Exterior de España	SPAIN	41,782,950.0	0.44	8.75
Dresdner Bank AG	GERMANY	252,176,685.7	0.44	12.44
Banco Central Hispano	SPAIN	79,466,541.0	0.42	8.03
Banca Commerciale Italiana SpA (COMIT)	ITALY	90,500,880.0	0.41	7.20
Bayerische Hypotheken- und Wechsel-Bank AG	GERMANY	173,600,112.2	0.41	13.00
Société Générale	FRANCE	277,542,732.5	0.39	11.15
Istituto Bancario San Paolo di Torino SpA	ITALY	117,709,080.0	0.37	8.65
Bayerische Vereinsbank AG	GERMANY	201,604,729.0	0.35	12.60
Gruppo Bancario San Paolo	ITALY	149,650,020.0	0.25	5.88
Banque Paribas	FRANCE	175,759,287.9	0.25	10.52
Banque Nationale de Paris (BNP)	FRANCE	271,626,902.1	0.21	5.30
Union Européenne de CIC	FRANCE	97,835,941.4	0.18	6.00
Banco Pinto & Sotto Mayor SA	PORTUGAL	9,320,148.0	0.14	3.36
Banca Nazionale del Lavoro (BNL)	ITALY	84,649,380.0	0.07	1.54
Banca di Roma	ITALY	91,296,480.0	0.06	0.85
Banco Español de Crédito (BANESTO)	SPAIN	43,077,804.0	-0.31	-8.40
Crédit Lyonnais	FRANCE	327,893,225.5	-0.57	-21.50

If one uses return on equity (ROE) instead of ROA as the measurement of profitability only minor changes are found. As shown in Table 4.4, again the UK and Portuguese banks are ranked at the top of the table while French and Italian banks appear concentrated in the lowest part. As for German banks they appear in the higher half of the table, and the Spanish banks are well spread out down the table between number 8 and number 29.

Table 4.4 Sample banks ranked by return on equity (ROE)

	Country	Total Assets	ROA (%)	ROE (%)
Lloyds Bank plc	UNITED KINGDOM	114,375,000.0	1.78	34.00
Midland Bank plc (Group)	UNITED KINGDOM	123,714,062.5	1.14	29.62
Barclays Bank plc	UNITED KINGDOM	249,004,687.5	1.17	28.64
Royal Bank of Scotland plc	UNITED KINGDOM	70,921,762.2	1.20	27.70
National Westminster Bank plc	UNITED KINGDOM	245,145,312.5	1.01	24.18
Banco Totta & Açores SA	PORTUGAL	17,753,560.0	1.05	19.60
Banco Espirito Santo e Comercial de Lisboa (BESCL)	PORTUGAL	13,694,168.0	1.19	18.30
Banco Santander SA	SPAIN	113,818,122.0	0.94	17.14
Commerzbank AG	GERMANY	217,637,832.6	0.51	16.95
Deutsche Bank AG	GERMANY	363,978,085.3	0.56	15.65
Banco Bilbao Vizcaya (BBV)	SPAIN	98,733,756.0	0.88	15.26
Banco Português do Atlantico (BPA)	PORTUGAL	22,667,660.0	0.80	13.69
Bayerische Hypotheken- und Wechsel-Bank AG	GERMANY	173,600,112.2	0.41	13.00
Banco Comercial Português SA	PORTUGAL	13,953,532.0	1.13	12.99
Bayerische Vereinsbank AG	GERMANY	201,604,729.0	0.35	12.60
Dresdner Bank AG	GERMANY	252,176,685.7	0.44	12.44
Société Générale	FRANCE	277,542,732.5	0.39	11.15

(continued)

	Country	Total Assets	ROA (%)	ROE (%)
(continued)				
Banque Paribas	FRANCE	175,759,287.9	0.25	10.52
Banco Exterior de España	SPAIN	41,782,950.0	0.44	8.75
Istituto Bancario San Paolo di Torino SpA	ITALY	117,709,080.0	0.37	8.65
Banco Central Hispano	SPAIN	79,466,541.0	0.42	8.03
Banca Commerciale Italiana SpA (COMIT)	ITALY	90,500,880.0	0.41	7.20
Union Européenne de CIC	FRANCE	97,835,941.4	0.18	6.00
Gruppo Bancario San Paolo	ITALY	149,650,020.0	0.25	5.88
Banque Nationale de Paris (BNP)	FRANCE	271,626,902.1	0.21	5.30
Banco Pinto & Sotto Mayor SA	PORTUGAL	9,320,148.0	0.14	3.36
Banca Nazionale del Lavoro (BNL)	ITALY	84,649,380.0	0.07	1.54
Banca di Roma	ITALY	91,296,480.0	0.06	0.85
Banco Español de Crédito (BANESTO)	SPAIN	43,077,804.0	-0.31	-8.40
Crédit Lyonnais	FRANCE	327,893,225.5	-0.57	-21.50

Even if one recognises that only data for one single year are used, and that profit ratios are not strictly comparable without considering country-specific features like the density of demand, the size of the branching network and the relative labour unit costs, an adequate size for a European bank does not appear clear in the data. Each country might have an adequate size of bank which corresponds with the size and degree of concentration of the domestic market, the degree of internationalisation and the type of banking activity that it performs. And even in this case, it is common to find more substantial differences in profitability that arise from different degrees of efficiency rather than from the distinct sizes of the banks. In order to shed some extra light on this issue further empirical analysis is required using a homogeneous sample of banks operating in the European financial market. A comparison of profitability and/or an efficiency score study could be performed to see if there is any evidence of an optimal size of European bank.

NOTE

1. Thanks are due to José Manuel Pastor for his valuable help and comments.

PART II

The response of banking systems to securitisation

CHAPTER 5
BANK LENDING AND THE SECURITISATION PROCESS:
A COMPARATIVE ANALYSIS

Andrea Landi and Giuseppe Lusignani

1. INTRODUCTION

The role and the importance of banks in providing funds to the economy
has been analysed from different perspectives with various possibilities for
the future of bank lending. On the one hand, the long-term evolution of
financial systems through securitisation and financial innovation processes
may decrease the importance of banks in the financing of the economy.
The introduction of new financial instruments traded in efficient open
markets increases, for borrowers, the possibility of raising funds direct
from private and institutional investors. Firms with high-quality standing
in the market are more capable of substituting bank loans with new
financial instruments which are subscribed directly by investors and are
traded in efficient secondary markets. This may result in a long-term
reduction in bank lending and an increasing role for financial markets in
providing funds to the borrowers (Rybczynski 1984).

On the other hand, some theories about financial intermediation claim
that bank lending provides a better service than direct access to securities
markets. Reductions in information costs of monitoring and efficiency
from pooling many loans into a diversified portfolio allow banks to offer
higher returns to savers, who are too small to evaluate borrowers and
diversify their assets. At the same time, banks provide lower credit costs
to borrowers who are unable to access securities markets. Finance theory
has also offered additional explanations in terms of control mechanisms
provided by banks to corporate managers of companies with very large
numbers of small shareholders. Furthermore, the key role played by
banks in the payment system and the implicit protection received by
central banks against liquidity problems allow them, with respect to other
intermediaries, to charge less for the liquidity risk of holding a loan
(O'Brien and Browne 1992).

From the point of view of corporate finance, too, several empirical
studies argue against the securitisation hypothesis. Taking some concise
facts about corporate finance and evaluating them in the context of
alternative theories of corporate finance, Mayer (1988, 1990) has disputed
the financial literature on securitisation by reaching the conclusion that in

91

no country do securities markets contribute a large proportion of corporate sector financing, while banks are the dominant source of external finance in all countries. These conclusions apply to both the bank-dominated systems and the market-orientated systems.

Recent trends in bank lending growth add evidence on the changing role of bank credit in financial systems. In particular, the analysis of the main factors that caused the evolution of bank lending in the 1980s and in the early 1990s seems to provide useful insights for the future prospect of bank lending and its role in financing economies. In fact, during this period of high competition and a high degree of financial innovation specific factors linked to the behaviour of banks and corporate firms emerge in almost all the main countries. The analysis of such factors may help to provide some answers to issues regarding: a) the importance of loans in financing the economy in relation to the growth of securities markets; b) the question of whether the high volatility shown by loans during the last decade was an exceptional event that will normalise in the near future or a structural characteristic that banks will have to manage; c) the effects of these prospects on banks' strategies in terms of growth, risk and profitability.

Through the analysis of both demand and supply factors in changing bank credit activity, this work puts forward some preliminary answers. The work is structured as follows: Section 2 describes major trends in bank lending in the main countries; in Sections 3 and 4 we focus respectively on bank credit market strategies and borrowers' financial decisions. In the last section we attempt to put together both supply and demand implications on the future of bank lending.

2. TRENDS IN BANK LENDING

Despite the increasing presence of other important sources of funds, in the 1980s the higher competition from securities and non-bank intermediaries did not reduce the important role of banks in financing economic activities. Banks were highly active in the credit markets during the 1980s, and bank lending grew at a very high rate until the economic slowdown of the early 1990s. By comparing the elasticity of both bank loans and broad monetary aggregate to gross domestic product for the main European countries (Germany, UK, France and Italy) and for the US and Japan from 1961 to 1994 (Figure 5.1), we can clearly see that, in almost all the countries, bank credit increased relative to output, particularly in the second half of the 1980s.

A long-term perspective might be useful to clarify the characteristics of bank credit expansion in the 1980s and the subsequent sharp contraction. First of all, we can see that, especially in the second half of the 1980s, in the UK, France, Italy and Japan bank loans increased at a higher rate than gross domestic product (elasticity of loans to GDP greater than one). In Germany growth rates of bank loans are closer to those of GDP, while in the US, elasticity of loans to GDP seems to follow a volatile pattern for all the period analysed. The result is a higher share of loans to GDP in the long term, particularly in Japan, the UK and Italy (Figure 5.2). Only at the beginning of the 1990s did the share of bank credit relative to GDP stop growing, and in countries like the UK, France and Italy it fell slightly. The non-decreasing trends of those ratios give support to the existence of a durable 'core' role for banks in financing spending.

Figure 5.1 shows that differences do exist between bank loans and broad monetary aggregate elasticities. When these differences are large and extended in time, structural changes in bank portfolios are likely to occur. The longer the periods of divergence, the more likely are the changes in portfolio composition of economic agents driven by structural changes in market conditions. This seems to be the case for France, the UK and Italy, which experienced wide and prolonged divergences between the two elasticities in the 1980s. In Germany and Japan, on the other hand, the increasing role of bank loans to GDP was accompanied by an increase in monetary aggregate that did not require changes in bank balance-sheets. In the US bank lending and broad money elasticity to GDP followed a different pattern with respect to the other countries: both indicators are characterised by wider divergences and higher frequency and are brief.

Evidence reported in Figures 5.1 and 5.2 suggests that in the UK, France and Italy loan growth in the 1980s presents characteristics similar to those of a 'bubble': a higher growth than the one experienced in other countries, more prolonged in time and followed by an intense reduction. In the US the credit expansion is less intense and shorter, with some characteristics that are similar to others experienced in the past. This evidence suggests that in European countries specific and not cyclical factors may have played a role. On the other hand, the higher volatility of bank lending in the US compared with that of the other countries analysed might be the result of cyclical and endogenous factors that reflect a closer relationship and integration between banks and financial markets.

Figure 5.1   Loans and money supply elasticities to GDP

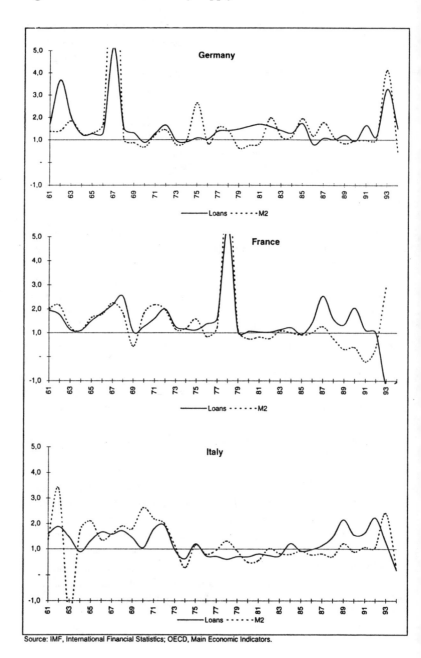

Figure 5.2   Loans to GDP ratios

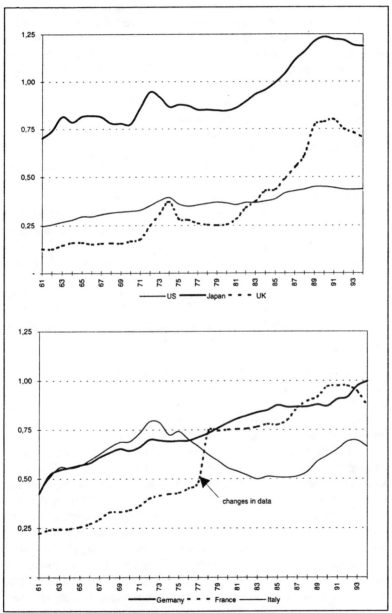

Source: IMF, International Financial Statistics; OECD, Main Economic Indicators.

3.   CHANGING STRATEGIES IN BANK LENDING

A crucial factor in growth patterns of bank lending in the 1980s was the deregulation process in financial systems that affected the main European countries. Deregulation and the removal of direct controls on bank lending allowed more borrowing from firms and households: the UK, Italy and France are examples of these processes. Banks were able to increase their loan portfolios, operating as they did without the direct control of the central bank and with the possibility of entering new markets, which before were restricted to specialised intermediaries.

Deregulation, which affected the main financial systems differently, forces banks to change strategies in order to be competitive in the new economic environment (Abraham and Lierman 1991; Gardener and Molyneux 1993).   In the UK, France and Italy, banks reacted to deregulation by increasing competition in their domestic credit markets. In order to enlarge their credit market shares banks responded to competitive pressures with new products such as adjustable mortgage rates, credit cards and other forms of consumer credit.   They also increased their loans to the commercial real estate markets, which were offering higher returns as a result of the rising prices of commercial buildings.   In Italy the removal of direct controls followed by the effects of the first European directive (EC Directive no. 77/780), which in 1985 liberalised the possibility for banks of entering new local markets by opening new branches, resulted in a sharp increase in the loan portfolio and in its importance in total assets.

The increasing competition in bank lending has shown its effects in loan pricing.   In the UK, France and Italy, the rate differential between loan and money market funds was very narrow in the second half of the 1980s.   The relative reduction in the cost of lending, therefore, also encouraged borrowers' demand for bank loans (Figure 5.3).

The effects of the aggressive strategies in the credit markets in terms of higher risk exposure and reduced profitability are well known. Competition forced banks to ease rationing procedures and to lower risk limits; furthermore, bank credit strategies have satisfied higher demands of loans from specific industries (for example, from commercial real estate, financial firms and households).   This resulted in a lower loan portfolio diversification and a greater exposure in high and volatile industries.   The reduction in the quality of loan portfolios was common to all the banks in the countries analysed. German banks too, which endured fewer shocks in bank lending, experienced an increase in risk exposure[1].

Figure 5.3   Bank loans real growth rate and spread between lending and money market rates

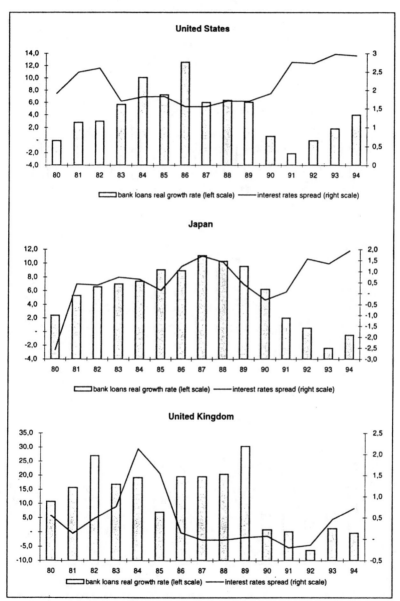

(continued)

Figure 5.3   (continued)

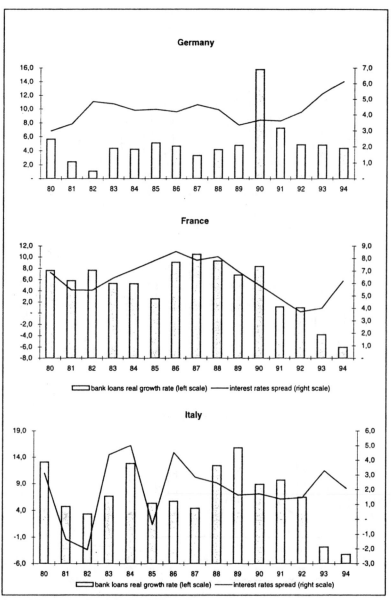

The downturn in the business cycle at the end of the 1980s resulted in unprecedented levels of bad loans and in stronger impacts on bank profitability compared with previous economic recessions. In the UK, France, the US and Japan the sharp reduction in asset prices, in particular those related to commercial real estates, exposed banks to unexpected losses. Existing loan loss provisions have also proved to be inadequate. Figure 5.4 shows the ratio of loan loss provisions to net interest income for the commercial banks of the countries analysed[2]. In all the banking systems, negative effects of increasing credit risk became evident at the end of the 1980s. In the UK and France, as well as in Germany, the effects on profitability have been very strong. In Italy the negative effects have been delayed until 1993 and 1994 (not in the figure) in relation to the downturn in the business cycle of 1993. As a result, the growth in loan provisions has reduced return on equity of commercial banks in all the countries (Figure 5.5).

Reduction in loans has been one of the first reactions of banks to the consumption of capital suffered from the rise in loan losses experienced at the end of 1980s. By tightening examination criteria banks were less willing to lend credit; this was accompanied by a voluntary reduction in risk by bank managers. The slowdown in bank lending was obtained by increasing lending rates and through non-price factors - such as collateral requirements and tighter lending standards - that were all used to reduce the amount of credit lent to riskier borrowers. Starting from the early 1990s the spread between bank lending rates and short-term money market rates increased substantially from the very low levels reached during the previous period of bank lending expansion (Figure 5.3). This was partly responsible for the bank credit slowdown of the 1990s. In other words, banks have modified previous strategies on bank credit markets that had resulted, for some countries, in mispricing of lending.

Bank lending has also been influenced by the introduction of capital requirements that might have had unintended effects on bank portfolio risks[3]. The high growth rates in bank lending in the 1980s might have been boosted by capital requirements; banks were looking at riskier opportunity sets in order to improve expected returns. Empirical evidence has found a positive relationship between average bank capital asset ratios and the subsequent average growth rate of bank loans.

The response of banks to unexpected drops in capital was more rapid in the early 1990s than in the late 1980s[4]. In particular, the changes in banking behaviour, together with banks' more conservative strategies in managing loan portfolios, were also driven by regulation on capital, even if empirical studies do not suggest that implementation of capital standards directly caused the large decrease in lending in the 1990s.

Figure 5.4   Loans provisions to net interest income ratio

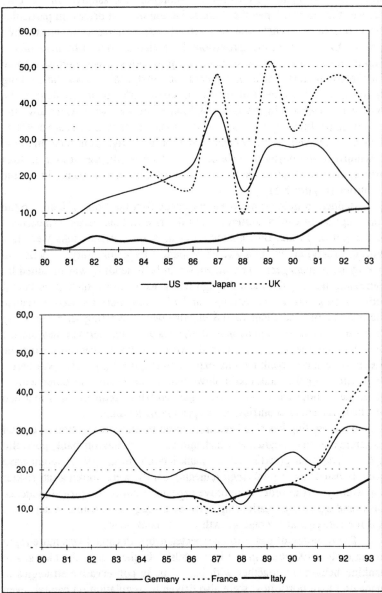

Source: OECD, Bank Profitability. Data refer to commercial banks; France: all commercial banks and credit co-operatives.
In UK, provisions (net) as a percentage of net interest income.

Figure 5.5   Return on equity

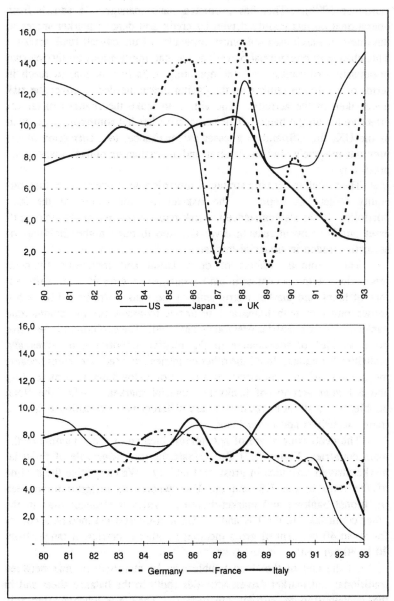

Source: OECD, Bank Profitability. Data refer to commercial banks; France: all commercial banks and credit co-operatives.

The increasing importance of bank capital has forced bankers to improve the return on equity offered to shareholders (Revell 1994; Gardener 1996). This has prompted bank managers to switch from operational targets mainly driven by credit and deposit market shares to the one that maximises the return on equity of the overall bank activity. This change in operational objectives has had implications on the internal organisation of banks. All the operating units have a goal to reach in terms of minimum returns on the capital that is needed to cover the risk undertaken in the activity. The aim is to make the changes in targets effective for all the banks. This perspective has led some countries, such as the UK, the US, and to a lesser extent France, to a correction of the previous mispricing in bank lending and to a reduction of bank loans in the portfolios[5].

The switch in banking strategies towards a more orientated return-on-equity target has improved the risk-return combination of the loan portfolio. It has also enhanced the risk-return combination of the overall asset portfolio by increasing diversification through higher holdings of securities traded in financial markets.

The combined effects of deregulation and increasing financial innovations with the change in bank strategies have resulted in a different mix of loans and market instruments in the bank portfolio. Figure 5.6 shows ratios of both loans and securities to assets for the commercial banks of the six countries previously analysed. The evolution of the ratios gives an idea of the change in the relative importance of loans and securities for banks. In all the other countries analysed, securities became more important in bank assets, as a result of a slowdown in bank lending and a higher activity of banks in financial markets. After the 'loan bubble' of the 1980s banks have a very different asset portfolio, with more traded securities and fewer loans.

The decreasing share of net interest income in gross income in the main countries (Figure 5.7) also signals the increasing role of financial market-driven activities in gross profitability. We can notice the decline of the ratio in the US and the UK, where the integration between traditional banking and market-driven activities is stronger than in the other countries. In the UK and the US non-interest net income accounts for about 40 per cent of gross income; in other countries, it ranges from 20 to 30 per cent.

At the end of the 'loan bubble', banks modified the mix between traditional and market-driven activities, both in the balance sheet and in the contribution to current profitability. They also changed the mix between credit risk and market risk exposure, with the result that bank

Figure 5.6 Loans and securities as a percentage of total assets

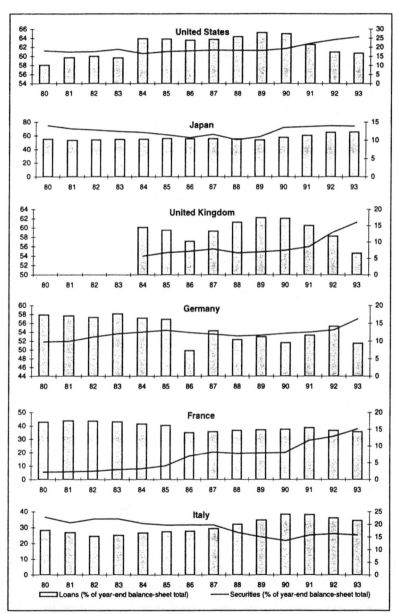

Source: OECD, Bank Profitability. Data refer to commercial banks; France: all commercial banks and credit co-operatives.

Figure 5.7   Net interest income as a percentage of gross income

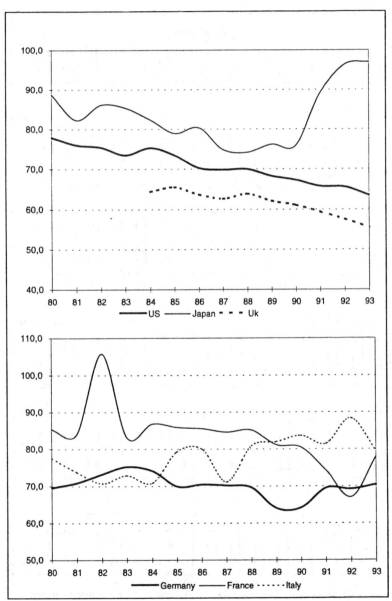

Source: OECD, Bank Profitability. Data refer to commercial banks; France: all commercial banks and credit co-operatives.

profitability is more concerned with financial market volatility today than it was in the mid-1980s.

After the experience of the 1980s, when deregulation effects and myopia in banking strategies increased the role of loans in all the financial systems, banks are showing more conservative behaviour. From the supply side of the credit markets we might expect more stability in bank lending and a lower probability of seeing other 'loan bubbles' in the near future. However, it becomes important to evaluate the effects of financial innovation on borrowers' decisions, in order to understand, also from the demand side, whether there are factors that might have changed the traditional role of bank loans in the economy and introduced more volatility in bank lending.

4. EVOLUTION IN CORPORATE FINANCING

In this section we compare the industrial investment and financing of the six countries and evaluate the evidence in the context of the relationships between firms, markets and banks. In this analysis we take as a 'benchmark study' the work of Mayer (1988, 1990), adopting the same methodological approach (flow of funds statistics)[6], delineating some stylised facts concerning real and financial choices of non-financial firms in some important systems and enriching the 'evidence-gallery' with some reference to the most recent research on firms' financial behaviour.

Firms' financial needs are affected to an ever increasing extent by merger and acquisition processes

Figure 5.8 represents the ratio between the flow of acquisitions of shareholdings and the increase in non-financial assets (tangible fixed gross assets and stocks). For the six countries taken into consideration, the increase in the holding of shares averaged nearly one quarter of the investment in real assets. Only German firms showed a lower percentage (nearly 10 per cent), although at the end of the period examined, the reorganisation of East Germany implied a consistent flow of takeovers by West German firms.

The wave of mergers and takeovers has been first and foremost the financial expression of the attempt by large firms to achieve leading positions in the arena of international competition. The external growth strategies pursued by the main European industrial groups seem to have been coherent with the lowering of national economic barriers and the

Figure 5.8   **Increase in holding of shares as a percentage of investment in non-financial assets**

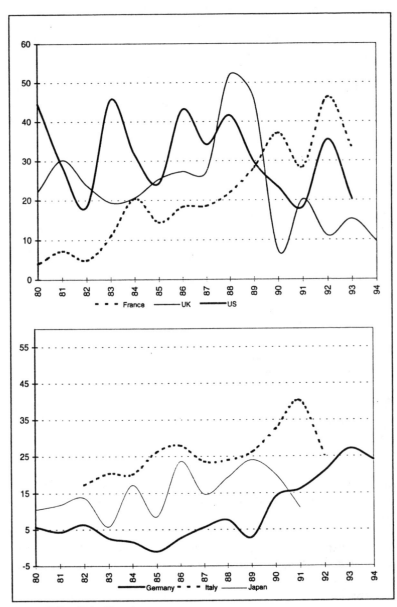

Sources: OECD and National Accounts

search for a dimensional threshold considered critical for the achievement and maintenance of a position of international leadership. The main aspects of this external growth process are:

■ in their strategic objectives, companies give less importance to profitability than to the maintenance of leadership in dimensional terms; the long-term effects of this leadership on profit appear to depend strongly on the competitive mechanisms triggered by growth. A recent study of the strategies of European industrial groups (Sassatelli 1993) states that two types of strategies dominate: on the one hand, the search for large size at the expense of good performance in terms of profit, on the other hand, a focus on good operating performance without particularly aggressive growth strategies

■ the speed with which growth strategies are implemented. The rule of competition which tends to apply in the largest oligopolistic markets is that the first move, which takes advantage of a takeover opportunity before it is grabbed by a competitor, is able to give a competitive advantage which is difficult to recoup

■ the considerable financial effort, which applies high pressure on the area of the sourcing of long-term funds in a manner compatible with parent groups' needs to maintain stability in their share distribution. This leads them to incur debts first, and then turn to the stock markets when economic conditions are favourable. The strategic nature of the investment, the speed of the takeover process and the associated need for large amounts of financing make it more difficult for financiers to assess the prospects for profitability and prevent the market from completely replacing banks as a source of finance.

The work of Davis and Mayer (1991) on corporate finance in the euromarkets stresses the role of banks in financing the riskier and larger-scale investments of large firms by virtue of their ability to monitor the borrower and to control companies moving towards bankruptcy. More specifically 'in the euromarkets loans tend to be used for large financing requirements such as project and acquisitions, while bonds were used for general financing needs'.

Retentions are the most important source of finance in all countries but with marked differences across systems and strong variability during the period analysed

In Figure 5.9 we report the ratio of self-financing in terms of total gross

Figure 5.9   Self-financing as a percentage of total sources

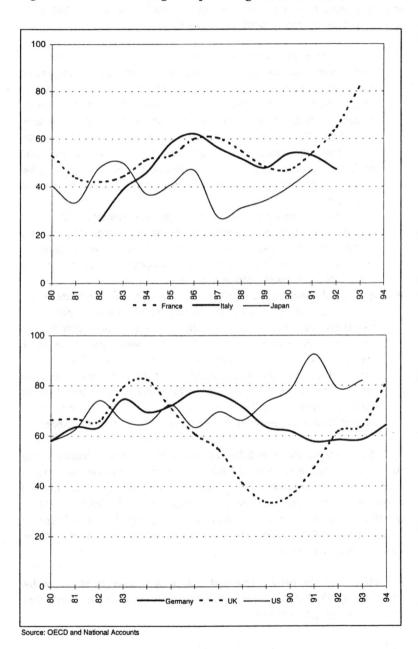

Source: OECD and National Accounts

sources. Comparing the different countries on the average during the period, German and US firms show the highest level of self-financing, while Italian and Japanese firms depend most heavily on external sources. In the case of France and the UK the ratio is extremely variable, falling below 50 per cent in some years in the second half of the 1980s. These observations confirm the pivotal role of retentions in financing firms' investment decisions and give support to the 'pecking order hypothesis' (Myers 1984) according to which internal resources are preferred to external ones in order to overcome costs associated with information asymmetries and with borrower control.

At the same time the ratio between retentions and total investment in fixed assets and shares also gives an idea of the importance of external finance (Figure 5.10). When we include the acquisition of shares in the definition of investment, it follows that in the long run earnings can provide only part of the resources needed for investment. Then a quantitative gap problem overlaps with the timing problem - internal resources may not be available just when investment opportunities come up. For medium and large firms competing in international markets and characterised by huge investment and a growth strategy which is focused on a few large acquisitions, a sequence of financing which sees most of this investment covered, temporarily, by banks which have an informative and liquidity advantage, makes sense. Later, these loans are paid back and replaced by retentions and some other more permanent source of finance such as equity issues (Sussman 1994). A rough indication which also reflects the role of the banks in financing acquisition processes is given by the high correlation between flows of bank credit and investments in fixed assets and shares not covered by internal funds (Table 5.1).

The situation for the large number of small firms is different, since they seem much more dependent on internal resources in their investment decisions. The recent literature on the impact of liquidity constraints on firms' investment underlines the importance of financial factors for smaller firms, in the sense that external capital is not a perfect substitute for self-financing. Fazzari *et al*. (1988) found that the inclusion of the cash flow in the investment function for a sample of US companies improved the results of the regression: the explanatory power of cash flow was greater in smaller firms. Similar results were obtained by Bonato *et al*. (1993) with reference to Italian firms: the cash flow variable has a negative effect on the corporate borrowing of large companies which, thanks to a greater availability of financial sources, can translate any increase of cash resources into a reduction of their stock of debt. For smaller firms the availability of cash is crucial to support their investments and any increase

Figure 5.10   Investment in real assets and shares covered by external funds, in percentages

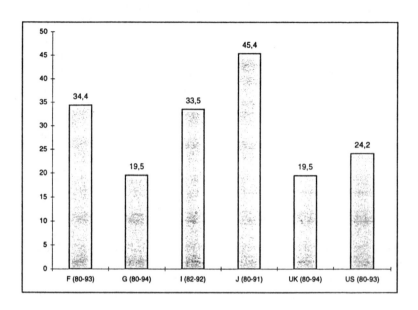

Table 5.1   Correlation indexes between investments financed by external funds and different sources of funds

Sources	France (80-93)	Germany (80-94)	Italy (82-92)	Japan (80-91)	UK (80-94)	US (80-93)
Banks	0.82	0.87	0.87	0.64	0.80	0.84
Bonds	0.78	0.32	-0.77	0.52	0.90	0.37
Shares	0.34	0.55	-0.56	0.59	0.27	-0.56
Other borrowings	0.05	0.81	0.84	0.65	0.83	0.55

in internal resources will be reflected in higher investment expenditure. Audretsch and Elston (1994) dispute the hypothesis that the institutional structure of finance in Germany has been able, since the mid-1970s, to avoid the impact of liquidity constraints: in particular this impact tends to increase systematically as firm size decreases. Less conclusive are the results of Devereux and Schiantarelli (1990) on the investment behaviours of 689 UK manufacturing firms over the period from 1969 to 1986. They find that cash flow has an economically important effect on investment decisions for all size classes of firms, even if the effects seem stronger for younger, smaller firms. The behaviour of larger firms could be explained in terms of their more diversified ownership and the related agency costs of finance.

Securities markets have increased in significance as a source of finance since the mid-1980s

The ratios of the shares and bond issues in relation to total sources of finance (Figure 5.11) show that the corporate securitisation process seems particularly strong for the majority of the countries (excluding Germany and Japan) but with particular reference to the share market (excluding US firms). This evidence contrasts sharply with Mayer's observations, according to which both stock and bond markets contributed little to overall corporate financing. The reason for the contrast can be attributed simply to the different periods under examination: Mayer's analysis covers the period 1970-85, while the development of the corporate securities market seems particularly intense in the late 1980s and 1990s. In this regard corporate finance patterns in the recent recession, if compared with the recession of the early 1980s, seem striking for Anglo-Saxon and French firms banks have notably retrenched and the securities market continued to provide finance (Davis 1994). Even in the recovery which followed, share issues continued to play a central role in the consolidation of firms' financial structure.

From a theoretical point of view the relevance of share issues does not accord with the 'pecking order hypothesis', which considers the stock market as the last convenient source of finance available for firms. Several factors are able to explain the distance between the theoretical aversion to new equity finance and the empirical evidence on the issue of shares. Firstly, the pecking order model is based on the distinction between owners and outside investors (Myers and Majluf 1984), and therefore it does not take into account the fact that a large proportion of the new issues is subscribed by owners themselves, as evidenced by the large

Figure 5.11 Composition of external funds

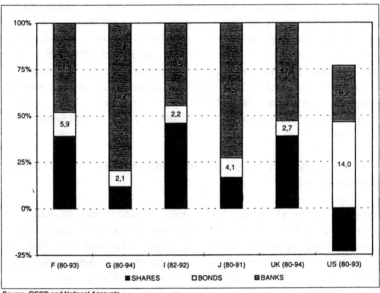

Source: OECD and National Accounts

widespread use of rights issues in several countries. Secondly, most share issues seem to have been concentrated by a few large issuers with well-known reputation in terms of solvency and recourse to the market, so as to reduce the premium new shareholders require to offset the losses arising from funding lemons. A third factor is related to the idea that equity finance is employed at high levels of gearing when debt becomes risky. In this regard, the overall changes in the level of gearing assume more relevance than the different structural levels of gearing between countries. Davis (1992), using the OECD data relating to the balance sheets of non-financial firms, identifies some sizeable changes in gearing in the US in 1982-89 and in UK and France since 1985. These shifts in the leverage levels seem to anticipate the re-equilibrium in the financial structure based on a huge recourse to the equity market which occurred in the early 1990s.

In no country, with the exception of the US, do companies raise a substantial amount of finance from the bond markets

Amongst debt instruments, bonds are in direct competition with bank loans, and there are several reasons - related to information and control problems - which imply a comparative advantage for banks in financing certain types of borrowers. Even for larger, higher-rated firms, the choice of bank versus bond financing could be affected by factors such as the timely availability of bank funds, the liquidity service associated with the drawdown of loans and the opportunity of keeping the information about the firm's strategic goals inside the direct, confidential relationship with the bank.

In addition to bank loans, the corporate bond is in strict competition with the securities issued by other borrowers - in order of importance the state and banks. In all countries securitisation has been induced or magnified by the placing of the state deficit on the bond market and by the financial innovations needed to guarantee the liquidity of the public debt. Also, banks found in the bond markets the funds needed to make long-term loans and to compensate for the relative disintermediation on the side of core deposits. The general superiority of state bonds in terms of rating and liquidity makes the issue of debt securities by non-financial firms difficult and relatively expensive.

Although debt securities have been seen to be the minority component of the total sources of funds, some recent trends regarding the market of commercial paper, which also seems to spread in strongly bank-orientated financial systems, cannot be neglected. Bertero (1994) observes that, as a consequence of the set-up of the money market in 1985 and of the availability of new instruments, French firms have been switching funding to market sources: for example, the development of commercial bills may account for part of the sharp decline in short-term bank borrowing registered since the end of the 1980s. The issue of Deutschmark commercial paper has enjoyed initial vigorous growth: the amount of CP outstanding reached an all-time high in October 1992, at a total of DM 19.5 billion (Deutsche Bundesbank 1995). On average over the period 1992-94 the recourse of German firms to the debt securities markets accounted for 5.5 per cent of total sources and for nearly 15 per cent of external funds.

The most extensive empirical evidence on the functioning of the commercial paper market and on the role played by the money markets in firms' financial decisions relates to the US corporate system. The importance and the prospects for growth of this kind of short-term instrument depend on different factors such as:

- the countercyclical nature of commercial paper. Kashyap *et al.* (1993) observe that bank loans and CP tend to move in opposite direction over the business cycle. Also Friedman and Kuttner (1993) find that tight monetary policy and the consequent decline in economic activity tend to be associated with an increase in outstanding non-financial commercial paper. The microeconomic data analysed by Calomiris *et al.* (1994) highlight an indirect counter-cyclical role of CP, which appears to be used to finance trade credit for firms without access to the debt market
- the short-term characteristics of the instruments which imply both i) incentive advantages over long-term debt in the form of limiting the increase in asset risks (Gertler and Hubbard 1993); ii) potential benefits in terms of renegotiation of debt when the quality of the firm increases (Diamond 1991); iii) a reduction in the liquidity premium outweighing the greater transaction costs of placing short-term debt (Gorton and Pennacchi 1990), also as the effect of a strong demand for CP from money market funds
- the complementarity between the CP market and bank loans implied by the requirement for 'backup lines' for commercial paper programmes, which give the banks a central role in the screening and monitoring process as well as in the supply of funds at times of difficulty in rolling over the paper

Banks are an important, sometimes dominant, source of external finance, but their role was also extremely variable over the period analysed

The international comparison gives prominence to the differences in the variability of the bank loans between countries. While German, Italian and Japanese firms show a significant and relatively stable dependence on bank lending, UK, US and French firms evidence a much more elastic use of bank debt (Table 5.2).

This evidence may support the idea that, where the markets play a significant role in corporate financing, the demand for bank loans becomes more volatile, with consequences in terms of liquidity and credit riskiness. The hypothesis that the banks and not the markets become a residual source of finance for firms is probably too strong, but surely the experience of the UK and the US seems to show a strong substitutability between loans and market securities.

Table 5.2   Standard deviation of the different external funds ratios

	Shares	Bonds	Banks
France (80-93)	5.3	1.4	15.1
Germany (80-94)	0.9	2.2	5.9
Italy (82-92)	5.4	2.5	6.3
Japan (80-91)	1.6	2.3	7.5
UK (80-94)	9.2	2.3	14.8
US (80-93)	11.4	6.2	10.7

5. CONCLUSIONS

Empirical evidence, in accord with financial intermediation theory, shows that bank lending continues to play an important role in financing the economic activity in all the countries examined, including those most orientated to securities markets. However, if we look both at the mix of firms' financial sources and banks' gross income, the growing role of securities markets cannot be neglected. In particular, securities markets become important for two reasons:

- they make a significant and increasing contribution to covering the financial needs of non-financial firms; not only is this true of traditionally market-orientated systems, but also of those countries where banks are firmly at the centre of financial intermediation flows
- with respect to bank loans, securities markets are a stable and, in some periods, counter-cyclical source of financing: the fact that in the recent recession in the UK and France, banks have notably retrenched and securities markets continued to provide finance is striking. In the US, during the 'credit crunch' of 1989-92 bank lending fell as a result

of the weakened conditions of banks, while commercial paper issuance increased

These characteristics of securities markets are destined to keep bank loan volatility up also in the near future. In other words, we believe that the behaviour of bank credit cannot be considered to be specific to the period analysed.   Both the combination of over-aggressive lending following deregulation and exceptionally high loan demand to finance merger and acquisition projects in the second half of the 1980s and the effect of firms' and banks' need to restore financial equilibrium in the early 1990s (O'Brien and Browne 1992) overlap with a structural development of the securities markets which, in the form of non-temporary funds, may introduce a natural variability in bank credit supply. The behaviour of US bank loans with respect to the monetary aggregate and to GDP may be a good 'benchmark' for the future evolution of bank lending in all those countries increasingly orientated to securities markets.

On the bank side the complementarity between loans and securities markets will become a strategic goal. In fact, even if loans reduce their share in bank asset portfolios, this will not necessarily lead to a reduction in the importance of banks in the financial system; more likely, it will result in a change in the mix of traditional intermediation and new activities in securities markets.

Factors related to bank risk and profitability targets are in favour of a hypothesis stressing the long-term shift in bank activity towards an increasing complementarity between loans and securities. Return on equity targets increasingly force loan pricing policies that are not compatible with a high growth in loans. When taking into account that higher competition among banks has reduced extra return from market segmentation, it follows that net profits from traditional bank intermediation may not be enough to reward all the capital banks that have increased in the 1980s, also as a result of capital requirements.

In some countries (the US and the UK) the introduction of capital requirements has led banks to price loans so as to reward the capital needed to take into account the underlying credit risk. This resulted in a reduction in credit demand and, therefore, in the lower loan portfolio weight to the total assets. In these countries banks have favoured the integration between bank lending and market-driven activities supporting borrowers and investors' financial decisions.

In other countries (see Italy) this process has been delayed by the larger contribution from deposit activities to return on capital compared with that from bank lending. In fact the higher segmentation of deposit markets has allowed for a higher spread; the increasing competition in these markets will induce banks to improve profitability by higher integration between non-tradeable and illiquid assets with tradeable securities in financial markets. This may lead to a stronger impulse towards securitisation.

Looking at the risks, different factors may affect the integration between loans and securities. Firstly, by increasing market activities banks augment their portfolio diversification (cross-section diversification); secondly, the rising weight of securities in the asset portfolio improves flexibility and liquidity as well as the possibility of reaching the desired risk-return combinations; thirdly, improvements in asset-liability and risk management systems allow for different combinations of credit and market risks and the attainment of desired targets of return on capital. However, this does not imply that credit and market risks cannot add up, thus highlighting the instability of banks; this result will depend on bank strategies and their ability to deal with changes both in financial markets and the economic scenario.

APPENDIX: STATISTICAL SOURCES

The dataset on corporate financing is based on the flow-of-funds national accounts, data and statistics sources for non-financial firms, and for some countries on companies' accounts. For French firms we use the 'Tableau simplifié d'emplois et des resources des sociétés' based on *Les Comptes de la Nation et Statistiques Monétaires de la Banque de France*. For German firms we refer to the statistics on 'Capital formation and financing of West German producing enterprises' which appear in the *Monthly Report* of Deutsche Bundesbank. The definition of producing enterprises sector included unincorporated businesses. For details see Deutsche Bundesbank (1988). Data on UK firms is drawn from Central Statistical Office, *Financial Statistics*, 'Sources and uses of capital funds of industrial and commercial companies'. US data make reference to the statistics 'Nonfinancial corporate business-sector balance-sheet' of the Board of Governors of the Federal Reserve System.

For Italy and Japan we use OECD, *Non-financial Enterprises Financial Statements*. The group of companies included in the Italian statistics covers almost all manufacturing companies with a net worth of up to 2.5 billion lire. The Japanese statistics cover all the incorporated companies with a net worth of up to 1 billion yen and a representative sample of small incorporated companies (with a net worth less than 1 billion of yen).

NOTES

1. A recent research on the credit risk exposure of the main European banks (Forestieri and Onado (eds) 1995) showed the negative effects of the easy lending strategies on the risk exposure and profitability of banks. The main European banks had insufficient credit risk control systems and incomplete evaluation procedures to choose the firms to be financed and to monitor the activities during the period of the loan contract.
2. Data come from OECD surveys on bank profitability from 1980 to 1993. For the UK we refer to the amount of net provisions as a percentage of net interest income.
3. The theoretical issue of how higher required equity ratios affect bank-risk taking is still unresolved. Koehn and Santomero (1980), Keeton (1988) and Kim and Santomero (1988) sustain that an increase in the required equity-to-assets ratio might either raise or diminish the portfolio risk chosen by banks. Bank failure models find that a higher equity-to-assets ratio is associated with a lower future probability of failure, but there is no clear evidence whether this positive relationship reflects a decrease in portfolio risk in addition to the reduction in leverage risk (Berger *et al*. 1995). However, there is a possibility that a bank, in response to a growth in its equity-to-assets ratio, might increase its portfolio risk.
4. Peek and Rosengreen (1995) find an explicit regulatory link to the shrinkage of both bank loan portfolio and bank capital. Thakor and Wilson (1995) show that an increase in capital requirements will cause banks to be less willing to renegotiate loans in the future; this anticipated contraction in the future supply of loans might have an effect in the quantity of loans issued at present. This might push borrowers to shift from bank loans to the issue of direct debt in the capital market.
5. The credit slowdown at the beginning of the 1990s has also been caused by changes in the loan demand related to the economic recession and changing preferences of borrowers because of the growth of alternative sources of credit. We will discuss the demand factors in the next section.

6. The starting point of our evidence is given by the flow of funds
statistics which offer a picture of the way the non-financial firms
cover real and financial investments with different sources of
financing. Even if the flows do not express the leverage of the firms,
nevertheless the interemporal analysis of the financial flows becomes
a useful (and largely used) approach to delineate the patterns of the
real and financial behaviour of the firms in the last decade (see
Appendix for details on the national statistics).

LIST OF REFERENCES

Abraham J.P. and F. Lierman (1991), 'European banking strategies in the
nineties: a supply side approach', IEF Research Papers in Banking and
Finance, RP 91/8
Anderson, R.W. (1994), 'An exploration of the complementarity of bank
lending and securities markets', mimeo (December)
Atkin, J.M. (1994), *Gestione del rischio di credito e ciclo economico:
alcune lezioni dal mercato inglese*, ABI (May)
Audretsch, D.B. and J.A. Elston (1994), 'Does firm size matter? evidence
on the impact of liquidity constraints on firm investment behaviour in
Germany', CEPR Discussion Paper, no. 1072
Bank for International Settlements, *Annual Reports*
Bank of England, *Large Exposures Undertaken by Institutions Authorised
under the Banking Act 1979*, Notice to Banks
Beattie, V., P. Casson, R. Dale, G. McKenzie, C. Sutcliffe and M.
Turner (1994), 'Loan loss provision by international banks: estimation,
determinants and evidence', Discussion Paper in Accounting and
Management Science, University of Southampton (December)
Berger, A.N., R.J. Herring and P.G. Szegö (1995), 'The role of capital
in financial institutions', *Journal of Banking and Finance* (June)
Bertero, E. (1994), 'The banking system, financial markets, and capital
structure: some new evidence from France', *Oxford Review of
Economic Policy*, **10**
Bonato, L., R. Faini and M. Ratti, (1993), 'Empirical determinants of
corporate debt decisions: some evidence for Italy', in V. Conti and R.
Hamaui (eds.), *Financial Markets' Liberalisation and the Role of Banks*
(Cambridge: Cambridge University Press)
Borio, C.E.W. (1990), 'Leverage and financing of non-financial
companies: an international perspective', BIS Economic Paper, no. 27
(Basle)

Calomiris, C.W., C.P. Himmelberg and P. Wachtel (1994), 'Commercial paper, corporate finance, and the business cycle: a microeconomic perspective', NBER Working Paper no. 4848

Corbett, J. and T.J. Jenkinson (1994), 'The financing of industry, 1970-89: an international comparison', CEPR Discussion Paper, no. 948

Dale, S. and A. Haldane (1993), 'Bank behaviour and the monetary transmission mechanism', *Bank of England Quarterly Bulletin*, (November)

Davis, E.P. (1992), *Debt, Financial Fragility, and Systemic Risk* (Oxford: Clarendon Press)

Davis, E.P. (1994), 'Banking, corporate finance, and monetary policy: an empirical perspective', *Oxford Review of Economic Policy*, **10**

Davis, E. P. and C.P. Mayer (1991), 'Corporate finance in the euromarkets and the economics of intermediation', CEPR Discussion Paper no. 570

Deutsche Bundesbank (1995), 'Trends towards securitisation in the German financial system and their implications for monetary policy', *Monthly Report* (April)

Devereux, M. and F. Schiantarelli (1990), 'Investment, financial factors and cash flow: evidence from UK panel data' in R.G.Hubbard (ed.), *Asymmetric Information, Capital Markets and Investment* (Chicago, Ill: University of Chicago Press)

Diamond, D.W. (1991), 'Debt maturity structure and liquidity risk', *Quarterly Journal of Economics*, **106**

Edwards, J. and K. Fischer (1994), *Banks, Finance and Investment in Germany* (Cambridge: Cambridge University Press)

Fazzari,S., R.G. Hubbard and B.C. Petersen (1988), 'Financing constraints and corporate investment', Brookings Paper in Economic Activity, **1**

Forestieri G. and M. Onado (eds) (1995), *La gestione del credito nelle banche europee* (Milano: Egea)

Friedman, B.M. and Kuttner, K.N. (1993), 'Economic activity and the short-term credit markets; an analysis of prices and quantities', *Brookings Papers on Economic Activity*, **2**, pp. 193-283

Gardener, E.P.M. (1996), 'The future of traditional banking' in J. Revell (ed.), *The Recent Evolution of Financial Systems* (Basingstoke and London: Macmillan)

Gardener, E.P.M. and P. Molyneux (1993), *Changes in Western European Banking: an International Banker's Guide* (London: Routledge)

Gertler, M. and R.G. Hubbard (1993), 'Financial factors in business fluctuations', *Financial Market Volatility*, Federal Reserve Bank of Kansas City

Gorton, G. and G.Pennacchi (1990), 'Financial intermediaries and liquidity creation', *Journal of Finance*, **45**

Kashyap, A., J. Stein, and D. Wilcox (1993), 'Monetary policy and credit conditions: evidence from the composition of external finance', *American Economic Review*, **83**

Keeton, W.R. (1988), 'Substitutes and complements in bank risk-taking and the effectiveness of regulation', Federal Reserve Bank of Kansas City, working paper (December)

Kim, D. and A.M. Santomero (1988), 'Risk in banking and capital regulation', *Journal of Finance*, **43**

Koehn, M. and A.M. Santomero (1980), 'Regulation of bank capital and portfolio risk', *Journal of Finance*, **43** (December)

Mayer, C. (1988), 'New Issues in Corporate Finance', *European Economic Review*

Mayer, C. (1990), 'Financial systems, corporate finance and economic development', in R.G.Hubbard (ed.), *Asymmetric Information, Capital Markets and Investment* (Chicago, Ill: University of Chicago Press)

Mayer, C. and I. Alexander (1990), 'Banks and securities markets: corporate financing in Germany and the UK', CEPR Discussion Paper no. 433

Myers, S. (1984), 'The capital structure puzzle', *The Journal of Finance*, **39**

Myers, S. and N. Majluf (1984), 'Corporate financing and investment decision when firms have information that investors do not have', *Journal of Financial Economics*, **13**

O'Brien, P.F. and F. Browne (1992), 'A "credit crunch"? the recent slowdown in bank lending and its implications for monetary policy', OECD, Working paper no. 107

Peek, J. and E.S. Rosengreen (1995), 'Bank regulation and credit crunch', *Journal of Banking and Finance* (June)

Revell, J. (ed.) (1994), *The Changing Face of European Banks and Securities Markets* (Basingstoke and London: Macmillan)

Rybczynski, T.M. (1984), 'The UK financial system in transition', *National Westminster Bank Quarterly Review* (November)

Salomon Brothers (1991), 'Bank asset-quality: a global profile', *International Equity Research* (October)

Sassatelli, M. (1993), 'Strategie di crescita ed evoluzione del posizionamento dei grandi gruppi europei', in **Nomisma**, Rapporto 1992 sull'industria italiana (Bologna: Il Mulino)

Shrieves, R.E. and D. Dahl (1995), 'Regulation, recession, and bank lending behavior: the 1990 credit crunch', *Journal of Financial Services Research*, **9**

Sussman, O. (1994), 'Investment and banking: some international comparisons', *Oxford Review of Economic Policy*, **10**, 4

Thakor, A.V. and P.F. Wilson (1995), 'Capital requirements, loan renegotiation and the borrower's choice of financing source', *Journal of Banking and Finance* (June)

CHAPTER 6
EFFICIENT RISK MANAGEMENT IN FINANCIAL SYSTEMS: UNIVERSAL BANK OR SECURITISATION?

Elisabetta Montanaro

From the early eighties onwards, two seemingly opposite tendencies have developed in financial systems. On the one hand there has been the great success of the securitisation process that resulted in the disintermediation of banks; this originated in the conversion of bilateral credit relations into marketable financial instruments. The main cause of securitisation has been the growing advantage for firms, investors and even banks in dividing complex credit functions into a series of elementary functions, each assigned to a different part of the market. Evidence of this can be seen in off-balance sheet securitisation, which is the most innovatory outcome of functional specialisation in financial markets (Bryan 1994).

On the other hand that functional and institutional specialisation which distinguished banks from other financial intermediaries, particularly those active in stock markets as brokers or dealers, has gradually declined even in systems, such as the US, the UK or France where securitisation is most widespread (Saunders 1989). The natural tendency of the bank to act as a multiproduct firm grew everywhere thus transforming traditional commercial banks, in fact if not by law, into universal ones (Steinherr and Huveneers 1994).

The model of banks today is no longer the original Anglo-Saxon one of the 'real bill doctrine', but the German universal bank. This is the model that the evolutionist theory of financial systems (of the transformation from bank-orientated to market-orientated financial systems) places at the initial and historically more backward stage, characteristic of underdeveloped or developing economies (Cameron 1972; Rybczynski 1984; Hellwig 1991). Commercial banks which specialised in short-term or self-liquidating loans developed, in fact, because they had the exclusive right to self-funding through monetary deposits. Like the central banks, from which they originated and with which they kept close relations of hierarchical dependence, the commercial banks were characterised by a close complementarity, or in present day terminology, by joint production economies between their monetary and credit functions.

The efficient management of liquidity, credit, and interest rate risks which these synergies involve allowed the commercial banks to establish themselves as the leading financial institution of Victorian Britain. This occurred in that country whose level of economic development was the highest and whose capital markets were the most efficient and international, thanks to the strength acquired by the pound as the standard means of payment in world trade (Hawtrey 1962). With the bank reforms of the thirties, the specialised commercial bank, which had seemed destined to survive only in economic textbooks with the mystique of credit creation '*ex-nihilo*', was on the contrary imposed by law both in the US and in many European countries.

Thus the distinction between credit and investment functions was concretised in different ways according to the individual countries' supervisory regulations. In Italy, where most large companies are state-owned and the financial market has been dominated by government securities (Montanaro 1980; Onado 1986), it took the form of the specialisation by maturity of loans to firms, since banks were allowed to make short-term loans only. In the US on the other hand, through the Glass-Steagall Act, this specialisation imposed strict separation of commercial from investment banks. By this law Congress hoped to protect the financial system from eventual conflicts of interest, which would stem from the banks abusing their fiduciary responsibilities. In particular the fear was that the banks might attempt to bail out bad loans by selling equity to the public, the proceeds of which would be used to repay the bank. In reality, however, this practice is the essence of several of the processes of securitisation (Kroszner and Rajan 1994).

The purpose of this regulation of the functional specialisation of banks was to guarantee financial stability while at the same time achieving two basically ideological aims:

- the safeguarding of depositors' 'unconscious savings'
- the principle of economic democracy, which was ensured by making industry independent of banks - the allocative neutrality of banks

Bank specialisation, in its various forms, was in the first place the outcome of a political project: one aimed at using government intervention to correct the social and economic disequilibria which resulted from market failures such as the Great Depression of the thirties (Confalonieri 1965; Saraceno 1981). Paradoxically this type of organisational model was founded more or less on the belief that banks, although necessary, were more risky or at least less efficient than free markets. This assumption legitimised regulation aimed at restricting both the activities and the size of banking intermediaries and that which favoured direct credit channels thought to be a valid and more efficient alternative.

The line of thinking according to which the virtuous functioning of banking specialisation would cause the more backward bank-centred financial systems to evolve towards more advanced market-orientated systems, such as that in the US, was widely agreed upon. Germany and Japan were not as yet first-rank economic powers and thus did not merit the attention of bankers and analysts.

Seen with hindsight the ideology behind banking specialisation appears to be coherent with the theory of credit intermediation which was dominant until the end of the seventies. The latter saw the specificity of banks with respect to other intermediaries as residing in the transaction function necessary to administer the payments system and its relative regulation. According to this theory, based on the perfect market postulate and the Modigliani-Miller theorems of the indifference of financial choices (Hellwig 1981), the role of the banks in the allocation system had to be tailored within the space left by the residual imperfections of financial markets, due to transaction costs, fiscal incentives to borrow, and also to the safety net which last-resort credit and bank deposit insurance provided to commercial banks.

Between the end of the sixties and the beginning of the seventies a series of factors altered, perhaps irreversibly, the coherence of the system of bank specialisation imposed by regulation. A vast literature has examined the endogenous and exogenous circumstances which have put an end to the 'good old times' in which bankers under the protection of regulation thought they could expand both the volume and profits of intermediation without appreciable risk and therefore without consistent capital investments and updating of know-how.

Tobin had clearly understood in 1963 that the moment would come when the specialised commercial bank would no longer be able to satisfy the needs of the market and could therefore no longer require 'a positive risk premium on loans and a negative premium on deposits' (Pyle 1971): he warned that 'there is at any moment a natural economic limit to the scale of the commercial banking industry' (Tobin 1963; Bertelli 1995). In reality the disintermediation of deposits, which began in the US at the end of the sixties and in Italy almost ten years later, was the first sign that the artificial balance created by specialised banking had been broken. It was no chance that this process of change, which sooner or later involved all those countries which had adopted specialisation, started with the long inflation of the seventies and gathered pace with the high degree of variability in interest and exchange rates which followed.

This coincidence is important because it allows us to underline empirically how those countries like Germany and Switzerland, characterised by a system of universal banks and a tradition of monetary stability, both necessary conditions to minimise risks and contain the cost of long-term indebtedness, remained on the whole immune from the upheaval of financial restructuring (Edwards and Fischer 1993). Moreover, financial innovation, the globalisation of markets and increasing competition in both wholesale and retail intermediation have all gradually worn away at the foundations of the artificial equilibrium created by specialised banking.

The Italian case is an example of this. Italy is among the countries which have defended the principles of functional and temporal specialisation of credit most tenaciously. The regulatory and operative canons, by which the rules aimed at pursuing the allocative neutrality of the bank were able to work without apparently generating financial imbalances, functioned up to the beginning of the seventies, or rather as long as the banks' capacity to provide credit was kept well above firms' demand for real short-term financing. The importance of banks in the financing of Italian firms was based on instruments such as the widespread use of current account loans, which although formally short-term were granted to firms as permanent credit lines, the practice of multiple bank credits, and double intermediation. Thus the boundaries of commercial credit were largely exceeded despite the fact that the orthodoxy of transferability was respected.

The financial crisis which hit large firms at the beginning of the seventies served to confirm what was already clear - that these technical artifices would, in the long run, bring about structural imbalances both for banks and firms if the growth of risk capital through self-financing or recourse to external financing through the market or the private or public fortune of the entrepreneur was insufficient to keep an arm's-length distance between banks and firms. During the eighties it became clear that all the premises upon which the idea that banks were allowed to operate the whole range of maturities without being transformed into universal banks was based, either had not happened or were no longer relevant. In particular:

- The Italian credit system has remained very 'bank-centred' to this day, despite disintermediation and the rapid development of financial markets in terms of both size and efficiency
- The transferability of credit, founded on the postulate by which 'credit capacity is earning capacity' has been disproved empirically. The statistical evidence showing a significant inverse correlation between indebtedness and self-financing in all financial systems,

which is particularly noticeable in Italy, should be interpreted in these terms (Banca d'Italia 1993). This is due to the close negative relation generated between cash flow and interest costs when the proportion of short-term, variable rate and unrenouncable debts is high among the firm's liabilities

■   Bank deposits have decreased compared with financing which is transferable only inasmuch as creditors can be substituted within creditworthiness relations, thus accentuating risks of maturity imbalances and the consequent variability in interest margins

Since the failure of the assumptions on which bank specialisation is based, two opposite processes have gained ground - securitisation and despecialisation.   The contradiction between securitisation and the tendency of the bank to become, or rather to go back to being, universal is obvious if we consider that securitisation empirically negates the existence of those economies of scale and scope upon which the competitive advantage of the universal bank is based.   Seen in these terms securitisation and the universal bank become an apparently insoluble dilemma for the microeconomic analysis of the financial industry.   They are two contradictory organisational solutions which financial systems adopt in carrying out their institutional functions.   These consist in satisfying at the same time and at the least cost for the community the portfolio preferences of those whose money is available today and those who think they will have it in the future.

The risks connected to this function are inevitable since they both arise from the asymmetrical distribution of information among the participants in the credit process. They can, however, be minimised either through dividing and spreading them between several operators in the credit process, or through integrated management exploiting the related information synergies and the compensation effects between different types of risks.   The application to banks of the analytical tools of industrial economics helps to explain why multiproduction and large size, faced with variable product mixes, operating size and market choice of banks, have not produced satisfactory results so far. This is due to the fact that 'productivity' measurements of their efficiency do not consist so much in the construction and distribution of specific products or services but in the transformation and management of variable risk mixes through the use of real and financial resources and above all professionalism and entrepreneurial skills, which can neither be created nor modified in the short run.   From the scientific point of view it would not be correct to consider the enlargement of the areas of intermediation as the necessary and sufficient condition to improve the efficiency of the banking industry, since the securitisation (in practice the most advanced form of specialisation) must be considered one of the most evident demonstrations that the opposite can be true.

This antithesis between securitisation and universal bank becomes even more obvious if seen in terms of an evolutionary analysis of financial systems. On the one hand securitisation would reinforce the superiority of the market in which the banks could survive as long as they maintained a competitive advantage in terms of monitoring technology. The latter would guarantee them the riskiest and non-liquid credits, such as those to small firms or new ventures, which are the most problematic from the information point of view. (Berger and Udell 1991). However these are credits which banks tend to avoid as much as possible.

On the other hand the general tendency towards a universal bank on the part of those systems which had imposed specialisation and the stability of financial structures of the German type of bank-orientated systems would seem to indicate the exact opposite. The superiority of indirect channels over market channels whose function would consist in minimising liquidity risks and those conflicts of interest typical of banking intermediation would make it more efficient and thus more capable of growth (Jensen 1986). The latest theories of intermediation give analytic support to this latter interpretation.

While economists' faith in the inherent superiority of the market is wavering, the strong points of intermediaries, particularly banks, are the efficiency of their information and regulation systems, especially the selection and control of loans through long-term client relationships. These deal effectively with problems of asymmetric information and free-riding typical of market financing (Greenwald and Stiglitz 1991). Moreover the informative efficiency of intermediaries tends to grow along with the consolidation of client relations with firms through the simultaneous provision of capital and credit financing and corporate governance services. It is, therefore, possible to see the German universal bank in the paradigms of the new theory of intermediation (Edwards and Fischer 1993). The situation in Germany, Switzerland and in part also Japan shows that the existence of this model of bank does not require the vast efficient stockmarkets necessary for a securitisation system.

The purpose of this paper has been to emphasise the contrast between securitisation and the universal bank, not to conciliate the two but rather to understand the scientific limits of the various financial theories. These seem to be better at giving an *a posteriori* explanation of prevailing tendencies than at proposing empirically verifiable scientific hypotheses.

We must be aware of these limits, especially since the legitimisation of new organisational structures and models of regulation of financial systems are based on these theoretical postulates. In my opinion the opposition between specialisation and despecialisation in financial risk management is more apparent than real, because they are so defined by the theoretical frameworks within which the complex determinants of financial structures is discussed today.

The close association which is observed systematically in the dynamic of bad loans and the economic cycle is coherent with the old saying that it is 'healthy industry which makes the bank healthy' and not *vice versa*. This confirms the hypothesis that the informative superiority of the bank, which lies at the heart of the modern theory of intermediation, is more ideological than scientific: the same is true of the opposite hypothesis of the allocative superiority of the market. The only certainty in all financial systems, however banal but no less evident, is that the type and size of banking intermediation is modified according to the type and size of the sources of financing, be that due to the prince's privilege or the trust of markets, and thus allows banks to incur debt at a lower cost than their customers. This observation could thus be the starting point for further research.

LIST OF REFERENCES

Banca d'Italia (1993), *Relazione Annuale*, Roma, p. 183

Berger, A.N. and G.F. Udell (1991), 'Securitisation, risk and the liquidity problem in banking', Finance and Economic Discussion Series, Federal Reserve Board, Washington, 181

Bertelli, R. (1995), 'Le determinanti dello spread bancario: il premio per il rischio e i coefficienti patrimoniali', *Bancaria*, 10, 18-30

Bryan, L.L. (1994), 'Structured securitized credit: a superior technology for lending' in D. Chew (ed.), *New Developments in Commercial Banking* (Cambridge, MA: Basil Blackwell)

Cameron, R. (1972), *Banking and Economic Development. Some Lessons of History,* (Oxford: Oxford University Press)

Confalonieri, A. (1965), 'Credito ordinario e a "medio termine": considerazioni sull'esperienza italiana', in A. Confalonieri (1970), *Aspetti dell' Attività Bancari* (Milano: Giuffrè 225-72)

Edwards, J. and K. Fischer (1993), *Banks, Finance and Investment in Germany*, CEPR (Cambridge, UK: Cambridge University Press)

Greenwald, B.C. and J. Stiglitz (1991), *Information, Finance and*

Markets: the Architecture of Allocative Mechanisms (Cambridge, MA: NBER)

Hawtrey, R.G. (1962), *The Art of Central Banking* (London: Frank Cass & Co.)

Hellwig, M. (1981), 'Bankruptcy, limited liability and the Modigliani Miller theorem', *American Economic Review*, **71**, pp. 155-70

Hellwig, M. (1991), 'Banking, financial intermediation and corporate finance', in A. Giovannini and C. Meyer (eds), *European Financial Integration* (Cambridge UK: Cambridge University Press)

Jensen, M.C. (1986), 'Agency costs of free cash flow, corporate finance and takeovers', *American Economic Review, Papers and Proceedings*, **76**, pp. 323-9

Kroszner, R.S. and R.G. Rajan (1994), 'Is the Glass Steagall Act justified? A study of the United States experience with universal banking before 1993', *American Economic Review*, **84**, 4, 810-32

Montanaro, E. (1980), 'Disintermediazione e despecializzazione bancaria: evoluzione del mercato del credito italiano', *Note Economiche*, 5/6, 140-63

Onado, M. (1986), 'Banche e altri intermediari: specializzazione of concorrenza?', *Note Economiche*, 3/4, 273-93

Pyle, D.H. (1971), 'On the theory of financial intermediation', *Journal of Finance*, pp. 737-52

Rybczynski, T.M. (1984), 'The UK financial system in transition', *National Westminster Bank Quarterly Review*, November, pp. 26-42

Saraceno, P. (1981), 'Salvataggi bancari e riforme negli anni 1922-1936' in AA. VV. *Banca e Industria fra le due Guerre. Le Riforme Istituzionali e il Pensiero Giuridico* (Bologna: Il Mulino pp. 15-61)

Saunders, A. (1989), 'Banks and securities markets', Salomon Brothers Center for the Study of Financial Institutions, Working Papers Series, 509

Steinherr, A. and C. Huveneers (1994), 'On the performance of differently regulated financial institutions: some empirical evidence', *Journal of Banking and Finance*, **18**, pp. 271-306

Tobin, J. (1963), 'Commercial banks as creators of money' in Hester, D.D. and J. Tobin (eds) (1967), *Financial Markets and Economic Activity*, Cowles Foundation Monograph 21 (New York, NY: J. Wiley)

CHAPTER 7
TRENDS IN GERMAN BANKING

Leo Schuster

1. CHANGES IN THE BANKING INDUSTRY

About ten years ago some new terms became common in the international banking industry, such as securitisation, disintermediation, globalisation, deregulation and computerisation. Only today, and certainly even more so in the future, will the consequences of these phenomena be fully understood. This is also true for some of the new catchwords which have had to be introduced into the banking vocabulary in the meantime: derivatisation, dehumanisation and cultural change. The scope of this article is to show the consequences of these developments on the German banking system.

2. CULTURAL CHANGE IN BANKS

The reasons for securitisation are well known and do not have to be explained in this context. The consequences, however, are far-reaching inside the financial industry and can be pinpointed with the following figures: in 1994 the traditional loan business amounted to US$113 billion, whereas capital market instruments exceeded US$400 billion and euronote facilities almost US$200 billion. Securitisation has sparked off a further development that is known as disintermediation, and this has led to a huge volume of off-balance sheet business. In some banks it accounts for almost double or triple the balance sheet volume. German banks having always had a strong loan culture, refrained from this development for a long time, but now there is some evidence for a certain shift to a securities culture: securities as a financing alternative are gaining momentum in Germany. Though the structure of personal German investments still shows a small proportion in securities of only 24 per cent compared with the US with a proportion of 37 per cent, the trend is obviously in favour of securities: forecasts say that in the year 2010 the share of securities in personal investments will be 50 per cent, corresponding to a total of DM7,000 billion. The same trend can be observed with German companies. They feature an average finance mix of 18 per cent equity, 0.1 per cent bonds, 20 per cent bank loans, 19 per

131

cent supplier credits and a significant proportion - 43 per cent - in pension funds, which is specific to Germany. In the US for a comparison two-thirds of total financing - namely 49 per cent in equities and 20 per cent in bonds - is raised on the capital market; bank loans sum up to 9 per cent only. The different circumstances are due to the more advanced securities culture in the US. It is said that the securities culture in Anglo-Saxon countries generally results from their specialised banking system; it is backed by superbly performing investment banks. Over the past decades, the Americans have thus become 'investors' whilst the Germans have always been 'savers'. This will have to change as the privatisation of state-owned companies such as Telekom progresses.

However, Deutsche Bank AG - which is the largest German bank - is only ranked tenth in the investment banks' league table. It does not have enough placement power to distribute all Telekom shares efficiently on its own. Consequently, a more high-profile investment bank is required to support the privatisation process. This role will be taken over by Goldman Sachs, which is ranked third in the investment banking league table.

Because of the current tendencies and developments the traditional loan business has already been declared as dead. Loan managers of German banks can no longer be considered as part of the banks' traditional 'prime function'. Nevertheless, a second humiliation has been dealt to the classic loan business. Modern capital market theory and sophisticated portfolio management techniques - state of the art in investment banking for a long time - are now influencing German commercial banking. The focal point still is credit risk. However, it is not the single risk - which is evaluated by traditional methods of creditworthiness, i.e. bottom up - that plays an important role any more. On the contrary, the total loan portfolio, i.e. the top-down strategy, prevails; it implies a daily assessment of the positions through a performance-orientated credit portfolio manager. This new approach stands in contradiction to the old way of doing credit business where confidence and a long-standing relationship with the customer played an important role.

A bank which is in a position to assess instantly its worldwide risk exposure and to avoid risk accumulation through rearrangement of its positions can easily optimise its risk-return profile. The idea behind this is known as the unbundling and repackaging technique of risks. The first step in this risk allocation process is the subdivision of risks into smaller parts. This method is also known under the idiom of 'particle finance'. The remaining risks are to be hedged by financial innovations such as futures and options. Only a few risky assets are kept within the banks, others are sold off. The marketability of risks enables banks to restructure their balance sheets or to concentrate on their respective trading. The new way of assessing and reallocating credit risks is regarded as 'non-traditional banking'. It is believed that it will gradually replace 'traditional banking'. This development will certainly lead to a new breed of bankers in Germany.

3. STRUCTURAL CHANGES IN GERMAN BANKING

The driving forces behind any structural change in market economies are national and international competition. Experts predicted that the German banking industry would become the steel industry of the 1990s because of overcapacities in the local market and a lack of competitiveness abroad. Indeed, several countries have witnessed a continuing concentration process in the banking industry: in Switzerland more than 130 regional and savings banks have disappeared since 1990. The largest bank in the world has emerged in Japan through the fusion of Bank of Tokyo - which has an international scope - and Mitsubishi Bank - which is a Keiretsu-type of institute with a national scope. The latest mega-merger was carried out in the US by the marriage of Chase Manhatten and Chemical Bank. The catchword behind these developments is no longer 'small is beautiful' but 'big is necessary'. German banks, however, are finding it difficult to generate size by external concentration. Unorganic expansion is restricted, especially in view of political barriers. No noteworthy national merger has occurred in the last few years. The loophole to this end is an increasing 'going abroad'.

Deutsche Bank was the first institute to concentrate investment banking in London and to use a 1989 merged investment house - now called Deutsche Morgan Grenfell - as its investment banking headquarters. Other German banks are planning the same 'going abroad' strategy. Internationalisation of investment banking is also triggered by the lack of efficiency in German stock and bond markets.

At the present time a very controversial debate between the German government and the Deutsche Bundesbank on the one hand and some big private banks on the other hand is going on. The point of controversy is whether the current escape to London is a blow against Frankfurt as the emerging European financial centre. Some bankers argue that the step to the London market is only in the interest of their customers. Additionally, it will have positive impacts on creating innovations, which otherwise cannot be introduced in Germany because of legal and central bank constraints.

As German tax laws are becoming increasingly stringent and as banking secrecy has *de facto* been abolished, German private banking will be increasingly carried out abroad. This trend has already been seen as Luxembourg investment funds have flourished, and it is now going to continue on a larger scale in Switzerland. Most German banks already have subsidiaries in Switzerland, founded several years ago; those that are not represented in this country are now setting up companies. Especially privileged private investors - so called high-net-worth individuals - who want to 'diversify' their portfolios are the centre of attention. Considering these developments, one must assume that shifting business under the umbrella of a holding company will be a major strategic issue for German banks in the future.

On a national scale, one goal is to make distribution channels more flexible and to exploit opportunities to design them as a customer-value-added component. Several German banks have introduced so-called discount brokers; this is a marketing channel which has been used successfully in other countries for several years. The final aim of this strategy is to facilitate investment banking on a more widespread basis. It remains to be seen whether this strategy will pay off in the end. Whilst transaction costs are lower for both parties the renunciation of advisory facilities, however, could cause various problems. German private investors are rather unaware of investment risks and usually need expert advice.

In summary, the German banking system is changing its face. It is increasingly becoming a conglomerate system of financial concerns consisting of many different - legally independent - companies. Financial and non-financial activities are based in different countries according to local comparative advantages. Following this process German banks will have to cope with diverging cultures.

Surprisingly, a similar development is taking place in countries with originally specialised banks such as the US and Britain. Accelerated by deregulation and mergers, many banks are in the process of developing into conglomerate financial institutions too. Considering these developments, an old academic question has to remain open however: will universal banking succeed specialised investment banking? My guess is both systems will meet after having changed in the same direction!

4.   DEHUMANISATION IN GERMAN BANKING

This topic is likely to cause some astonishment at first sight. Dehumanisation, however, is an obvious trend in German banking, and it contains two aspects: the first concerns the business relation to customers, whilst the second involves the role of bank employees.

German financial institutions are very effectively managed in the domestic context. Business acquisition through an extensive branch system, as well as sound controlling systems and human resource management, have traditionally been an asset for German banks. However, the branch system turns out to be of minor advantage. It is criticised because of its density and its operating-leverage risk. Furthermore, the German domestic banking system is obviously overbanked with one outlet for every 1,300 customers.

Forecasts predict that 15,000 branches will be closed in the next few years and substituted by home banking, telephone banking, multimedia and Internet banking. The implications of this development are far reaching both in respect of customers and employees. The bank-customer interface will be increasingly characterised by electronic, impersonal means of communication. This is certainly a change compared with common methods. It has to be analysed on the background of traditionally strong competition amongst German banks in the retail segment.

For many years banks did have to try very hard to attract potential customers. For this reason they built representative lobbies for having personal contact. Thereby, opportunities for cross-selling could be exploited. Nowadays, on the contrary, bankers are increasingly happy if customers use electronic media for routine business transactions. This is, of course, due to cost reasons.

The most extreme example of a branchless computer bank is 'Bank 24', a subsidiary of Deutsche Bank AG. It was founded in 1995 and is located in Bonn; this virtual bank can only be reached by telephone or computer, consequently bankers and customers will never have personal contact with each other. Deutsche Bank AG is speculating on the young generation which it hopes will increasingly take advantage of the new electronic sales channels. 'Bank 24' is regarded as a lucrative investment - mainly for the future. However, the new distribution methods imply that bank personnel is going to be increasingly redundant. All German banks have announced plans to make people redundant and to reduce their personnel capacity by 10-15 per cent. This trend can also be observed in other countries. After the merger of Chase Manhatten and Chemical Bank the new management released the information that 15,000 people will be outplaced.

Any long-standing observer is likely to be amazed about these latest trends. One can remember numerous statements of bankers saying that 'Banks are People' and that qualified people are the most valuable asset of each bank. All of a sudden the same bankers pretend that banking meanwhile has become a 'technology-driven business'. It is no longer reputation which counts; the only important performance criterion in the eye of the customer is customer value. Under the bottom line, it will not be surprising, however, if these 'dehumanisation' trends lead to problems in those banks which face fundamental employee relationship difficulties. Furthermore, it must be clear that banks still depend on qualified employees. It still happens that the prospects of banks are dramatically changed by the loss of 'knowledge teams' who leave banks and thereby take away expertise and know-how. This takes place especially in the areas of financial engineering and derivative instruments.

5.   THE PROBABLE CONSEQUENCES OF THE EUROPEAN MONETARY UNION FOR BANKS

The introduction of a single European currency, the Euro, will not only have a strong impact on the whole economic and political system but also on the banking industry. The latter will be more affected than any other sector as banks are intermediators of money and credit. This impact will also be strong on the central banks of those countries that fulfil the convergence criteria and therefore become members of the Monetary Union. Their importance will decrease, as they will become 'outlets' with technical functions within the European Monetary System.

It has to be seen which instruments and tools the EMS will dispose of in future. Moreover, it is not clear nor yet decided if the forthcoming European Central Bank is going to manage the money supply in the way successfully practised today by the German Bundesbank. It is also not known if there will be an inflation-orientated target such as in the UK or an exchange rate policy such as in the Netherlands.

It should be clear, however, that in any case the main objective will have to be the stability of the Euro, thus protecting personal and institutional wealth from inflation. The forthcoming European Central Bank should also consider that every tool used has to be neutral in terms of competition. Ideally, no European financial centre should be preferred and its policy should not accelerate concentration within the various banking sectors. Moreover, the payment settlement system used should also be a task of the European Central Bank at the Currency Union level. For this purpose a new lump-sum payment system has been developed which is called 'Target'. It will be set into operation with the beginning of the third phase of the European Currency Union.

Major commercial banks hope to realise advantages in international business after the implementation of the single currency. Not all of them, however, seem to be prepared for the European Currency Union. Their long-term portfolio management is still aimed at the present multi-currency system. Some banks also do not consider that they will be confronted with a loss in turnover of up to 40 per cent in their payment transactions, travellers cheque, credit card and foreign exchange business resulting from the fact that there will no longer be currency exchange fluctuations between EU countries. On the other hand, the whole situation is not as dramatic as it seems to be. The position of German banks in forex dealing has always been very weak despite the strong DM, which is still the second most important currency after the US dollar. Not a single German bank is to be found in the top-ten ranking by the *Euromoney* FX Surveys. These are filled by American, British and Swiss banks. However, these are three countries that will not, or cannot, join the Currency Union. Therefore, they will not suffer from diminishing business.

Finally, 90 per cent of all bank accounts in retail banking are managed by savings and co-operative banks, and these two banking groups will probably suffer most from the costs of change resulting from the EMU. Costs will occur from the necessary adaptation of computer software, the change of automated teller machines and many other currency-related systems. Some banks estimate that these costs will amount to DM100-200 million, depending on the size of a bank.

6. PROBLEMS IMPOSED BY LAW AND REGULATIONS

One tendency seems to be quite clear: the worldwide deregulation of the past fifteen years has been replaced by a striking reregulation within the EU countries. German banks - similar to those of other EU countries - have to deal with more than fifty European rules and regulations. What makes it worse for the Germans is that national legislation based on these regulations is often more stringent, thus imposing an additional burden on German banks.

Besides legislation further legal problems are imposed by German law courts. A considerable obstacle is put in the path of the banking system by jurisdiction in so far as banks have been sentenced for supposedly false advice in portfolio management. The second Capital Market Enhancement Law prescribes that bankers should advise customers according to their individual risk-return preferences. These have to be assessed through special questionnaires, and if a customer can testify to any shortcoming in this procedure, banks are likely to be sentenced to pay compensation in case of any losses occurring from the customer's investments.

Furthermore, banking secrecy - known and observed in every country - has become a special issue in Germany. The backbone of banking secrecy, which is not legally defined in Germany, has become very weak. The reason for this is that Germany today is one of the countries with the highest taxes in the world. As a natural consequence citizens and entrepreneurs tried to invest their savings (respectively their profits) abroad where taxes are more moderate in the belief that banking secrecy would cover up those procedures. The favourite countries for such transactions are within the EU Luxembourg and outside the Common Market Switzerland, Liechtenstein and, to some extent, the Channel Islands. *Nota bene*, experts assert that the real reason why Switzerland cannot join the EU is the fact that one consequence would be that it would lose invested capital from member countries to an extent that would ruin domestic banks.

The only possibility for the German government to secure tax-evading money is *de facto* to abolish banking secrecy. This enables advanced investigations in which every paper trail resulting from transactions can be tracked and thus people who have committed tax fraud or even money laundering can be prosecuted. Tax authorities have already initiated intensive investigations into banks at the slightest suspicion of fraud. Recent examples which highlight this development are provided by investigations into some leading German banks. These 'raids' have resulted in thousands of customers being screened in detail by German tax authorities. Many of them are already sentenced, some of them even put into jail.

7.   THE GERMAN BANKS IN AN EVER-CHANGING ENVIRON-MENT

Banks have always been the focus of individual and public criticism, and German banks are no exception. This is shown in the results of periodical opinion polls: for example, fewer than 50 per cent of the German population believe that banks enhance economic development, and only one-quarter of the population of the new Bundesländer (new federal states) is of this opinion; 60 per cent have confidence in banks and 37 per cent do not trust banks at all; about 20 per cent believe that banks do not look after their customers' money correctly.

The banks' image has always been very fragile, and whenever special 'cases' (e.g. the bankruptcy of the real estate entrepreneur Jürgen Schneider, or the quasi failure of Metallgesellschaft or Balsam) have occurred, the banks' image is at its lowest level. Banks spend a lot of money on public relations in order to improve their corporate images, usually without long-lasting success. Sometimes, criticism of the banks overshoots the mark. One prime example is the role of West German banks after the fall of the Iron Curtain and the reunification of both parts of Germany.

West German banks were absolutely prepared to penetrate the eastern part of Germany, which they finally did in a very short period of time. This is a good example of the strategic principle that chances have to be exploited immediately. Because of the lack of adequate buildings West German banks established their branches in imported container boxes, from which the term 'container banking' arose. Telephone calls had to be made by satellite telephones using a special western net because the eastern telephone system was completely unusable. After all, West German banks were the pacemakers of East German integration and upswing. Sadly, they are not regarded as beneficial pioneers, having a worse image in East than in West Germany.

German banks not only penetrated the East German market, but they also set up branches and joint ventures in other former communist countries. All major German banks are represented in the Czech Republic, Poland and Hungary and some of them also in other eastern markets today. They follow industrial corporations that increasingly establish plants in the so-called 'low wage' countries in order to remain competitive *vis-à-vis* the east Asian industries. Germany has become too expensive as a location and is therefore of restricted economic attraction. Only high-tech and sophisticated service industries have a chance of surviving domestically. All other industries will gradually have to go abroad, with banks following close behind. German banks will have to remain flexible, market-orientated and innovative. Only by demonstrating these qualities will they also fulfil their responsibility to society.

LIST OF REFERENCES

Breuer, Rolf-E. (1995), 'Der Weg der deutschen Investment-Banken nach

London ist eine Befruchtung des deutschen Kapitalmarktes',
Kreditwesen, Nr. 29, 1196 ff.

Büschgen, Hans E. (1995), 'Den Banken ist es nicht gelungen, den
Privatanlegern die Eignung von Aktien als Anlageform zu Vermitteln',
Kreditwesen, Nr. 29, 1180 f.

Flesch, Johann Rudolf (1995), 'Visionen zur Bank der Zukunft', *Bank
und Markt*, Heft 1, January, pp. 37-40

Huber, Paul (1995). 'Vom Monopol zum Wettbewerb', *Der Monat in
Wirtschaft und Finanz*, April, 4 ff.

Lamfalussy, Alexandre (1993), 'Ist die Finanzielle Revolution zu weit
Gegangen?', *Börsen-Zeitung*, 11.09.93

Priewasser, Erich (1994), *Die Priewasser-Prognose; Bankstrategien und
Bankmanagement 2009* (Frankfurt/Main)

Schmid, Beat (1994), 'Electronic Banking - Strategien der Zukunft',
Geldinstitute, 7/8-94, pp. 46-56

Schultze-Kimmle, Horst-Dieter (1994), 'Zehn Thesen zur Bank der
Zukunft', *Die Bank*, 2/94

Weibel, Peter F. (1994), 'Risiken und Chancen Bewirtschaften',
Schweizer Bank, 94/6, pp. 38-41

CHAPTER 8
UNIVERSAL BANKS, OWNERSHIP AND EFFICIENCY:
A STOCHASTIC FRONTIER ANALYSIS OF THE GERMAN
BANKING MARKET

Yener Altunbas, Lynne Evans and Philip Molyneux

1. INTRODUCTION

Within Western Europe the structure of the banking industry is changing rapidly, and one motivation for these changes is a drive for greater efficiency. However, whilst scale and scope efficiencies have been fairly extensively studied both in the US and the European contexts, surprisingly little attention has been paid to measuring what appears to be an important source of inefficiency - X-inefficiency - particularly in the European context[1]. This paper starts to redress this imbalance by measuring deviations from the efficient cost frontier for specific bank types and organisational forms in the German market. Moreover, the paper extends the literature on the merits and demerits of universal banking systems by focusing on the technical efficiency of banks operating under these systems.

The existing literature evaluating universal banking systems gives little empirical attention to the efficiency of banks operating under these systems; see, for example, Benston (1994), John *et al.* (1994), Steinherr and Huveneers (1994), Saunders (1994) and Saunders and Walter (1994)[2]. Sheldon and Haegler (1993) and Sheldon (1994) have investigated the Swiss market and found that banks with diversified product mixes are more inefficient than specialised banks. In contrast, Lang and Welzel (1994) and Altunbas and Molyneux (1994) find evidence of scope economies for the German market, especially for the largest banks. This paper uses a stochastic cost frontier analysis to calculate technical inefficiencies for banks in the German market. We find that private commercial banks, public (local government-owned) savings banks and mutual co-operative banks have similar levels of mean inefficiency around the 25 per cent level. Specialist institutions of mixed ownership appear to be significantly more inefficient around the 45 per cent level. The paper is set out as follows. Section 2 outlines the stochastic cost frontier methodology. Data and results are discussed in Section 3, and Section 4 is the conclusion.

2.   METHODOLOGY

Previous studies on cost inefficiency and bank organisational form have focused on the stock versus mutual ownership debate in the US savings and loans industry[3]. For example, recent studies by Mester (1993) and Cebenoyan *et al.* (1993) estimate stochastic cost frontiers and analyse the inefficiency scores to determine whether stock or mutual firms are systematically closer to the 'efficient cost frontier' (ECF)[4].   In this approach the cost function of the most efficient producers (the ECF) is estimated, and an institution's deviation from the frontier consists of random error and inefficiency.   The part of the error term representing random deviations from the frontier is assumed to be drawn from a two-sided distribution, while the part representing inefficiency is assumed to be drawn from a one-sided distribution because inefficiency raises costs.

Following Cebenoyan *et al.* (1993) we estimate a single stochastic cost frontier and derive inefficiency scores for five categories of German banks: private commercial banks; public (local government-owned) savings banks; mutual co-operative banks; central organisations; and mortgage banks. Inefficiency scores for individual banks are estimated using the stochastic frontier approach as   introduced by Aigner *et al.* (1977), Meeusen and van den Broeck (1977) and Battese and Corra (1977).

The single-equation stochastic cost function model can be given as:

$$TC = TC(Q_i, P_i) + \varepsilon_i \qquad (1)$$

where TC is observed total cost, Q_i is a vector of outputs, and P_i is an input price vector. Following Stevenson (1980) we assume that the error of the cost function is:

$$\varepsilon = u + v \qquad (2)$$

where u and v are independently distributed. u is assumed to be distributed as a truncated normal with mean μ, that is, a one-sided positive disturbance capturing inefficiency, and v is assumed to be distributed as two-sided normal with zero mean and variance σ_v^2, representing the effects of the statistical noise[5].   Furthermore, it can be assumed that u and v are distributed as:

$$h(u) = \frac{1}{(1 - F(-\mu/\sigma_u))\sqrt{2\pi\sigma_u}} \exp\left[-\frac{1}{2}\left\{\frac{u-\mu}{\sigma_u}\right\}^2 \right] \; for \; u>0, \qquad (3)$$

and $= 0$ otherwise,

$$f(v) = \frac{1}{\sqrt{2\pi}\sigma_v} \exp\left[-\frac{1}{2}\left(\frac{v}{\sigma_v}\right)^2\right] \text{ for all } v, \tag{4}$$

where $F(.)$ is the distribution function for a standard normal random variable. The joint density function $\epsilon = u + v$ can be written as:

$$g(\varepsilon) = \sigma^{-1}f\left(\frac{\varepsilon - \mu}{\sigma}\right)\left[1 - F\left(-\frac{\mu}{\sigma\lambda} - \frac{\varepsilon\lambda}{\sigma}\right)\right]\left[1 - F\left(-\frac{\mu}{\sigma_u}\right)\right]^{-1} \tag{5}$$

where $\sigma = (\sigma_u^2 + \sigma_v^2)^{\frac{1}{2}}$, $\lambda = \sigma_u/\sigma_v$, f is the standard normal density calculated at $((\varepsilon - \mu)/\sigma)$.

The log-likelihood function for a sample of N observations can be shown as:

$$\ln L = \frac{N}{2}\ln\sigma^2 - \frac{N}{2}\ln 2\pi - \frac{1}{2\sigma^2}\sum_{i=1}^{N}\left((Y_i - \beta'X_i) - \mu\right)^2 +$$

$$\sum_{i=1}^{N}\ln\left[1 - F\left(\sigma^{-1}\left(-\frac{\mu}{\lambda} - (Y_i - \beta'X_i)\lambda\right)\right)\right] - N\ln\left[1 - F\left(-\frac{\mu}{\sigma} - (\lambda^2 + 1)^{\frac{1}{2}}\right)\right] \tag{6}$$

where N is the number of observations, $Y_i = \beta'X_i + \varepsilon_i$ with β and X_i being [1 x K] vectors. Jondrow *et al.* (1982) have shown that the ratio of the variability (standard deviation, σ) for u and v can be used to measure a bank's relative inefficiency, $\lambda = \sigma_u/\sigma_v$ where a small value for λ indicates that uncontrollable factors dominate controllable inefficiencies. Estimates of this model can be computed by maximising the likelihood function directly (see Olson *et al.* 1980).

Observation-specific estimates of technical inefficiency, u, can be calculated by using the distribution of the inefficiency term conditional on the estimate of the composed error term, as proposed by Jondrow *et al.* (1982). The mean of this conditional distribution for the half-normal model is shown as:

$$E(u_i/\varepsilon_i)=\frac{\sigma\lambda}{1+\lambda^2}\left[\frac{f(\varepsilon_i\lambda/\sigma)}{1-F(\varepsilon_i\lambda/\sigma)}+\left(\frac{\varepsilon_i\lambda}{\sigma}\right)\right] \quad (7)$$

where $F(.)$ and $f(.)$ are the standard normal distribution and the standard normal density function, respectively. $E(u/\epsilon)$ is an unbiased but inconsistent estimator of u_i, since regardless of N, the variance of the estimator remains non-zero (see Greene 1993; 80-82). However, Stevenson (1980) has analysed the case in which u, has a truncated normal distribution with parameters μ, which is allowed to differ from zero in either direction, and variance σ_u^2. Greene (1990) has shown that the conditional distribution for the truncated normal model, which we use in this paper, can be obtained by replacing $\varepsilon_i\lambda/\sigma$ in equation (7) with:

$$\mu^*=\frac{\varepsilon_i\lambda}{\sigma}+\frac{\mu}{\sigma\lambda} \quad (8)$$

To get estimates of the technical inefficiencies, u_i, a standard translog cost function (see Noulas *et al.* 1990; Mester 1993; Cebenoyan *et al.* 1993; Kaparakis *et al.* 1994) incorporating a two-component error structure is first estimated using a maximum likelihood procedure. This is specified as follows:

$$\ln TC=\alpha_0+\sum_{i=1}^{2}\alpha_i\ln Q_i+\sum_{i=1}^{3}\beta_i\ln P_i+\lambda_b\ln B+$$
$$\frac{1}{2}\left[\sum_{i=1}^{2}\sum_{j=1}^{2}\delta_{ij}\ln Q_i\ln Q_j+\sum_{i=1}^{3}\sum_{j=1}^{3}\lambda_{ij}\ln P_i\ln P_j+\lambda_{bb}\ln B\ln B\right]+ \quad (9)$$
$$\sum_{i=1}^{3}\sum_{j=1}^{2}\rho_{ij}\ln P_i\ln Q_j+\sum_{i-1}^{2}\lambda_{bi}\ln B\ln Q_i+\sum_{i=1}^{3}\tau_{bi}\ln B\ln P_i+\varepsilon$$

where
TC = total cost, comprising operating cost and financial cost (interest paid on deposits)
Q_1 = total loans
Q_2 = total securities
P_1 = average annual wage expenses per branch
P_2 = average interest cost per Deutschmark of interest-bearing deposits

P_3 = average price of capital, calculated as the ratio of total capital expenses to total fixed assets

B = the number of branches

ε = stochastic error term and

α, β, δ, γ, ρ, λ and τ are coefficients to be estimated. The estimation yields a set of parameter estimates describing the characteristics of efficient production technology by means of the shape of the cost frontier. To get estimates of inefficiency we evaluate $\hat{E}(u/\epsilon_i)$ at the estimates of σ_u and σ_v.

Since the duality theorem requires that the cost function must be linearly homogeneous in input prices, the following restrictions are imposed on the parameters of equation (9):

$$\sum_{i=1}^{3} \beta_i = 1; \quad \sum_{i=1}^{3} \lambda_{ij} = 0; \quad \sum_{i=1}^{3} \rho_{ij} = 0 \quad \text{for all } j \qquad (10)$$

Furthermore, the second order parameters of the cost function in equation (1) must be symmetric, i.e.:

$$\delta_{ij} = \delta_{ji}; \quad \lambda_{ij} = \lambda_{ji} \quad \text{for all } i, j \qquad (11)$$

3. DATA AND RESULTS

The empirical approach to output definition used in this study is consistent with Sealey and Lindley's (1977) model of production in depository financial institutions. Given the chosen intermediation approach (see Kaparakis *et al.* 1994), we use two categories of outputs, three variable inputs (with input prices P_i) and the number of branches as a control variable. Bank outputs (Q_i) are measured as total loans and securities, in accordance with Kolari and Zardkoohi (1987) and most other cost studies. The three inputs are labour, deposits and physical capital[6].

Our study uses balance sheet and income statement data from 1988 for a sample of 196 German banks, obtained from the London-based International Bank Credit Analysis Ltd (IBCA) database. Data on the number of branches were obtained from *Bankers' Almanac* (1989). Overall the sample represents around 80 per cent of the German banking industry in assets terms, and the descriptive statistics are shown in the Appendix. Kempf (1985), Gardener and Molyneux (1990) and the Deutsche Bundesbank (1989) provide us with our bank classification model. Bank types and organisational forms are cross-checked in the *Bankers' Almanac* (1989), which gives information on banks' ownership characteristics. Five categories of banks are identified having four ownership types: private (or joint-stock) commercial banks; public (local government-owned) savings banks; mutual co-operative banks; central organisations and mortgage banks, both of which have mixed ownership[7]. Table 8.1 reports the maximum likelihood parameter estimates of the stochastic cost frontier for German banks and Table 8.2 shows the inefficiency scores. The mean inefficiency score for all banks at 35 per cent suggests that German banks could produce the same output with 65 per cent of the current inputs if they were operating efficiently[8].

Both the mean and median inefficiency scores suggest that the mixed ownership specialist banks - the mortgage banks and central organisations - are less efficient than the other groups of banks in our sample. In fact the statistics for the private commercial banks compared with the public savings and mutual co-operative banks appear to be similar[9]. To evaluate whether the inefficiency scores pertaining to different bank groups were significantly different we used the Kruskall-Wallis (1952) test to evaluate differences between sample medians. The Kruskall-Wallis test statistic at 27.38 (to be compared with a critical chi-squared value of 9.48) leads us to reject the null hypothesis that median inefficiency scores were equal[10]. Since we have found that there are significant differences between inefficiency levels for the various types of banks, a natural follow-up question is to ask which groups statistically differ from each other. This can be tested by using Dunn's (1964) non-parametric statistic. If there are k groups then there are $k*(k - 1)/2$ paired comparisons to be made. To perform the test, we calculate the 'absolute difference' between the mean ranks and the standard deviation as given by $\sqrt{[N*(N+1)/12]*[1/n_i)+(1/n_j)]}$. Pairwise comparisons using Dunn's (1964) method for the different bank types are shown in Table 8.3.

Table 8.3 indicates that the inefficiency scores for public savings banks and mutual co-operative banks are not significantly different from each other. On the other hand, inefficiency levels for private commercial banks appear to be significantly different from those of the aforementioned banks even though mean and median technical inefficiencies for all three groups are around the 25 per cent level. These three categories of banks, despite having different ownership characteristics, are universal in nature. The mortgage banks and central organisations (with mixed ownership characteristics and yielding inefficiency scores which are not significantly different) are more specialist in their operations. Therefore our results tentatively suggest that specialist banks operating in the German banking

Table 8.1 **Maximum likelihood parameter estimates of the translog stochastic cost frontier**

Parameter	Estimate	Parameter	Estimate
α_0	5.66 (5.011)	γ_{33}	0.01 (0.0418)
α_1	0.51* (0.0798)	ρ_{11}	0.01 (0.0195)
α_2	0.38* (0.0581)	ρ_{12}	-0.08* (0.0254)
β_1	0.78* (0.1704)	ρ_{21}	0.04* (0.0138)
β_2	0.27 (0.1999)	λ_b	0.44* (0.0568)
δ_{11}	0.09* (0.0257)	λ_{bb}	-0.06 (0.0674)
δ_{12}	-0.05** (0.0171)	λ_{b1}	0.04 (0.0224)
δ_{22}	0.13* (0.0273)	λ_{b2}	-0.08** (0.0302)
γ_{22}	-0.06* (0.0257)	σ_u/σ_v	1.22 (0.7061)
γ_{13}	0.06 (0.0323)	$\sqrt{(\sigma_u^2+\sigma_v^2)}$	0.49** (0.2310)

Notes: Standard errors of estimated parameters are shown beneath in parentheses
* significantly different from zero at 0.01 level
** significantly different from zero at 0.05 level
The parameter estimates for the average price of capital and other second order input prices can be estimated using the restrictions in equation (10). In estimating the model we exclude three variables, that is the interactive variable between the average deposit price and total loans and the interactive variables between input prices and the number of branches due to high multicollinearity among the explanatory variables

Table 8.2   Technical inefficiencies according to bank types and ownership status

Owner-ship	Mean	Median	Std.Dev.	Minimum	Maximum
Private commer-cial	0.300	0.267	0.130	0.059	0.628
Mortgage	0.470	0.435	0.248	0.112	0.935
Public savings	0.269	0.241	0.192	0.059	0.884
Mutual co-operative	0.238	0.220	0.075	0.163	0.364
Central organisa-tions	0.480	0.436	0.293	0.155	0.703
All banks	0.351	0.291	0.134	0.059	0.935

Table 8.3   Ownership and technical inefficiency: pairwise comparisons using Dunn's (1964) statistic

Groups	G_2	G_3	G_4	G_5
G_1	3.213*	2.530*	2.437*	3.334*
G_2		4.514*	4.066*	0.707
G_3			0.384	2.382*
G_4				2.390*

Note: At the 5 per cent level, if the difference divided by the standard deviation is larger than $Z=2.33$, we reject the null hypothesis that there is no significant difference between the two group of banks. If not then we infer that there is no significant difference in the inefficiency levels between the two groups.

G_1 Private commercial banks
G_2 Mortgage banks
G_3 Public savings banks
G_4 Mutual cooperative banks
G_5 Central organisations

market are significantly less efficient than their broader-based universal bank counterparts. In addition, different ownership characteristics - whether private, publicly-owned, or mutual - do not appear to have a large effect on the *absolute* level of bank inefficiencies in the German market, although the inefficiency scores for banks in private ownership are found to be significantly different from those of all other bank types[11].

4. CONCLUSION

This paper uses the stochastic cost frontier approach to evaluate technical inefficiencies for specific bank types and organisational forms in the German market. We find that private, public and mutually-owned banks have mean inefficiencies around the 25 per cent level. Specialist institutions of mixed ownership appear to be significantly more inefficient around the 45 per cent level. This result broadly supports the view that in terms of cost efficiencies universal banks appear to have some advantage over specialist banks. Indeed it seems that, in the German market, diversified banks (which follow the precept of finance-diversification) are more efficient than specialist banks (which follow the precept of economics-specialisation). These results do, however, conflict with the Swiss findings of Sheldon and Haegler (1993) and Sheldon (1994). With regard to ownership types, there do not appear to be substantial differences in the *absolute* levels of technical inefficiency between private, local government-owned and mutual banks in the German market. This surprising finding perhaps deserves further investigation to identify the extent to which ownership type affects bank efficiency in other banking markets.

Appendix   Size distribution and bank type

Total assets ($ million)	Private commercial banks	Mortgage banks	Public savings banks	Mutual co-operative banks	Central organisations	All
0-1000	52	1	4	10	1	68
1000-3000	33	0	20	7	0	60
3000-5000	8	2	10	0	0	20
5000-10000	2	9	9	0	0	20
10000-50000	8	5	2	0	6	21
50000 <	7	0	0	0	0	7
All	110	17	45	17	7	196

NOTES

1. In their review of research on the efficiency of (largely US) financial institutions, Berger *et al.* (1993) indicate that, whilst scale and product mix inefficiencies are found to account for less than 5 per cent of costs in banking, X-inefficiency accounts for some 20 per cent of costs.

2. Saunders and Walter (1994) find evidence of super scale (at around the $25 billion asset range) but no evidence of economies of scope for the top 200 banks many of which have a universal banking focus.

3. See Verbrugge and Goldstein (1981); Verbrugge and Jahera (1981); Blair and Placone (1988) and Mester (1989).

4. Mester (1993), as in her (1989) study, chose to estimate separate cost frontiers for the two different categories of banks. In this paper we follow the single technology analysis as indicated in Cebenoyan *et al.* (1993). This is because we assume all banks have the same opportunities to combine inputs and produce outputs and the choice of differing technologies is a management decision. It should also be noted that our sample could not be split as in Mester's studies because of the small sample size.

5. See Bauer (1990) for an excellent review of the frontier literature and how different stochastic assumptions can be made. Cebenoyan *et al.* (1993), for example, use the truncated normal model as we do in our analysis. Mester (1993), in common with many (non-banking) studies uses the half-normal distribution. Stevenson (1980) and Greene (1990) have used the normal-gamma model, and a normal-exponential model has also been used. Altunbas and Molyneux (1994) find that efficiency estimates are relatively insensitive to different distributional assumptions when comparing the half-normal, truncated normal, normal-exponential and gamma distributions.

6. Berger and Humphrey (1992) argue that the Sealey and Lindley (1977) approach may be inappropriate because deposits should be included as an output term. This is based on the view that because deposit services usually account for a substantial proportion of total costs, they should be included as outputs. We re-estimated efficiency scores with deposits as a third output and overall the parameters of the new cost function were remarkably similar to the two output models. Efficiency scores were slightly higher, but the general findings of the two output models were

not substantially affected. The inefficiency differences between specialist institutions and the other banks were further exaggerated with the three-output model. See Pulley and Humphrey (1993) for a recent example of cost function estimation using deposits as an output term.

7.   Public savings banks are governed by their own national public law and are owned by local government. Mortgage banks have a mixed ownership; some are owned by the private commercial banks and others have mutual status. Central organisations undertake wholesale business for their savings bank or co-operative bank owners. For our purposes we regard them as having mixed ownership. Deutsche Bundesbank (1989) noted that at the end of 1988 commercial banks had 23.4 per cent of total volume of business, compared with 21.4 per cent for the savings banks, 12.2 per cent for the co-operative banks, 20.9 per cent for the central organisations and 13.8 per cent for the mortgage banks.

8.   These inefficiency scores are relatively high when compared with those found in US studies. For example, Evanoff and Israilevich (1991) surveyed the productive efficiency results for ten US studies and found inefficiency levels ranging between 13 and 51 per cent. Cebenoyan *et al.* (1993), Berger (1993) and Bauer *et al.* (1993) find mean inefficiency levels in commercial and savings banks in the 21 to 52 per cent, 10 to 40 per cent and 15 to 17 per cent ranges, respectively. Kaparakis *et al.* (1994), using a sample of 5,548 US banks, estimate mean inefficiencies of 9.8 per cent and find that banks generally become less efficient with increasing size.

9.   Provisional estimates using the exponential error distribution yield similar results, where we also find that the inefficiency scores are considerably larger for the mortgage banks and central organisations.

10   We use a non-parametric test because this is the appropriate test given the non-normal distribution of $E(u/\epsilon)$. The inefficiency measure ranges from 0 to 1. This is a technical violation of the assumption that variables are required to be normally distributed over the range $-\infty$ to ∞ for the parametric test. The Kruskall-Wallis (1952) test is the natural extension of the Wilcoxon rank-sum test for two to more than two statistical populations. The purpose of the non-parametric test is to determine whether the relative frequency distributions of populations of interest are

identical to or different from one another. The null hypothesis can be written as (see Conover 1971, 257): H_0. There are no differences between the medians (H_0: $\mu_1 = \mu_2 = \ldots \mu_k$); H_1: At least two μ's differ.   To perform the test, the observations contained in the various groups are pooled and ranked from 1 to N ($N = n_1 + n_2 + \ldots n_k$). The test statistic H is given as follows:

$$H = \left[\frac{12}{N(N+1)} \left(\sum_{i=1}^{k} \frac{R_i^2}{n_i} \right) \right] - [3(n+1)]$$

where n_i is the number of observations in each group and R_i the sum of the ranks from the ith group. The statistic is asymptotically chi-square-distributed with k-1 degrees of freedom.

11.   Bearing in mind the limitations as identified in Mester (1993), we also undertook a Tobit analysis regressing inefficiency scores against ownership types, and this highlighted significant differences between the groups. This suggests the need to explore these issues further in other banking markets. It may be that ownership type and style of governance affect bank efficiency in some systematic way.

LIST OF REFERENCES

Aigner, D., C. Lovell and P. Schmidt (1977), 'Formulation and estimation of stochastic frontier production models', *Journal of Econometrics*, **6**, pp. 21-37

Altunbas, Y. and P. Molyneux (1994), 'A comparative analysis of scope and scale economies in EC Banking Markets', Paper presented at the European Economics Association, 3-5 September, Maastricht, The Netherlands

Bankers' Almanac (1989), Volumes 1 and 2 (London: Reed Information)

Battese, G.E. and G.S. Corra (1977), 'Estimation of a production frontier model: with application to the pastoral zone of Eastern Australia', *Australian Journal of Agricultural Economics,* **21**, pp. 169-79

Bauer, P. (1990), 'Recent developments in the econometric estimations of frontiers', *Journal of Econometrics*, **46**, pp. 39-56

Bauer, P.W., A.N. Berger and D. Humphrey (1993), 'Efficiency and productivity growth in US banking' in H. Fried, C.A.K. Lovell and S.

Schmidt (eds), *The Measurement of Productive Efficiency: Techniques and Applications* (Oxford: Oxford University Press), pp. 386-413

Benston, G.J. (1994), 'Universal Banking', *Journal of Economic Perspectives*, **8**, pp. 121-43

Berger, A.N. and D.B. Humphrey (1992), 'Measurement and efficiency issues in commercial banking' in Z. Grilliches (ed.), *Output Measurement in the Service Sectors*, National Bureau of Economic Research (Chicago: University of Chicago Press), pp. 245-79

Berger, A.N., W.C. Hunter and S.G. Timme (1993), 'The efficiency of financial institutions: a review and preview of research past, present, and future', *Journal of Banking and Finance,* **17**, pp. 221-49

Berger, A.N. (1993), 'Distribution free estimates of efficiency in the US banking industry and tests of the standard distributional assumptions', *Journal of Productivity Analysis,* **4**

Blair, D.W. and D.L. Placone (1988), 'Expense preference behaviour, agency costs, and firm organisation: the savings and loan industry', *Journal of Economics and Business,* **40**, pp. 1-15

Cebenoyan, A.S., E.S. Cooperman, C.A Register and S.C. Hudgins (1993), 'The relative efficiency of stock versus mutual S&Ls: a stochastic cost frontier approach', *Journal of Financial Services Research,* **7**, pp. 151-70

Conover, W.J. (1971), *Practical Nonparametric Statistics* (New York: Wiley)

Deutsche Bundesbank (1989), *Monthly Report of the Deutsche Bundesbank,* **41**, 3, table 13, 32-33

Dunn, O.J. (1964), 'Multiple comparisons using rank sums', *Technometrics,* **6**, pp. 241-52

Evanoff, D. and P. Israilevich (1991), 'Productive efficiency in banking', *Economic Perspectives*, Federal Reserve Bank of Chicago, July/August, pp. 11-32

Gardener, E.P.M. and P. Molyneux (1990), *Changes in Western European Banking* (London: Allen Unwin)

Greene, W.M. (1990), 'A gamma-distributed stochastic frontier model', *Journal of Econometrics,* **46**, pp. 141-63

Greene, W.M. (1993), 'The econometric approach to efficiency analysis', in H.O. Fried, C.A. Lovell and P. Schmidt (eds), *The Measurement of Productive Efficiency: Techniques and Applications* (Oxford: Oxford University Press)

John, K., I.A. John and A. Saunders (1994), 'Universal banking and firm risk-taking', *Journal of Banking and Finance,* **18**, pp. 307-24

Jondrow, J., C.A. Lovell, I.S. Materov and P. Schmidt (1982), 'On estimation of technical inefficiency in the stochastic frontier production function model', *Journal of Econometrics*, **19**, pp. 233-38

Kaparakis, E.I., S.M. Miller and A.G. Noulas (1994), 'Short-run cost inefficiencies of commercial banks', *Journal of Money, Credit and Banking*, **26**, pp. 875-93

Kempf, U. (1985), *German Bond Markets* (London: Euromoney Publications)

Kolari, J. and A. Zardkoohi (1987), *Bank Cost, Structure and Performance*, (Lexington MA: Lexington Books)

Kruskall, W. and W.A. Wallis (1952), 'Use of ranks in one-criterion variance analysis', *Journal of the American Statistical Association*, **56**, pp. 293-98

Lang, G. and P. Welzel (1994), 'Efficiency and technical progress in banking. Empirical results for a panel of German co-operative banks', Institut fur Volkswirtschaftslehre der Universitat Augsburg, Working Paper No. 117, August

Mester, L.J. (1989), 'Testing for expense preference behaviour: mutual versus stock savings and loans', *The Rand Journal of Economics*, **20**, pp. 483-98

Mester, L.J. (1993), 'Efficiency in the savings and loan industry', *Journal of Banking and Finance*, **17**, pp. 267-86

Meeusen, W. and J. van den Broeck (1977), 'Efficiency estimation from Cobb-Douglas production functions with composed error', *International Economic Review*, **18**, pp. 435-44

Noulas, A.G., S.C. Ray and S.M. Miller (1990), 'Returns to scale and input substitution for large US banks', *Journal of Money, Credit and Banking*, **22**, pp. 94-108

Olson, R.E., P. Schmidt and D.M. Waldman (1980), 'A Monte Carlo study of estimators of stochastic frontier production functions', *Journal of Econometrics*, **13**, pp. 67-82

Pulley, L. and D. Humphrey (1993), 'The role of fixed costs and cost complementarities in determining scope economies and the cost of narrow banking proposals', *Journal of Business*, **66**, pp. 437-62

Saunders, A. (1994), 'Banking and commerce: an overview of the public policy issues', *Journal of Banking and Finance*, **18**, pp. 231-54

Saunders, A. and I. Walter (1994), *Universal Banking in the United States: What Could We Gain? What Could We Lose?* (New York: Oxford University Press)

Sealey, C. and J.T. Lindley (1977), 'Inputs, outputs and a theory of production and cost at depository financial institutions', *Journal of Finance*, **32**, pp. 1251-66

Sheldon, G. and U. Haegler (1993), 'Economies of scale and scope and inefficiency in Swiss banking' in N. Blattner, H. Genberg and A. Swoboda (eds), *Banking in Switzerland* (New York: Weidelberg), pp. 103-34

Sheldon, G. (1994), 'Economies, inefficiency and technical progress in Swiss banking', paper presented at the Société Universitaire Européenne de Recherches Financières (SUERF) Colloquium on The Competitiveness of Financial Institutions and Centres in Europe, 19-21 May, Dublin

Steinherr, A. and C. Huveneers (1994), 'On the performance of differently regulated financial institutions: some empirical evidence', *Journal of Banking and Finance,* **18**, pp. 271-306

Stevenson, R.E. (1980), 'Likelihood functions for generalised stochastic frontier estimation', *Journal of Econometrics,* **13**, pp. 57-66

Verbrugge, J.A. and S.J Goldstein (1981), 'Risk, return and managerial objectives: some evidence from the savings and loan industry', *Journal of Financial Research,* **4**, pp. 45-58

Verbrugge, J.A. and J.S. Jahera (1981), 'Expense-preference behaviour in the savings and loan industry', *Journal of Money, Credit and Banking,* **13**, pp. 465-76

CHAPTER 9
THE RESTRUCTURING OF BANKING GROUPS IN ITALY: MAJOR ISSUES[1]

Elisabetta Gualandri

1. FOREWORD

Over the last decade Italian banks have achieved growth and diversification by establishing group structures; they had no alternative since, by strictly limiting the activities of the banks themselves, the 1936 Banking Law forced them to found subsidiaries if they wished to operate in all the different financial service fields. However, in many cases the group mentality and strategic co-ordination were sadly lacking, and there was a signal failure to exploit the synergies and interrelations between the various areas of operation. Groups were merely collections of isolated subsidiaries, with no clear unifying strategic design, and this had obvious repercussions on efficiency. The last few years have seen the re-organisation of the largest groups: the primary objective has been the solution of problems of various kinds linked to the way in which the groups have grown. New links have been established between operations in different geographical areas and fields of business, with takeovers and mergers followed by group restructuring intended to rationalise and/or simplify structures, which have often grown up without any identifiable strategic logic.

This process has been stimulated and facilitated by the 'Amato' Law 218/90, which redefined the legislative framework for banking groups and introduced consolidated supervision. This far-reaching overhaul of Italian financial legislation was followed by the new banking law, the 1993 Testo Unico, which implemented the second EC Banking Directive, introducing the model of the universal bank and allowing Italian banks to engage directly in activities formerly closed to them (such as leasing and factoring) and to work in the medium term without the previous restraints.

Naturally, the magnitude of the resulting changes has depended on the one hand on the development history of the various groups and the stratification of the existing diversification and expansion into new areas of business, and on the other on the strategic objectives pursued by the management. In all cases the processes of change have been the response to the need to achieve greater efficiency and the changing requirements and growing financial sophistication of the clientele of savers and businesses. The principal aims are to create efficient structures allowing more effective internal co-ordination, ensure that the results actually achieved are truly in line with the strategic objectives, increase profitability and improve risk control. Changes have been implemented in different ways, which can be summed up as described in Table 9.1.

Table 9.1   Group restructuring: possible forms

Sale of subsidiaries	In this case the parent bank decides to sell minority holdings considered non-strategic, concentrating on its core business and thus reducing the range of activities engaged in through its subsidiaries. In some cases, such sales have been dictated by a strategy of cutting back operations in foreign markets in general or in some specific geographical areas. In other cases, they have followed takeovers which left groups with two companies operating in the same fields - a common occurrence with leasing and factoring firms
Mergers	Here again the main aim is to avoid duplication. In a few cases, mergers have been between companies with contiguous activities, such as different types of medium- and long-term credit
Creation of sector/product subholdings	The objective is to define responsibility for management and co-ordination of activities of the same kind, either geographically, as in the case of foreign holdings, or in relation to a type of business, as in the case of financial firms. However, in some cases subholdings are disposed of to allow more effective control of subsidiaries by the parent bank

(continued)

Table 9.1 (continued)

Creation of service companies common to more than one company in the group	Outsourcing has been developed by removing a number of functions, normally technical or in the training area, from the bank, and concentrating them in *ad hoc* companies, still within the group, offering their services to various group firms, and sometimes to customers outside the group. Outsourcing has two main aims: on the one hand to stop the duplication of functions within the same service covered by more than one group company, thus reducing costs, and on the other to sell such services where possible to smaller operators in order to optimise the use of the human and technical resources available. In contrast, some groups have opted to buy in these services from outside, with the same objectives of rationalisation and cost cutting
Internationalisaton of companies	Using the opportunities offered by the new legislation, some parent banks have taken over a number of their subsidiaries; in some cases the trigger factor has been the parent bank's awareness of the need for greater control over its subsidiaries' activities. Internationalisation offers a number of advantages, which makes it preferable in some cases to the maintenance of independent structures. There are pluses of a fiscal nature, since transfers of goods and services within the

(continued)

Table 9.1 (continued)

group are taxed while those between the
between the different divisions of a
universal bank are not. Furthermore,
where the subsidiary's products are
contiguous with those of the parent bank
itself, joint production becomes possible,
allowing optimisation of both production
processes and information flows. In fact,
the higher the degree of differentiation, the
more unlikely it is that the activity will be
internalised, as in the case of industrial
leasing. The internationalisation of
activities covered by the second EC
Directive normally occurs when the
subsidiary is much smaller than the parent
and its share of the domestic market is
small

This paper sets out to analyse the main management problems which
have emerged during group restructuring. These depend first and foremost
on the type of operations carried out, which may have varying impacts on
existing structures and be traced back to the types of relationships
established between the parent and its subsidiaries, and to the degree of
centralisation or decentralisation of the processes of decision-making and
control. Where restructuring follows mergers of two or more banks, the
principal problem is one of interpenetration between the existing structures
or the complete assimilation of one or more of them.

Bearing in mind these important differences, three broad areas of
management are crucial in restructuring processes:

- planning and control
- management of human resources
- information systems

My analysis of these three areas, which draws partly on meetings and interviews with operators in the sector, makes no claim to cover all the implications of an organisational, management and operational nature intrinsic to group restructuring processes or to propose reference models. Much more simply, my aim is to provide an overview of the current situation with regard to the above factors, identified unanimously by all the professionals interviewed as vitally important. It is also essential to remember that the scenario is constantly changing, and many banks are still working to perfect their new structures.

2. PLANNING AND CONTROL

Any analysis of the problems related to planning and control must start with an examination of the role assigned to the parent bank with regard to consolidated supervision, a factor of considerable importance at the management level too. This role is summed up by article 25, subsection 4 of legislative decree 356/90, which assigns the parent bank strategic and management control over the group:

■ strategic control over the evolution of the various areas of activity in which the group operates and the risks posed to the portfolio by the activities engaged in

■ management control intended to assure the maintenance of economic, financial and capital equilibria both within the individual group companies and across the group as a whole. These control requirements should preferably be satisfied through plans, programmes and budgets and periodic analysis of statements, quarterly and monthly accounts, and individual and consolidated balance sheets, both for homogeneous sectors of activity and with reference to the entire group (Banca d'Italia, cap. LII, Sezione III)

The parent bank is also responsible for reporting to the Banca d'Italia with regard to three forms of consolidated supervision: prudential, informative and inspective. The parent is required to collect the significant information data and statements from the group companies and verify that the supervisory regulations are complied with. Subsidiary administrators are obliged to supply data and information, and to implement the instructions given by the parent bank. The law also envisages that to allow control of the group's risk level, the parent bank will establish mechanisms for the exchange of information between the individual companies and the parent itself. To achieve this, group risk control centres will obviously have to be formed.

Direct inspection of individual subsidiaries by the parent bank is also explicitly envisaged. This has interesting implications worthy of note: while on the one hand such controls are necessary for monitoring of the level of risk of the group overall and its individual members, on the other hand they give the parent considerable powers over the subsidiary, seriously limiting the latter's autonomy. The main instruments of prudential supervision implemented for consolidated supervision are capital adequacy, the limitation of risk of various kinds (credit risk, interest rate risk and exchange rate risk) and permitted holdings.

Two aspects of risk control appear of particular interest for the purposes of this paper. Firstly, the notion of risk is expanded from credit risk to include other types of risk which may be encountered by a financial intermediary, above all with regard to dealings in securities. This implies the introduction or reinforcement of suitable means of monitoring and controlling these risks. Secondly, with regard to credit risk, control of the degree of risk is introduced at the group level for both the provider and the receiver of funds. As we will see later, by expanding risk control at the level of both the industrial/trading and the banking/financial group, this aspect of consolidated prudential supervision has interesting implications of an organisational nature for the parent bank.

The new legislation places organisation amongst the key factors in prudential supervision, indicating the importance which organisational structures and internal controls are assuming in assuring the efficiency and stability of intermediaries and groups. The need to establish or reinforce risk control at a group level has emerged, above all to limit the various types of risk, and because of the parent bank's responsibilities in relation to the Banca d'Italia. If it considers the organisation responsible for screening and monitoring of major borrowers inadequate, the Banca d'Italia may also fix individual and global capital limits more stringent than those envisaged by the new law. The parent bank is thus forced to organise structures and assure information flows allowing monitoring of the activities of the various group members and the relative degree of risk. Orientation towards group asset and liability management (ALM) is therefore becoming more and more important.

2.1 Reference models

The introduction of the new banking legislation has led to an interesting debate about the ability of multi-functional group structures to provide a unified mission and centralised strategic management, which will make full use of the interrelations and synergies between the various activities (Baravelli 1992a; Mottura 1992). One of the main aims of the debate has been to decide whether and how it is possible to achieve a balance in a structure where the parent company is responsible for orientating, co-ordinating and controlling the other group companies, thus limiting their management autonomy, while still maintaining their legal and capital independence and their specific operational nature, one of the strong points of the group structure. The advantages and disadvantages of the institutional models and organisation structures of the universal bank and the multi-functional group have been compared and assessed. Doubts have been expressed in particular with regard to the ability of the parent bank to provide effective, efficient planning, co-ordination and control for the entire group, essential for implementation of a unified strategy, and this has led to some decisions to internalise areas of activity.

It thus becomes important to check the extent to which the theoretical reference models are actually compatible with the supervisory regulations, in order to analyse how the control systems of Italian groups are developing. For banking and financial groups these reference models have not yet been developed to the same extent as for industrial groups. Reference is often made to the theories applied to the latter, but adaptation to the financial sector is required. Moreover, Italian groups still have relatively little experience in this field, and so further verification will be required as the restructuring process continues.

Regardless of the type of group and its activities, group control consists of the provision of guidance and co-ordination, through which members are orientated along lines appropriate to the group's own institutional objectives (Beretta 1990, 5). The structure of the control system inevitably depends on the characteristics of the group, particularly the role of the parent bank, the type and degree of affinity of the activities of the various members, and the after-effects of earlier growth and diversification. These factors are especially important for banking and financial groups (Patalano 1992). Within control systems the role of the parent company and the type of relations it establishes with its subsidiaries are crucial. At one end of the scale, the parent simply manages a portfolio of holdings, while at the other its interventions are becoming increasingly heavy-handed (Di Antonio 1994).

In an initial scenario the parent company is the strategic head of the group with the primary aim of pursuing its institutional objectives. In a second phase it also takes on co-ordination and control functions, assigning economic and financial objectives to the various units, participating in preparation of the budget, monitoring short-term performance and taking corrective measures if targets are not achieved.   In a subsequent development the key resources such as finance, technology and management are centralised and then allocated to subsidiaries on the basis of the strategic objectives set for them and for the group overall.

We then come to the situation where group management staff at the parent's headquarters provide services common to the various companies. This has obvious advantages in terms of costs but limits the autonomy of the subsidiaries.   In the specific case of a banking group accentuated centralisation meets various requirements, above all the activation of co-ordination mechanisms essential if the parent is to meet its obligations with regard to supervision.   It therefore appears logical to centralise management and accounting control, the inspection function and organisation. At the same time, centralisation of services such as treasury and marketing may be advantageous from the operational point of view. Last but not least, the advantages in terms of lower costs of centralising activities such as research and the legal department, as well as EDP, are obvious.   The management of human resources merits separate discussion since it is a critical factor in restructuring processes, as described in the next section.   Finally, the parent company may handle interrelations between the various members in order to exploit their synergies trying to strike a balance between integration and autonomy. (The exploitation of synergies by corporate strategy is analysed by Ansoff 1968.)   This development is of great interest for banking groups, since the optimisation of operating synergies is the main justification for their existence.

Group control structures may be of various kinds, depending on the different combinations of environmental, strategic and organisational variables. Here again industrial models have to be adapted to suit the special nature of the activities carried out by the member companies of banking groups, with the varying degrees of synergy and interrelation between conventional banking activities and those in other, more or less innovative, sectors (Di Antonio 1994).   The banking group requires a model which will give the parent adequate management and co-ordination powers, while still leaving the subsidiaries a certain amount of autonomy. A model which seems to fit this bill envisages a complex role for the parent, which thus sets out to exploit the various interrelations between traditional banking and the new sectors of intermediation in which the group operates. In this model, rarely found in industry, the parent participates in definition of the strategic plans of the group members, allowing exploitation of their synergies, while competitive and operational management is decentralised, allowing the subsidiaries to handle the specialised aspects unique to their own activities.

2.2 The lines followed in recent experience

I will now attempt to describe the lines recently followed by Italy's largest groups in the establishment of planning and control systems. The aim is to assess the extent to which they comply with the theoretical models and meet the supervision requirements discussed above. Once again we must remember that the theory is still in flux. The first factor for consideration is the amount of control exercised by the parent bank over the various group members, whether through appointees on administrative bodies or the definition of strategies and policies. The second concerns the organisational means of centralising a number of functions.

In most cases parent banks co-ordinate the activities of their subsidiaries by traditional means such as the appointment of their own administrators to the key functions in the various companies. The problem of the conflicts of interest which may emerge with regard to safeguarding the interests of the minority shareholders of the subsidiaries must be remembered here; it may affect directors who sit on the boards of both the parent and the subsidiary and do the parent's bidding on the latter, leading to disputes with minority shareholders over board decisions at general meetings.

At a second level, co-ordination is achieved by placing management staff or heads of functions in subsidiaries, establishing a kind of osmotic flow from the parent bank to the other companies in the group. As we will see in the next section of this paper, staff of the subsidiary may resent such appointments, leading to problems in the management of human resources. Dedicated functions or staff serving as interface between the holding company or parent bank and the subsidiaries are reported in only a few cases. In the context of management strategic control, staff structures are intended to improve internal information circuits, thus permitting the parent bank to obtain more information about general topics and develop aggregated analyses and strategies for individual functions or companies.

These observations seem to confirm the general poor development of management control systems, already reflected in an ABI (Italian Banks Association) survey in 1991 (see ABI 1991 and the comment by Di Antonio 1994). In Italy much progress remains to be made in acquiring a group culture, in the sense of a capacity for management. All the various cases suggest a delicate problem of striking a balance between the needs for integration and for maintenance of margins of autonomy in the subsidiaries in a scenario which is constantly changing, partly as a result of past decisions and partly in response to the organisational strategies chosen. Recent experiences, and particularly the consequences of the current restructuring phase, give the impression that common structures intended to exploit operational and information synergies and cut costs within the group are starting to be defined. These structures may be separate companies or functions within the parent bank, depending on the specific areas concerned.

Establishment of separate companies. Some activities are concentrated in specially created group companies, with the aim of achieving greater efficiency and solving problems of a technical/technological nature or concerning management of personnel during the restructuring phase. In such cases, comments about control, information systems and the management of human resources already made elsewhere again apply. Moreover, interesting considerations about the internal market are also implied, particularly with regard to the problem of determining the costs of the services offered by these companies to other group members. The establishment of independent companies rather than use of a multi-divisional structure has the advantage of assuring greater transparency during evaluation processes, for example by limiting the level of freedom enjoyed by management in the definition of transfer prices because of the rules enforced by civil and fiscal law.

Ad hoc companies are most often created to provide computer technology services, such as the design and production of software packages and data processing for the various companies in the group. In some cases, as we will be seeing in greater detail in the section discussing the restructuring of this sector, the aim is to offer the company's services not only to the captive market but also to other operators, particularly small banks. However, this strategy has occasionally proved disappointing because the newly formed company has failed to win a share of the non-captive market.

Training is another field in which specialist service companies may be formed. Such companies supply services both to group companies (with the objectives of cutting costs by rationalising resources, spreading a unified group culture and transferring know-how) and to the external market. New companies have also sometimes been established to ensure standardised management of property obtained through mortgages.

Centralisation of functions in the parent bank. Both operational and back-up functions are concerned. In the case of non-operational functions, one of the major needs is to develop management and accounting control at a group level, both for internal purposes and in order to comply with the requirements of the supervisory authorities. There is still a great deal to be done in this area, but the way ahead has already been marked out by the supervisory regulations. Research, generally intended to provide backup for strategic decision-makers, is another function which tends to be centralised and in some cases incorporated in management accounting. The problem of centralising marketing, which becomes more important as the group's synergies are increasingly expressed through a single commercial network, has been tackled in a number of cases. In this case the delicate problem of overlapping of similar products or identifying different market segments has to be solved. One field in which such difficulties may arise is the mortgages industry, offered both by banks themselves and by former special institution subsidiaries. Another commonly centralised service is the management of information about credit customers, which permits the establishment of a group risk-monitoring service in line with the control requirements set out in the regulations. Similarly, the construction of a unified customer data base will be an important aid in the marketing activity of the sales networks.

The operational function most often centralised is funding on the international markets, since it allows operation with smaller spreads, exploiting the reputation and bargaining power of the parent bank. Significant synergies can also be generated by creation of a team dedicated to the development of financial engineering, which responds effectively both to the internal need for derivatives to cover interest rate and exchange rate risks and to the growing demand for innovative products from the clientele of businesses and savers. Although they are the declared aim of many groups, most centralised treasury services are still in the embryo stage. There are, in fact, many technical and operational problems to be overcome in this field, linked to the wider problem of establishing an integrated finance area and clearly defining which functions should be subject to central and which to local control.

Finally, the problem of ALM (asset and liability management) at group level merits separate discussion, although it is also linked to the comments given above on the problem of centralising the treasury and the finance area. The need for a group ALM system is increasingly pressing, partly with a view to assuring risk control at a group level, but there are large obstacles in its way. We have already noted the importance given by the supervisory regulations to individual and consolidated risk control which reaches beyond credit risk to include capital adequacy, exchange rate, interest rate and market risks. Supervision consists of the measuring and monitoring of these risks and the assurance of adequate capital cover, as well as control of the suitability of the organisational structures responsible for overseeing them. Obviously, the responsibility for development of a system of ALM for risk control lies with the intermediaries and, in the case of a group, with the parent bank.

In an integrated context risk control has many operational advantages beyond the requirements of the supervisory authorities. Supervisory constraints are, however, extremely important since they require large investments for the establishment of integrated management systems at a group level, while Italian banks have been slower than their foreign counterparts in taking such steps even at the individual bank level. The need for integrated management techniques actually reaches beyond the objective of monitoring and control of the various types of risk, since they will also assure optimum allocation of assets where the regulations establish different degrees of capital cover for the different categories of risk. A problem is emerging of the return on activities which allows banks to cover the remuneration of their own funds in relation to the capital adequacy appropriate to the risk. The development of models for this process has recently become an important objective in ALM (Proust 1993). The introduction of integrated systems also has implications requiring careful evaluation across the area of information technology systems, with regard to the installation of suitable hardware, the selection of the necessary information and the definition of the appropriate procedures.

3.   THE MANAGEMENT OF HUMAN RESOURCES

During restructuring, banking groups have had to deal with the problem of the management of human resources in all its various aspects: channels for communication with staff, relations with trades unions, review of contracts and pay scales, design of new career structures, calculation of staffing levels and management of their consequences for job numbers, and the definition and implementation of transfer and re-training plans. Recent experience, both in Italy and abroad, has shown that the problem of the management of human resources is one of the crucial points in growth and restructuring in the banking and financial sector, since the human factor plays a vital role in the success or failure of such operations. This occurs at various levels, starting from the managers responsible for defining and implementing strategies, moving down through those who have to apply these strategies on a day-to-day basis, and finally reaching the retail network staff who transmit the bank's image directly to the public. It is therefore essential that all staff identify completely with the mission of the new intermediary or the group (Huret 1993).

The most thorny problems derive from the tendency of staff to resist organisational changes, mainly because of the suspicion with which most people view anything new (Colombo 1992 and Raggetti 1992). There is also frequently a fear that the new balances of power may bring disadvantages for individuals and undermine the positions they have achieved. When the individual assesses the possible costs and benefits to himself or herself of the changes in progress, the costs relate above all to job loss, transfers as a result of organisational restructuring, and modifications which may damage career prospects and pay levels. The benefits are linked to the acquisition of new skills, improved career and salary prospects, and the gradual reduction in automatic increments, providing greater incentives. Further possible benefits may lie in investments in training.

Staff may also resist changes because they feel inadequate to the new roles proposed for them. In many cases, resistance of this kind is based not so much on objective grounds as on a lack of information about the processes taking place, and a cultural gap between the banks which are merging or forming the new group. In Italy, as abroad, the most critical areas of human resources management for restructuring processes have proved to be information about the changes taking place, the management of any problems of overstaffing, the staff management systems and the problem of overcoming the individual company mentalities and creating a new group culture (see Rock 1990, in particular contributions by Jacobs, Shapiro and Morse, and Feldman and Martin). The way in which relationships with trades unions are handled is crucial in avoiding serious tension. Far-sighted management of these factors has made a large contribution to the success of some operations, while failure to recognise their critical nature has placed others in serious difficulties.

In the Italian banking system the critical aspects outlined above have coincided and interwoven with the more general problems of the continuing transformation of the way human resources are managed in the financial sector. A number of factors, such as fiercer competition, the expansion of the range of products and services offered to a more and more sophisticated clientele, and the increasingly large-scale introduction of automation and computerisation, are demanding the more productive, efficient use of a better qualified, more professional workforce. The next sections of this paper will analyse the critical areas identified above, bearing in mind that their relative significance depends on the positions from which the banks involved start the transformation process, particularly the level of differentiation in personnel management procedures, the level of efficiency, the size of the cultural gap and any conflicting management philosophies and strong individual mentalities.

3.1 Information about processes taking place

It is essential that all personnel be made aware of the guidelines with regard to the objectives of the restructuring process taking place and the mission of the new bank or group and receive information about the consequences the operation may have for them as individuals. Good communications prevent the spread of rumours, which may create wrong impressions and damage future working relations, generating active and/or passive resistance to the changes (Colombo 1990). All information processes must be based on a clear definition of the strategic design of the operation in progress, in all its organisational and operational details. Information in this field requires a uniformity of language and full cover of the entire organisation to prevent the emergence of informational imbalances. It must also be two-way, allowing its managers not only to communicate effectively with the staff of the various structures, but also to identify any weak points in the information process and highlight points of conflict between the company's objectives and the positions of individual staff members or groups of staff.

The systems through which information is channelled may be of various kinds, depending on the target staff levels. The main channels include:

- conventions for management staff
- meetings targeting specific figures within the organisation, such as branch managers
- newsletters and targeted articles in company magazines addressed to the workforce in general
- talks on the subject by management or other staff during training courses

In all cases, management staff are responsible for maintaining a dialogue on the changes with their respective departments, while branch managers do the same with the network.

Further measures are taken to standardise operating procedures and customer relations throughout the retail network, particularly in case of mergers/take-overs between banks, where the problems relating to the management and/or transfer of human resources combine and interweave with those linked to the standardisation of information systems, to be covered in the next section.

3.2 Personnel management systems

When banks merge, one very difficult question is how to eliminate any differences in conditions of employment between the employees of the various companies involved. These disparities derive from existing employment contracts with different pay scales, rankings, pension funds, assessment processes and career structures. (For the relevance of these problems in the financial sector, see Ruozi 1984.) The many risks involved in standardising these factors require careful preliminary evaluation, since initial personnel management practices may vary widely. Differing mean staff costs must be aligned upward leading to higher overheads, different average employee ages may cause a concentration of early retirement in a specific institute or area, and differences in employment contracts may require prolonged negotiations with trade unions.

Within group restructuring processes there is no doubt that the maintenance of different employment contracts in the various banks slows down the amalgamation of personnel management and standardisation procedures in general. Resistance to change is definitely greater in the case of companies working in sectors other than the banking operations of the parent bank. The situation is even more sensitive in the case of highly specialised companies, particularly in the securities industry, where more favourable terms of employment are an important factor for specialist staff providing a product with high added value. In such cases pay scales and career structures different from those of the parent bank and other group companies are often maintained. One interesting debate in this area concerns the hypothesis of internalising trading activities in banking firms, in response to the forthcoming implementation of Directive 93/22/EEC on investment services, which allows banks to engage directly in this activity. While in some cases internalisation is favoured as a cost-cutting measure, in others the maintenance of a separate company is preferred by those who believe it is advisable to retain different terms of employment, or at least clearly distinct career structures and incentive mechanisms.

3.3 Management of overstaffing

Concentration and restructuring processes, and the consequent reorganisation, have more often than not led to problems of overstaffing within banks and groups, both overall and with reference to individual sectors. Mergers between banks tend to generate overstaffing particularly in two specific sectors:

- in retail networks, when the areas covered tend to overlap, and when there is a need to rationalise or streamline the network
- in central services, where the more similar the size of the original banks, the greater the duplication of functions will be. Problems may arise in operational areas such as treasury, securities, foreign exchange and loans, and amongst general management staff, such as research and legal departments or in personnel management and training.

The degree of overstaffing encountered will depend on the level of restructuring intended gradually to centralise functions and services with a view to reducing costs and/or intensifying co-ordination and control by the parent bank.

Where possible, overstaffing is dealt with through early retirement or transfer to expanding services, in which case retraining is necessary. When expansion of the retail network is required, branches prove a useful relief valve for disposing of excess staff from other areas. This has become possible thanks to the liberalisation of branching within Italy's retail banking sector, which began in the late 1980s. Coping with overstaffing by means of transfers becomes difficult when the vacancies are for highly specialised posts, for which the existing staff would not be suitable even after re-training. In this case new staff have to be employed from outside. Re-training plays a very important role, but there will inevitably be some staff who cannot be transferred to new functions because of age or lack of the necessary skills.

3.4 Creation of a new group culture

Particularly in the case of mergers and takeovers, the predominant mentalities created by the previous history of the various companies must be modified to suit the mission of the new firm or group. Cultural differences are linked to many factors, including size: the company style is often more informal in small organisations, while the decision-making process is slower and more complex in larger ones. Management teams may be more or less orientated towards risk-taking, innovation, profit, people, quality, the market and delegation of tasks, and have different general strategic orientation. These attitudes will help or hinder interaction between the various companies and thus the integration process as a whole. As we have already seen, different company mentalities may lead to tensions and lack of collaboration. In some cases the problems of communication caused may even lead to professional jealousy, which impairs the circulation of information flows intended to improve knowledge of the clientele and thus optimise the commercial potential of the new intermediary or group.

There are four alternative ways in which a new group mentality may be created, depending on the level of osmosis established between the existing cultures:

- integration: the purchaser/parent company does not push for rapid standardisation, and the new subsidiaries aim to retain their own cultural identities, while respecting that of the purchaser/parent
- assimilation: adoption of a single cultural model which other group members acknowledge as superior to their own
- separation: a company retains its own cultural identify and rejects assimilation
- marginalisation: the various group members consider their own cultural models worthless but do not wish to acquire those of others, and thus lose their specific cultural identities.

The last two processes are definitely undesirable, as they derive from strong conflict between the various mentalities and/or a lack of ability to formulate and get across the new group or bank mission on the part of the management.

When applying this framework to the banking and financial sector, it is essential to remember that here mergers and aggregation processes are intended to optimise the management of information flows relating to clientele and achieve economies of scale and purpose. The most suitable model therefore seems to be integration, but of a more intensive kind than described above. Conversely, it is preferable for highly specialist companies to retain their specific and clearly distinct cultural identities. Consider, for example, the case of takeovers of British companies working in the securities industry by retail banks from the UK or abroad; their identity has been maintained, partly to exploit the reputation they enjoy within the international financial community. The same has not occurred in Italy because the recent takeovers have not involved highly specialised companies with a long tradition. Examples of processes of integration and assimilation, intended to create a new group culture, have been witnessed. However, the problem of establishing a new group culture which supersedes existing company identities sometimes encounters resistance within the retail network. In some takeovers, the nature of the customer relationship and territorial status may make the retention of existing identities advisable, at least in the short term. Conversely, the acquisition of a new image is extremely important if the reputation of the bank taken over has recently fallen.

In the context of group restructuring, cultural standardisation has been achieved both through internal information throughout the organisation, by the means already listed, and through training intended to eliminate cultural disparities within the new company or group and to provide a clear appreciation of the group's mission, strategies, style and rules, with a view to mutual professional growth. These operations have not always met with success, and in some cases barriers to integration, pointing to cultural conflicts, have persisted. In many cases, a flow of parent bank staff towards key points in the structure of the subsidiary has played an important role in transmitting the new group philosophy. These processes are very sensitive and some cases subsidiary staff have viewed them as a form of colonialism.

4.   INFORMATION SYSTEMS

Information requirements and the procedures by which the relative information flows are managed have become extremely important for banks, and even more so within groups. Information systems, consisting of information, procedures, equipment and organisational structures, are intended to produce and process the information needed to work within and manage the company. They must therefore provide an effective, efficient solution to needs for the collection of information about the activities engaged in, inside and outside the bank and group.   After acquisition the necessary data must be processed, combined and then distributed to the appropriate people at the right time and in the right place.

The importance of information systems and information technology for credit intermediaries is the direct result of the need to acquire higher levels of efficiency, owing to the modifications now taking place in credit and financial markets.   (For interesting contributions on the role of information technology in the financial industry see IBM 1993.) Banks and financial intermediaries are being forced to look for greater efficiency and flexibility in their various operational and management areas by a number of factors, mainly the growing competition and the consequent pressure on profit margins, the continuing process of financial innovation and the expansion of the range of products and services offered, the increasing sophistication of the clientele and the demand for higher quality standards, and the requirements of informative and prudential supervision, with regard to risk management and the maintenance of compulsory minimum capital adequacy coefficients. Furthermore, as we have already mentioned, the scenario in which banks are now operating, with rising involvement in the securities industry, and the resulting significance of market risks, requires the introduction of asset and liability management systems for which efficient information systems are essential.

Efficient, standardised structuring of the flow of information from the subsidiaries to the parent bank is thus essential in order to provide reliable data, permitting monitoring of the various companies and the group as a whole, both for the company's own purposes and in order to comply with consolidated supervision obligations. For internal purposes these flows must be mainly directed towards the allocation of costs and revenues to the appropriate headings in the accounts and preparation of individual and consolidated balance sheets; strategic planning and management accounting; risk control and monitoring; the implementation of a group asset and liability management system in order to minimise risks and maximise the profitability of assets; feeding the customer database with information about transactions, terms and statements; the creation and maintenance of the group central risk control unit; and supplying the internal control system.

To fulfil consolidated supervision obligations, information must be collected and processed in order to prepare annual and quarterly or monthly reports for the Banca d'Italia, calculate and verify compliance with individual and consolidated capital adequacy coefficients, and last but not least, carry out risk control. Clearly, information systems must be capable of collecting data correctly and then passing the necessary information quickly to the various internal centres of responsibility and to the external supervisory authority.

The problems which have arisen in this area during group restructuring vary in nature and merge with the more general problems of the implementation of efficient group information systems, along the lines briefly outlined above. A first group of problems relates to the management of information flows. One particularly problematic factor in this area has proved to be the standardisation of the information generated by the various group members, with special reference to reporting systems; measures have thus had to be taken to assure this. A second important aspect is the collection of the data necessary for the various forms of compulsory reporting, such as the consolidated balance sheet required by civil law; planning and control; the supply of information to the group ALM unit; and the information necessary for consolidated supervision: regular reporting on asset data, the assurance of capital adequacy and risk monitoring. It is important to remember that the parent bank is responsible to the Banca d'Italia for the reliability of the data supplied under this last head. As for planning and control, the various forms of supervision, particularly with regard to reporting, have provided considerable stimulus for more efficiency in information systems.

As things now stand, the implementation of group ALM systems appears an especially difficult area, where many groups still have a long way to go. However, the preparation of an efficient group information system is certainly an important step forward in solving the problems linked to the introduction and operation of integrated management systems.

Other problems in the restructuring process refer to information technology as such, since various companies in the group may have different computer systems, which must be able to communicate with each other and particularly with the system of the parent bank. Information and technology constraints are even more significant in the case of mergers/take-overs between banks (Rubin 1992). Here these problems are amplified, varying in complexity in proportion to the gap between the various systems at the time when a single information system has to be established. The decision taken depends both on the relative dimensions of the banks involved in the merger, and thus the costs of any conversions, and on technical considerations with regard to the efficiency and adequacy of the existing systems. It is often difficult to make such evaluations because, except for their hardware, information systems are invisible and intangible. However, the top priority must be the standardisation of information flows in procedures and reporting in the short term. The tendency is to limit, if not to eliminate, decentralised computer systems in favour of standardised, centralised solutions. This process also has implications for organisation and staff training and information, if operatives need to learn new procedures.

In this area of information systems the observations deriving from the restructuring processes now in progress vary widely. In some cases one of the two systems has been chosen and then imposed on one of the companies involved in the operation. In other cases, particularly mergers between banks of more or less the same size, a combination of the best elements of the existing systems has been adopted, and this seems to have aided the introduction of a group mentality amongst the computer staff of the two companies, avoiding passive resistance, although the economic costs have been quite high. The problems encountered during redefinition of information systems have generally been dealt with by mixed working groups consisting of experts from the various companies.

In the case of mergers EDP is generally standardised by sacrificing the system of the smaller bank. This solution is not painless; there are technical, logistical and staff constraints, proportional to the size of the EDP centre to be sacrificed, and problems in the quality of the service which may deteriorate in the smaller bank if its existing system worked to a high standard.

Some groups have resorted to outsourcing and delegated this activity to *ad hoc* companies within the group, independent firms, or consortia formed by a number of banks. (Outsourcing in the banking sector is analysed by Crone 1994.) The aim, obviously, is to optimise the service and minimise costs by exploiting economies of scale and large investments in the latest technologies. *Ad hoc* companies within the group also allow further reduction of costs and optimisation of technical resources, since computing services can be offered to the non-captive market consisting mainly of small banks. However, the outsourcing of information and data processing services does not relieve the bank of its responsibility for optimum management of its information processes. Moreover, in view of the close links between information technology and the entire administrative system, outsourcing of technological aspects may limit the bank's strategic flexibility in this field (Revell 1993), although this problem should be less significant if the company concerned belongs to the banking group.

5. CONCLUSIONS

My analysis of the restructuring processes in progress in the Italian banking and financial system, triggered by the growth of the groups themselves and the options made available by legislation introducing the option of the universal bank, has highlighted the problems encountered in three main areas: planning and control, the management of human resources and information systems. Although the process is not yet complete and some conflicting signals are emerging, some brief comments are possible. Firstly, once again the financial sector has tried to use models derived from industry for its organisational and functional development, with considerable problems of adaptation. Secondly, it is evident that efficient restructuring requires a clear strategic design, with definition of the mission of the group or the new bank created by the merger. The rapid provision of information about the main features of the restructuring process is of vital importance in dealing effectively with the sensitive question of human resources and achieving the objective of a group culture.

As we move on to more specific considerations, risk control is expanded in two directions: from the individual intermediary to the group as a whole and from credit risk alone to the entire range of risks typical of financial intermediation. From another angle risk control concerns the interface between the banking/financial group on the one hand and the client industrial/trading group on the other. This across-the-board approach has important implications for management and reorganisation, with special reference to monitoring and operational control of risks, and the development of appropriate information systems.

The growing attention focused on risks and the relative capital adequacy coefficients means that capital must be considered as a scarce resource, which must be efficiently allocated within the group and the bank in relation to the risk and return factors of the various types of activities engaged in.   The problems of risk control and optimum allocation of capital have obvious effects on the degree of autonomy of subsidiaries, which will probably be increasingly limited because of the strategic and management control functions of the parent bank.

It is also important to focus on problems related to the optimisation of information flows, essential for exploitation of the synergies within the group, including the possibilities for cross-selling. The exchanges of information may generate conflicts of interest which penalise the clients of the various companies in the group, or divisions of the same bank, particularly with regard to securities dealings and conventional loan operations. In this case the advantages deriving from centralised management of information may conflict with the need to safeguard the weaker bargaining partner, meaning the customer.   Problems in organisation, the management of human resources, and information systems also arise.

Finally, we must not underestimate the conflicts of interest which may occur between various companies or areas of operation within the group. Once again, it is essential for the parent bank to strike a balance in the delicate strategic control and management mechanism between the concentration of strategic co-ordination functions in the hands of the parent company to ensure unified group management and the need to maintain some decentralisation of functions in the subsidiaries in order to exploit their specific areas of expertise and safeguard their legal autonomy. In some cases, activities are internalised in the parent bank to increase efficiency and the level of control.

NOTE

1. The paper originated from a research project carried out at Newfin, Università Bocconi and also received funds from the CNR (Centro Nazionale delle Ricerche) and from Ministero dell'Università e delle Ricerca Scientifica.

LIST OF REFERENCES

AA. VV. (various authors) (1992), *Il controllo nell'ambito del gruppo polifunzionale*, Atti del convegno organizzato dal gruppo Banca Nazionale del Lavoro e dall'Associazione Italiana di Internal Auditors in collaborazione con l'ABI, Roma, 1 April 1992, Editoriale Lavoro

ABI (1991), Gruppo di lavoro interbancario per un censimento ed approfondimento delle problematiche inerenti l'attività delle holding nei gruppi bancari plurifunzionali, *Rapporto del sottogruppo controllo di gestione*, March (Roma: ABI)

Ansoff, H.I. (1968), *Corporate Strategy* (New York, NY: McGraw-Hill)

Banca d'Italia, *Istruzioni di vigilanza per gli enti creditizi*

Baravelli, M. (1992a), 'Le implicazioni organizzative della disciplina dei gruppi creditizi', *Il Risparmio*, no. 5 (September-October)

Baravelli, M. (1992b), 'La gestione strategica delle risorse umane nelle istituzioni creditizie' in G. Costa (ed.), *Manuale di gestione del personale*, (Torino; Utet)

Beretta, S. (1990), *Il controllo dei gruppi aziendali* (Milano: Egea)

Bottiglia, R.A. Baldassari, E. Gualandri and F. Vella (1995), *Ristrutturazione dei gruppi bancari e rapporti tra capogruppo e controllate* (Milano: Egea)

Camussone, P.F. (1990), *Informatica aziendale*, 53 (Milano: Egea)

Capriglione, F. (ed.) (1994), *Commentario al Testo Unico delle leggi in materia bancaria e creditizia* (Padova: Cedam)

Colombo, G. (1990), 'Introduzione. Fusioni e acquisizioni: operazioni di amministrazione straordinaria' in M. L. Rock, *Fusioni e acquisizioni. Aspetti strategici, finanziari e organizzativi* (Milano: McGraw-Hill Libri Italia)

Colombo, G. (1992), *Fusioni, acquisizioni e scorpori. Economia delle concentrazioni aziendali* (Milano: Egea)

Costi, R. (1994), *L'ordinamento bancario*, Il Mulino, Bologna

Crone, R.K. (1994), 'Management commitment: the key to successful outsourcing', *Bankers Magazine* (January/February)

De Marco, M. (1992), 'I sistemi informativi' in M. De Marco, G. Bruschi, E. Manna, G. Giustignani and C. Rossignoli, *L'organizzazione dei Sistemi Informativi Aziendali*, Il Mulino, Bologna

Di Antonio, M. (1994), 'I sistemi di programmazione e controllo nei gruppi bancari' in *Banca Impresa Società*, no. 1

Erzegovesi, L. (1990), *Il controllo del rischio di interesse nei gruppi bancari* in *Zenit*, no. 4

Gualandri, E. (1991), 'The approaches to interest rate risk of supervisory authorities and financial institutions', *Revue de la Banque/Bank-en Financiewezen*, January

Huret, J. (1993), 'Building trust after a merger', *Bankers Magazine*, July/August

IBM (1993), *Banca e informatica. Mercato risorse tecnologie*, Atti del Convegno, Bologna 7-8 October

Marchi, L. (1988), *I sistemi informativi aziendali* (Milano: Giuffrè)

Mottura, P. (1992), 'Aspetti aziendali e organizzativi dei gruppi creditizi', *Banca Impresa Società*, no. 3

Patalano, C. (1992), *Un modello di controllo interno per il gruppo polifunzionale bancario* in AA. VV.

Proust, J. (1993), 'Peut-on allouer les fonds propres en fonction du risque?' *Banque*, no. 537, May

Raggetti, G. (1992), 'Alcune riflessioni sul ruolo della risorsa umana nelle aziende di credito pubbliche che applicano la legge no. 218/90', *Il Risparmio*, no. 3

Revell, J.R.S. (1993), 'L'evoluzione delle istituzioni finanziarie: analisi delle tendenze alla luce dei recenti cambiamenti in Europa' in IBM

Rock, M.L. (ed.) (1990), *Fusioni e acquisizioni, Aspetti strategici, finanziari e organizzativi* (Milano: McGraw-Hill Libri Italia)

Rubin, H. (1992), 'The intricate process of merging two banks' information systems', *Bankers Magazine*, September/October

Ruozi. R. (ed.) (1984), *La gestione delle risorse umane nelle banche* (Milano: Giuffrè)

Testo Unico del Credito, (1994) (Milano: Giuffrè)

Turati, C. (1990), *Economia e organizzazione delle joint venture* (Milano: Egea)

CHAPTER 10
RECENT DEVELOPMENTS IN RETAIL BANKING IN SCANDINAVIA: NARROW V. UNIVERSAL BANKING

Ted Lindblom and Martin Andersson

INTRODUCTION

Traditionally, banks have had a dominating role in the financial markets in Scandinavia[1]. There are at least two strong reasons for this. One is that banking has been a way of dealing with asymmetric information. Banks as financial intermediatries have a competitive advantage against individuals and the securities market in gathering information. The other reason, and perhaps the more important one, is that regulations have protected banks from competitive pressure. As a response to this banks are expected not to expose deposits to any large risks, to finance corporate investments, to handle a well functioning payments system and to be a channel for the implementation of the central bank's monetary policy (Blomberg and Blix 1995). This has not been a specific situation for the Scandinavian countries, but rather the common practice throughout the world. In the mid-1980s, however, this situation began to change in many countries. The financial markets were at the time undergoing a deregulation phase.

The deregulation of the financial markets in Scandinavia during the 1980s led to major changes of banks' business strategies. In order to improve competitiveness and increase market shares, banks developed customer-orientated strategies. In retail banking, this implied that most banks were offering a broadening range of products and services which were often bundled together and priced as a unit. Many established banks regarded universal banking as the appropriate concept for keeping customers and attracting new ones. In the last few years, however, several other financial institutions, and some non-financial corporations, have been permitted to start banking activities through subsidiaries. This represents a systemic change. In the past, the authorities were reluctant to permit new banks to start operating[2]. These new banks are applying a different strategy from the one implemented by traditional banks, namely specialising in a narrower range of banking products and services. This study focuses on the competition between 'narrow banks' and traditional universal banks[3]. The main focus will be on the Swedish situation, but analogies with the other Scandinavian countries will also be made.

STRUCTURAL CHANGES IN SCANDINAVIAN BANKING

The banking structure in the Scandinavian countries has been largely unchanged for many years. The concentration ratios have traditionally been very high (Vesala 1993). The normal way of analysing this ratio is to study the market shares of the largest actors. If we look at the four largest Swedish banks, their total market share in terms of balance of account has increased during the last decade. During the 1980s their market share was approximately 50-60 per cent, but it increased significantly in the early 1990s through structural changes: in 1993 it was 86 per cent. This ratio should be compared to the ratio in Finland, which was 90 per cent for the three largest banks. (Two of the four largest banks have merged earlier this year [1995].) The concentration ratio in Norway is 85 per cent, if the savings banks are aggregated; otherwise it is just 55 per cent, which shows the importance of the savings banks in Norway. Denmark differs somewhat from the other Scandinavian countries in that it has many more banks. This is to some extent reflected in the concentration ratio, but even in Denmark a few large banks dominate the banking industry. The market share for the four largest banks is approximately 75 per cent.

The concentration ratio measure has its obvious disadvantages. To study different parts of banking activities and the industry's potential competitive pressure in the future, as well as the existing barriers to entry and exit, adds to the analysis of the banking system[4].

In all the Scandinavian countries there are signs of increasing competition in the banking industry, even though the signs differ. In Denmark, Finland and Sweden interest rate margins have decreased since last year, while in Norway the interest rate margins began to decrease as early as the late 1980s and continued to do so during and after the banking crisis. This is quite the opposite from what happened in Finland and Sweden. In both of these countries there were very sharp increases of the interest rate margins during and immediately following the bank crisis. Figure 10.1 shows the interest rate margins in Swedish banks on an aggregated level for the period 1989-1994. The X-line shows the interest margin between average lending rates and the market rate, illustrated by the Swedish six-month T-bill rate, and the O-line shows the interest margin on deposits.

One explanation for the strengthened competition and the reduced interest rate margins in the banking industry is the establishment of new retail banks. It is important to study these banks as a group. Even though individually very small, their total impact on the banking industry will

Figure 10.1   Banks' interest rate margins in Sweden

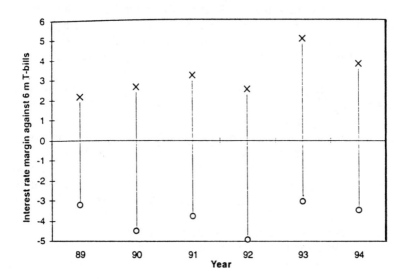

Source: The Swedish Central Bank
Note: The average figures for 1992 reflects only the first 9 months, because of a statistical change. This change also has a minor impact on the figures from 1993 and 1994

show signs of a structural change. The small retail banks that have recently been entering the Danish and the Swedish markets are taking market shares from the established banks. A majority of these banks are specialising in a narrow product and service range. In Sweden the new specialised or narrow banks have in common that they are primarily focusing on consumer deposit products and services. Of course, they also offer consumer credit products, but it is the liability side of the balance sheet and the payment services that are emphasised by these banks.

We cannot find the same development in Norway and Finland. The bank crises have led to major reconstructions of existing banks. While the independent provincial savings banks have increased their market shares in Norway, the savings bank sector has almost disappeared in Finland. Here, the only narrow bank, the independent Interbank, started before the bank crisis. Interbank is a telephone bank focusing on deposit products. Recently, it has also begun to supply lending products. The bank is not engaged in any payment services. The telephone banking concept is also provided in the other Scandinavian countries. In Denmark and Norway the concept has been adopted by some of the established universal banks as an integrated part of the existing bank. This is the case also in Sweden, but here we can find independent telephone banks as well.

Regarding the ownership of the new specialised or narrow banks it is interesting to notice that some of the new Swedish banks are owned by non-financial corporations like, for example, retail chains. We cannot find this kind of ownership in the other Scandinavian countries - at least not yet. Another difference is that some of the new banks in Sweden are owned by insurance companies. In Norway, for example, the situation is reversed; the Norwegian banks are now starting insurance companies, as was the case in Sweden in the beginning of the 1990s.

The observed changes of the banking structure in the Scandinavian countries give rise to some interesting questions regarding the establishment of specialised or narrow banks. Why are narrow banks being established now? How have they managed to obtain market shares from the existing universal banks? May the reason be that the economies of specialisation are greater than the economies of diversification? Do we in fact see the beginning of another major restructuring of the banking industry - a decomposition of universal banks? We will not be able to answer these questions in this paper. Our aim now is only to provide a setting for further research and to contribute some exploratory results. We will start with a discussion of the rationale for establishing narrow banks. This discussion is followed by a closer study of their applied strategies and the responses from universal banks. Finally, we will discuss what implications the recent development might have for the future retail banking structure. Since the establishment of independent narrow banks hitherto has been most common in Sweden, we will use the Swedish experience as a reference point.

THE RATIONALE FOR ESTABLISHING NARROW BANKS

The deregulation of the financial markets in Sweden started in the mid-1980s. The process made the market more open for new competition. It even became possible for non-financial corporations to compete with the traditional financial institutions in the financial market. Some of the major changes in the deregulation process in Sweden were the following three, of which the first two were domestically driven and the third was an EEA/EU driven change (Blomberg and Blix 1995):

- Lending caps, interest rate regulation, liquidity quotas and 'placement quotas' were abolished in the middle of the 1980s. These regulations had obviously restricted the traditional banking activities.
- The currency regulation, which limited cross-border capital flows and foreign investments, was to a large extent repealed in 1989. This regulation had, for example, prohibited Swedes from buying foreign money market instruments and foreigners from buying Swedish instruments.
- Barriers to entry were lowered as a result of the EEA/EU harmonisation process starting in the late 1980s and in the early 1990s. Before then, these barriers were significant, with a rigourous means test (*behovsprovning*) that, for example, did not allow banks with foreign owners in Sweden. It should also be noted that there was one group of actors in the financial market that was much less regulated, and that was the finance companies (*finansbolag*).

In Table 10.1 some factors that influenced the competitive arena for the years 1990 and 1993 are shown. When foreign banks were allowed to establish subsidiaries in Sweden in 1986, twelve banks were opened. These banks had their main focus on the corporate sector, and mainly on trading and lending. Even though there were no legal obstacles for them, the entry barriers were significant - mainly on a cultural basis. Consequently, almost every one of them was soon closed down. This had much to do with the high level of trust[5] for the well-established Swedish banks. A similar conclusion can be seen in many of the studies of the competitive change of the EEA/EU, which show that the possibility of improved competition has often been overestimated[6]. This is probably because *ex ante* analysis has focused on reduced regulatory barriers, and neglected the cultural barriers such as preferences for home country products and trust. This was especially true in retail banking.

Thus, apart from the changes in the legal system from the deregulation of the financial markets, there have most likely been other changes of the market affecting the climate and conditions enabling new actors to be successful in establishing bank activities. In our opinion there are at least two additional important changes or forces that have had a major impact on the banking structure and on the conditions for

Table 10.1   Access to the Swedish banking market

	Jan-90	Jan-93
Freedom of establishment		
■ Subsidiary	yes	no
■ Branch	no	yes
■ Acquisitions	no	yes
Freedom of cross border trade		
■ Payments	no[1]	yes
■ Securities trading	no	yes

Source: Blomberg 1994
Note: 1.   Payments were free, but restrictions on intermediaries and payment channels discriminated against foreign competition

establishing new banks.   These other main driving forces are the rapid technological development and the bank crisis.

■   The technological development has, in short, lowered the transaction and information costs. This has made it possible for the securities market to compete with banks, in other words traditional intermediation has become less important. For retail banking the electronic technology development regarding telecommunications has led to more efficient distribution channels
■   The bank crisis emerged in the early 1990s. As mentioned earlier, the deregulation process meant that the lending caps were removed. This started a new era in Swedish banking with an almost explosive increase in bank lending, mainly with real estate as collateral. In this climate an adverse banking culture arose. Some banks were managed with the main objective of increased volume of lending instead of

long-term profitability - increasing market shares was the most important target. It was even possible to use the expected future increase in the market value of real estate as collateral when borrowing from finance companies, which in turn were financed by banks. The sharp drop in inflation in the early 1990s, as a result of a weakened economy, worsened the crisis in the real estate sector and the financial system as a whole. In this situation the government enacted a guarantee that all banks should be able to fulfil their obligations. Today, in the aftermath of the bank crisis, the state subsidies for this government guarantee amount to just over SEK 60 billion. Including guarantees which have not (yet) resulted in any payments for the government, this figure rises to about SEK 90 billion (Ministry of Finance 1994)

There are several reasons why the bank crisis has led to structural changes in the Swedish banking sector:

- In their efforts for higher profitability and for attaining capital adequacy requirements, banks increased the interest rate margins, which made it possible for new actors to enter the market. The development of interest rate margins was shown earlier in Figure 10.1
- Banks stopped their international expansion, and tried to consolidate themselves in their home market instead
- The cultural barriers to entry were reduced when the public trust in banks was sharply decreased, and the established Swedish banks were seen as something very negative (see Figure 10.2, where the X-line shows the trust index for Swedish banks and the O-line shows the average trust index for Swedish public services institutions). As is shown in Figure 10.2, the public trust for the established universal banks in Sweden was very high until the bank crisis in the early 1990s. Thereafter banks have had an extremely low trust figure, even though they have broken their downward trend in 1994. Of course, this situation has made it easier for new actors to break into the banking market now than in the mid-1980s when the deregulation process started[7]
- The government bank guarantee, which ensured that all banks could fulfil their obligations, was introduced to protect the Swedish financial market from a major breakdown. However, it also included newly established banks, which meant that new banks could enter the market without any risk of default

Figure 10.2   Public trust index

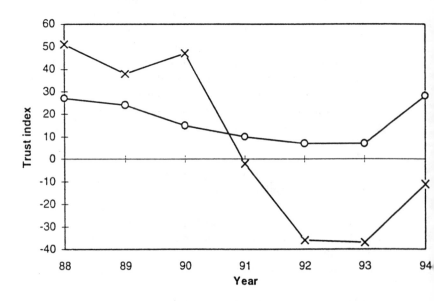

Source: Elliot 1994

The poor reputation of traditional banks evidenced by the lack of public trust, together with the bank guarantee, provides new banks with an extraordinary opportunity to establish themselves. Furthermore, these new banks may extensively use new technological and cost-effective equipment.   Even though this possibility is open to the established universal banks, one cannot disregard the fact that they have already invested a significant amount of money in systems based on yesterday's technique.

One result of this structural change can be seen in the figures regarding consumer savings. Even though total consumer savings have increased in the last few years, traditional bank depositing has levelled out, and in the last year even decreased. The decreasing money supply (M3) in Sweden can to a degree be explained by this weak development in the traditional bank depositing in favour of other sources of savings. From mid-1994 to mid-1995 savings in 'private' bonds increased from 50 to 120 billion Swedish Crowns. This should be compared with the SEK 400 billion that Swedish households have in banks deposits[8].

THE STRATEGIES OF NARROW BANKS

As mentioned earlier, the new banks that have entered the Swedish financial market have specialised in a narrow range of banking products and services. Hence, the narrow banks do not have the ambition to become their customers' main bank.

Although there are many similarities between these narrow banks, one does not have to study them too carefully in order to distinguish some major differences. According to a study by Petterson and Zetterberg (1995), the banks could be divided into two main groups: *the time deposit banks* and *the demand deposit or payment services banks*. Bearing in mind that this division is not clear cut (most of the banks are offering both kinds of products and services), we find the classification reasonable as a starting point for our analysis. When looking more carefully, it is obvious that the banks are quite heterogeneous within these groups as well.

The group of *time deposit banks* consists of seven banks. Two of them originate from universal banks. One bank, Credit Lyonnais Bank Sverige (CLBS), is a subsidiary of a foreign bank, while the other one (JP Bank) is the product of a merger between a provincial bank (Folkbanken) and PM Capital Markets. Both of these narrow banks were already established in the 1980s, but it was not until 1993 that CLBS was reorganised and restricted its business to the household market[9]. The remaining five time deposit banks were established in 1994-95 by other financial institutions and a non-financial corporation. Three of them (Skandia Banken, WASA Banken and Trygg Banken) are owned by insurance companies, while one (Hagströmer and Qviberg Bank) is owned by a securities trading company. Finally, the last bank (IKANO Banken) is closely linked to the furniture company IKEA.

The three insurance company-owned banks apply a similar strategy. Their target group is their present insurance customers. Two of the companies (Skandia and Trygg) have for a length of time offered financial leasing products and/or advisory services through subsidiaries. These businesses are now incorporated in the new banks. This enables the insurance banks to offer a broad range of financial products and services, although only a few regarding banking. The banking business is divided into three business units: the telephone bank for consumer depositing and lending; the financial service unit for car leasing and financial advisory services; and the insurance account unit for the administration of customers' insurance premium payments. Both banks have only one branch office. Consequently, 'bank customers' are normally obliged to use the telephone or ATMs. Cost-effective distribution channels are one of the banks' competitive advantages. However, the use of ATMs is not inexpensive for them. The two existing ATM networks in Sweden are owned by the established universal banks. They have been making, and still are making, efforts and attempts to prevent new banks from being connected to these networks. Hitherto, a solution for new banks to get round this reluctance of established banks has been to use the card company VISA's access to the ATMs. For this service the insurance company-owned banks are being charged a transaction based fee, which they pass on to their customers. Hence, customers to Skandia Banken are charged SEK 7,50 for each ATM withdrawal. On the other hand, they receive rather high interest rates on their savings accounts.

The situation for the third insurance company-owned bank, WASA Banken, is slightly different. This bank is the result of an acquisition of Bohusbanken, a provincial bank from the western part of Sweden. The strategy is that Bohusbanken is to continue its operations in its existing branch network under its own name, while the remaining or new part of WASA Banken, like other insurance banks, is primarily to operate as a telephone bank and only have one branch office. This new part specialises in only a few depositing and lending options. Generally, a minimum balance is required on its savings accounts. Against a fee, customers may use ATMs but they are more or less encouraged by the bank to turn to another (traditional) bank for payment services.

IKANO Banken also applies a customer relationship strategy. Its few banking products are more or less directed towards present customers and potential future customers of IKEA. Customers who deposit money in the bank for more than two years, for example, will get a discount on their purchases at IKEA. Likewise, borrowers are offered a lower interest rate if they use the loan to pay for purchases[10]. Furthermore, the bank also has a credit card, which is only valid at IKEA. Like the insurance banks, IKANO Banken has only one branch[11]. However, it does not offer any ATM services, hence, most customers are obliged to use other bank or giro accounts in order to deposit and/or withdraw money. Another possibility for them is to connect the IKEA card to a savings account in the bank and use it as a debit card when purchasing. Transaction fees are charged in neither case.

The remaining three 'time deposit' banks seem to be more product-orientated. Unlike the insurance company-owned banks (especially Skandia Banken and Trygg Banken), they do not target a certain customer category by cross-selling banking products and financial services with the purpose of utilising the synergy between the different businesses. The securities-company-owned bank is just about to start its banking activities and declares that it will be operating mainly in the field of financial advisory services and traditional stock and bond broker services. The organisational structure of CLBS and JP Bank is similar to that of banks owned by insurance companies. CLBS has two branch offices, and JP Bank has one. As complements, the latter bank has also seven 'bank shops' located in the three largest cities in Sweden. However, it is not possible to bank in these shops. Especially, CLBS tries to avoid ordinary payment services and does not offer any transaction deposit products. The bank concentrates on savings deposits, certificates and other time deposits with favourable interest rates. In order to stimulate long-term savings, for example, it offers a savings product with an extra interest rate premium that increases step-wise ($+0.5$ per cent annually) for three years.

Although JP Bank does include demand deposit products in its product and service range, the bank explicitly recommends its customers to utilise a traditional bank for payment services. Most of its deposit products are linked to STIBOR (STockholm InterBank Offered Rate). There are no stipulated minimum balances. The business concept is to offer simple and low-risk savings products with an apparent consumer surplus.

The group of *demand deposit or payment services banks* consists of five banks. However, three of them (ICA, KF and VIVO) are owned by large nationwide merchant companies and are not yet real banks in the sense that they have received a concession by the government to start banking activities. We have, however, chosen to regard them as narrow banks because they already offer several bank products and services within certain limits. The two other banks in the group have concessions. The largest one (Postgirot Bank) is a subsidiary of the Swedish Post Office, and began banking activities (for example, to offer interest on customers' balances on giro accounts) in 1994. The last one, SESAM Banken, is a subsidiary of the universal bank, Skandinaviska Enskilda Banken.

The three 'banks' owned by non-financial institutions can be characterised as (plastic) card banks. They offer their customers a combined debit and credit card that may only be used in the companies' own shops. Thus, they are comparable to the IKEA card and also to petrol company cards, which are administered by external financial institutions. The card banks try to attract customers to deposit money by offering high interest rates. However, customers are by law only permitted to have a maximum balance of SEK 8,000 on such accounts. Hence, these card banks are not time-deposit-orientated - at least not yet[12]. They are not completely demand-deposit-orientated either, since customers cannot withdraw money from their accounts unless they are buying something or clearing the account. The banks' apparent strategy is to tie customers' purchases of perishables to their shops. Often customers are offered a discount on some selected commodities, provided they use the card when paying. Thus, the card may be used for tie-in sales. It may also be regarded as a way of putting a price-bundling strategy into practice. In order to receive an offered discount on a commodity, a customer without a card must apply for one. Hence, we have a case of mixed-leader bundling, where the commodity is the 'leader'[13]. When the card is widely spread among customers, it will then be possible for companies to use the card as the 'leader'. Card customers may receive either an interest premium on deposits or an interest discount on credits, for a certain time period, when they are making their purchases in any of the company's shops and stores[14].

Postgirot Bank and SESAM Banken, finally, offer a broad range of payment services. The former postal giro had a dominant position regarding giro payments: it took care of about two-thirds of all giro transactions[15]. The strategy of Postgirot Bank is not only to defend this position, but to utilise its possibilities to offer interest and allow credits on giro accounts in order to increase its market share. Furthermore, it has the ambition to improve its other payment services, like ATM withdrawals, direct debits and cross-border payments. The bank has no branches of its own, but customers are welcome to use postal offices for ordinary cash (giro) payments and withdrawals. Still, the dominant product of the bank is giro payments orders. It offers two different giro payments order products to consumers. One is launched as a giro account with a favourable interest rate and a superior service to customers. Giro payments orders are cleared within one (working) day and customers receive a statement of account within a few days. However, they are charged a transaction fee on each order, and the interest rate offered is not comparable to that of time deposits. The other product offers a low interest on balances, and it takes four to five days to receive the statement of accounts. On the other hand, no transaction fees are charged.

SESAM Banken is basically a telephone bank, like Skandia Banken and Trygg Banken. However, it's primary focus is on payment services. Each customer receives a transaction account from which invoices and bills may be paid on their due day. The customer just has to send the bills to the bank. The bank charges a monthly fee of SEK 40, but on the other hand customers are not charged any transaction fees. Furthermore, customers receive relatively favourable interest rates on deposits. Hence, SESAM Banken applies another kind of price-bundling strategy - *pure bundling*.

RESPONSES FROM UNIVERSAL BANKS

Apart from offering higher interest rates on savings and time deposits, the starting of SESAM Banken is perhaps the most apparent response from the universal banks in order to meet the new competition from narrow banks. The bank operates more or less independently from its parent company. It has been launched as a new retail bank, which uses cost-effective distribution forms without any costly branches, but still with an instantaneous around-the-clock accessibility for customers. The fact that it is a subsidiary of Skandinaviska Enskilda Banken (SE-Banken) is seldom mentioned in its marketing campaigns.

The other three large universal banks in Sweden apply more conventional approaches. They have telephone banks as well, but as an integrated part of the bank. One of the banks (Svenska Handelsbanken) seems to be rather unaffected by the occurrence of the narrow banks. As opposed to most of the these banks, it has a relatively strong position in the rural parts of the country. But even more important, the bank has for several years been rather profitable and, above all, it managed extraordinarily well during the bank crisis. Hence, Svenska Handelsbanken continues its customer-orientated strategy and its successful concept of decentralisation. This concept means that it is the local branch managers who determine and decide on actions to be taken in order to meet the increase in competition[16].

The largest bank (Nordbanken) appears to have been occupied with its organisational changes in connection with the acquisition of the former Gota Bank, an acquisition that may be seen as a direct consequence of the disastrous results of the banks during the bank crisis. Both Nordbanken and Gota Bank made significant credit losses, and they have cost the taxpayers nearly SEK 60 billion[17]. The intervention by the government led to Gota Bank becoming a state-owned bank and it was later on acquired by the already state-owned Nordbanken. In spite of the huge credit losses, Nordbanken has preserved its customer relationship concept that was implemented five years ago. This concept favours customers who do all or most of their banking within the bank. After the acquisition of Gota Bank the concept has been further developed. This has nothing to do with the establishment of narrow banks, but is rather an endeavour to keep and incorporate the most appealing parts of Gota Bank's customer service concept. The latter concept was to target certain customer segments. Customers with high balances on their accounts were given financial advisory services by a 'personal' bank man. Considering the fact that Nordbanken has always been a mass-market bank regarding consumer products and services, the refinement of its customer relationship concept may be seen as an attempt to change its main focus away from the most transaction-intensive segments of the market.

Sparbanken Sverige (the savings bank) has recently become a public bank. It was created in 1992, when eleven large regional savings bank foundations were merged into a national savings bank foundation. Not surprisingly, Sparbanken Sverige is even more focused on the consumer mass market than Nordbanken. Like Nordbanken, Sparbanken also suffered severely during the bank crisis. Undoubtedly, this circumstance has accelerated the process of the banks going public.

Regarding the strategy of Sparbanken Sverige, it is evident that the bank is determined to achieve a better balance between its income-generating activities; it cannot maintain its 'cross-subsidising' price-bundling policy any longer. Two years ago it implemented charges on certain payment services; for example, the bank is now charging a transaction-based fee of SEK 15 on cheque payments and an annual fee of SEK 150 on its private giro order services. As a 'compensation' to the customers the interest rates on savings accounts were raised. At the same time the bank launched a new customer relationship concept, which is very close to the one that Nordbanken has applied. Customers who fulfil certain requirements regarding their use of the bank's products and services are favoured. They, for example, receive a 30 per cent discount on the annual fee of private giro orders and five cheque payments per year free of charge. The bank has also started a telephone bank, which is called Sparbanken Direkt. Unlike SESAM Banken, though, Sparbanken Direkt is neither an independent subsidiary nor a (giro) payment services bank.[18] It has two kinds of services - a 24-hour automatic service and an 18-hour personal service. The automatic service is free of charge and only offers straightforward services, such as the possibility to transfer private balances between different accounts and to get statements of accounts. The personal service costs SEK 100 every half-year, but it offers customers a broad range of products and services. However, neither the starting of telephone bank services nor the implementation of a new customer relationship concept and fees on certain payment services seem to have been a direct response to the increasing competition from narrow banks only; these actions were rather a response to the overall increase in competition within the banking industry. The bank can no longer afford to use inefficient distribution channels for ordinary banking.

IMPLICATIONS FOR FUTURE RETAIL BANKING

There are reasons for believing that the markets for retail banking in Scandinavia will see a significantly larger competitive pressure in the future. The established universal banks have already been forced to search for new business areas by falling interest rate margins and lower depositing and lending volumes. Examples of these new businesses are pensions savings, capital funds management and different activities off the balance sheet. In the long run they must probably imitate specialised institutions in the respective markets in order to survive competition, which means they have to change their business strategy and their organisational structures (Shaw 1990, Abraham and Lierman 1991, and Conti and Maccarinelli 1992). One of the challenges for universal banks is therefore to try to adapt to this change and to find new tasks which they can fulfil[19]. The change over the past ten years has mainly been in *the way* of performing the banking activities, not so much the activities as such. But lately there have been signs of new banking activities, and we believe that we are seeing the beginning of a new trend of universal banks developing new banking activities.

Regarding the competition between the established universal banks and the new narrow banks, it is obvious that the narrow banks in Sweden have contributed to decreasing interest rate margins and a vitalisation of the bank pricing strategies regarding payment services. Today, we can observe a development of product-orientated as well as customer-orientated pricing strategies in order to finance system capacity costs. Another observation is the cross-selling of products and/or services that is applied by the insurance company-owned banks and the non-financial institutions' banks. Furthermore, our survey shows that the new banks are able to begin banking activities with a small staff and cost-effective equipment based on the latest techniques. The established banks have already invested a significant amount of capital in personnel-demanding distribution systems based on yesterday's technique. Hence, even though we can expect the concentration ratio to remain high within the banking industry - at least in the near future - it is evident that the barriers to entry are decreasing. This is especially true in Denmark and Sweden, where new actors are entering the traditional banking market, while established banks are trying to expand their banking. In Sweden new banks also benefit from a decrease in public trust in the established banks, which has led to less loyal customers. In combination with universal banks' traditional reliance on income from interest rate margins, this has been an extraordinary opportunity for narrow banks to exploit the more profitable segments of the retail banking market. Universal banks have often used these segments in order to subsidise less profitable segments by their strategy of bundling. Therefore, we will probably see more transaction- or product-orientated banking in the future, instead of the more customer-orientated banking observed during the past ten years. There are clear signs of prices becoming more important than relations.

Vesala (1993) points out that there is no strong evidence for the assumption that there are economies of scale in (retail) banking. Empirical research in Europe shows no strong support for that hypothesis[20]. According to Conti and Maccarinelli (1992) a higher level of specialisation of employees and technology in specialised institutions is an effective competitive advantage in the absence of significant economies of scale in universal retail banking. This implies that narrow banks are more than just a temporary trend, and that we may very well be observing the first signs of a major structural change in banking.

It will be noted, however, that some of the new banks, like the insurance company-owned banks and the IKANO bank, use another form of price bundling. Banking products are bundled with non-banking products. In regard to insurance products and banking products, there may very well be significant cost advantages both in gathering information about customers and in distributing (standardised) products to customers. In case the economies of gathering information really are substantial, these narrow banks may enlarge their banking product and service range and, thus, become a universal financial conglomerate[21]. Recent advertising by Skandia Banken about additional products and services indicates that Skandia is heading in this direction. Hence, this may be a future strategy for other insurance companies as well. On the other hand, as we already have mentioned, this cross-selling concept has also been applied by many universal banks, although only to a certain degree. In the longer term, when banks have overcome their current problems with sunk costs and low public trust, it is therefore almost impossible to predict which of these financial institutions will triumph.

It seems easier to express more tenable opinions about the future for other narrow banks, those banks that are owned by non-financial institutions. We find it hard to distinguish any scope economies for them. Their competitive advantage is related to their cost-effective distribution of banking products and services, hence, they will never develop into universal banks.   The question is whether they will survive at all. Certainly, the kind of price bundling that, for example, IKANO Banken is applying, allows IKEA to discriminate between customers, which in turn may lead to increased sales volumes. However, it is evident that not only marginal customers will receive a discount on their purchases: many customers would have bought furniture at IKEA anyway. Assuming that IKANO Banken's interest rates are competitive, these customers are in fact increasing their consumer surplus on behalf of IKEA's producer surplus. Thus, it may be regarded as a case of 'cannibalisation'. But even the increased sales volumes to marginal customers would probably be obtainable at a lower cost in co-operation with an external financial institution. Is there really any reason to believe that an inexperienced narrow bank will be more efficient than an established financial institution in the long run? A similar question may be put regarding the price-bundling strategy applied by merchant chains when they offer special discounts or favours to customers using the companies' debit and/or credit cards. On the other hand, the merchant companies may gain cost reductions in this way since they are avoiding the newly implemented transaction charges by universal banks on card payments[22].

Regardless of the outcome of the 'battle' between traditional banks and insurance companies, and irrespective of whether or not narrow banks owned by non-financial institutions will survive, the vitalisation of pricing strategies is sustainable. For long, traditional banks have faced an almost unanimous general opinion against the implementation of explicit charges on payment services[23].   Especially so-called mass-market banks have suffered from this resistance. Certainly, the resistance has not disappeared with the entry of narrow banks, but these banks have been able to demonstrate that their charges on payment services really mean higher interest rates on deposits. In the longer run, every step towards a general acceptance of such charges will be of great value for 'mass-market' banks. It will enable them to abandon their cross-subsidisation of payment services and thus compete with other financial institutions for depositing and lending customers on more or less equal terms.

CONCLUSIONS

Even though our study is of an exploratory kind and aims at deriving reasonable explanations to the recent developments in retail banking in Scandinavia, we still believe it is possible to draw some important conclusions from the discussions. Evidently, these conclusions are primarily and conditionally in a typically 'academic' sense. The main conclusions of the study could be summarised in the following paragraphs:

- Specialised or narrow banks may have a future in the market, provided they maintain a focused strategy, continue to use cost-efficient distribution forms and straight product pricing. Their competitive advantage lies in the economies of specialisation. Naturally, the most severe threat will come from those universal banks that apply a segmentation strategy and, like SE-banken, start an independent subsidiary focusing on the same customer categories

- Narrow banks that are owned by other financial institutions and are developed as a means of cross-selling different financial products and services, will also fullfil the requirements enabling them to remain in the market, provided the economies of information gathering are significant. However, they will most likely be faced with strong competition from the established universal banks

- Narrow banks that apply a price-bundling strategy, meaning that non-financial products or services are subsidised, will presumably have difficulties surviving unless they abandon this strategy or, in some way, manage to make it more selective. Otherwise, the risk is obvious that the 'wrong' customers will benefit from this subsidy, customers who would otherwise have bought the subsidised products at full price

- The established universal banks must in the near future concentrate on recovering from the repercussions of the bank crisis and try to re-establish their former reputation of being serious and reliable financial institutions. They have to become still more business-orientated and search for new business opportunities that will add to the economies of scope. Furthermore, they must adapt to the new efficient distribution forms and considerably reduce their branch network. This is especially true for the mass-market banks.

- Finally, banks have begun seriously to develop their pricing on payment services. The new banks have shown in practice that interest rate margins may be reduced when payment services are charged for. To implement charges successfully on payment services is of utmost importance for (mass-market) banks. However, although such charges may be regarded as more or less indispensable for them in a competitive environment, the existence of explicit charges is by no means a sufficient guarantee for improved efficiency. It is also necessary for the bank to understand both how its cost structure will be affected by changes in transaction volumes in space and time and how sensitive revenues are to different price levels and price structures. Whether variable transaction charges or fixed annual charges (or a combination) are preferable is still to be proved

NOTES

The views expressed in the article are the responsibility of the authors and are not to be regarded as representing the view of the Sveriges Riksbank.

1. We include Denmark, Finland, Norway and Sweden in Scandinavia.
2. At least this was the common impression, even though very few banks actually applied for a bank concession.
3. As Revell (1994) points out the term 'universal bank' has a number of different meanings. We have chosen to regard a bank as a universal bank if it (1) undertakes both retail and wholesale business and (2) offers a broad range of banking products and services (including foreign services) to its customers. Accordingly, we regard a narrow bank as a bank that (1) has its main focus on either retail or wholesale business and (2) is specialising in only a few banking products and/or services.
4. Cf. the discussion of contestable markets by Baumol *et al.* (1982).
5. For a discussion of the trust concept see Luhmann (1979).
6. See e.g. Cecchini (1988) and Browaldh (1989)
7. For a further discussion on the effects of trust and reputation see Dowd (1992), Steinherr and Gilbert (1989), and Dixon (1991).
8. See *SvD* 15 August 1995.
9. The commercial customers were thereafter served by a newly established branch to Crédit Lyonnais S.A.
10. A necessary condition is that they have been saving in the bank for at least one year.
11. This branch lies in Almhult, where the head office of IKEA is located.
12. Two of the 'banks' have applied for a bank concession. These banks might develop their savings deposits, if and when they are permitted

200   *Ted Lindblom and Martin Andersson*

to start banking activities.
13. See Guiltinan (1989) for a more detailed overview of price-bundling strategies.
14. In principle IKANO Banken already applies this kind of price-bundling strategy, since lenders get a reduced interest rate on 'purchasing' loans.
15. Including payments by the State, municipal and public companies, see Affarsvarlden nr 36/93. Postgirot Bank will not limit its services to consumers only. It will continue the services to institutions and other organisations as well.
16. Of course these actions must be in accordance with the overall strategy of the bank.
17. Ministry of Finance (1994).
18. A similar concept is applied by Nordbanken. Its telephone bank is called NB Direkt.
19. Merton (1993) talks about the innovation spiral.
20. For a summary of results from a number of studies regarding economies of scale and scope, see Clark (1988).
21. Cf. Bergendahl's (1994) study of allfinanz in Germany.
22. Recently, some universal banks in Sweden have begun to charge shopkeepers for their customers' use of debit and credit cards. This summer the shopkeepers were permitted by the authorities to pass on these transaction charges to the customers. The merchant companies have recommended them to discriminate between customers paying with a card from another bank and customers paying with the company card. The latter customers should not have to pay any transaction fee. As a result the applications for the merchant companies' debit and credit cards have increased dramatically (see, e.g. *Fri köpenskap*, 23 June 1995, p. 4)
23. See Lindblom (1990).

LIST OF REFERENCES

Abraham, J. and F. Lierman (1991), 'European banking in the nineties: a supply side approach', IEF Research Papers in Banking and Finance, RP 91/8
Baumol, W.J. Panzar and R. Willig (1982), *Contestable Markets and the Theory of Industrial Structure* (New York, NY: Harcourt, Brace and Jovanovich)

Bergendahl, G. (1994), 'Allfinanz, bancassurance, and the future of banking', IEF Research Papers in Banking and Finance, RP 94/7

Blomberg, E. (1994), 'Banking' in Ems (ed.), 'EEA and the financial services sectors in Sweden' Sveriges Riksbank, Occasional Paper 9, Stockholm

Blomberg, E. and E. Blix (1995), 'Erfarenheter fran tillömpningen av den finansiella lagstiftningen', Working Paper, Sveriges Riksbank, Stockholm

Browaldh, T. (1989), 'Bankstrategi infor 90-talet' in G. Bergendahl (ed.), *Bankernas roll pa de finansiella marknaderna* (Stokholm: Norstedts)

Cecchini, P. (1988), *The European Challenge 1992: The Benefits of a Single Market* (Aldershot: Gower)

Clark, J. (1988), 'Economies of scale and scope at depository financial institutions: a review of the literature', Federal Reserve Bank of Kansas City, Sept/Oct

Conti, V. and M. Maccarinelli (1992), 'Bank profitability, capital adequacy and optimal size in modern banking: three studies', IEF Research Papers in Banking and Finance, RP 92/20

Dixon, R. (1991), *Banking in Europe - The Single Market* (London: Routledge)

Dowd, K. (1992), 'Is banking a natural monopoly?', *KYKLOS*, **45**

Elliot, M. (1994), 'Fornyat samhallsfortroende' in Holmberg and Weibull (eds.), *Det gamla riket*, SOM-rapport nr 13, Goteborg 1994

Fri köpenskap (1995), 23 June

Guiltinan, J.P. (1989), 'The price bundling of services: a normative framework' in Bateson (ed.), *Managing Service Marketing* (Chicago: The Dryden Press)

Lindblom, T. (1990), 'Pricing strategies on payment services', IEF Research Papers in Banking and Finance, RP 90/16

Luhmann, N. (1979), *Trust and Power* (Chichester: John Wiley and Sons)

Merton, R. (1993), 'Operation and regulation in financial intermediation: a functional perspective' in Englund (ed.), *Operation and Regulation of Financial Markets*, Economic Council, Stockholm

Ministry of Finance (1994), *The Swedish Financial Crisis*, July

Petterson, M. and M. Zetterberg (1995), *Sparbanken Sverige i konkurrensen med de nya nischbankerna*, Gothenburg School of Economics

Revell, J. (1994), 'Strategies of major British banks since Big Bang' in Revell (ed.), *The Changing Face of European Banks and Securities Markets'* (Basingstoke and London: Macmillan)

Shaw, R. (1990), 'Changes in organisational structures in banking', IEF
    Research Papers in Banking and Finance, RP 90/21
Steinherr, A. and P. Gilbert (1989), *The Impact of Freeing Trade in
    Financial Services and Capital Movements on the European Banking
    Industry*, European Investment Bank
Svenska Dagbladet (1995), 15 August
Vesala, J. (1993), *Retail Banking in European Financial Integration*, Bank
    of Finland

Other sources

Annual Reports

Interviews with:

- Jukka Vesala, Bank of Finland
- Jens Dalsgaard, Danmarks Nationalbank
- Hans-Petter Vilse, Norges Bank

CHAPTER 11

UNIVERSAL BANKING IN CENTRAL AND EASTERN EUROPE

Sándor Ligeti

INTRODUCTION

The term 'universal banking' does not have a precise definition, therefore it is not engraved in stone. In general, universal bank implies that banking organisations go beyond traditional banking activities into others, which can be selling and buying securities, underwriting securities and in some countries holding shares of non-bank (industrial and commercial) companies. We can see the term universal bank has at least two meanings: on one hand a multiproduct firm, on the other hand, a bank which carries out not only commercial bank activities but investment bank activities and recently insurance activities as well.

According to the present Hungarian Banking Act a commercial bank may perform the following activities:

- accepting customers' deposits
- granting credits
- providing payment transactions, as well as at least nine other financial institution activities

It means that a Hungarian commercial bank is universal because it is a multiproduct firm, but underwriting and trading with some types of securities are forbidden.

An investment bank:

- may not accept saving deposits
- accept deposits only over one-year maturity
- may define the minimum amount of a deposit accepted from one depositor
- may not provide current accounts
- may grant loans longer than one-year maturity

There is a controversy about the meaning of universal banking among the Hungarian economists. But there is a great controversy about the merits of universal banking as well. The proponents of universal banking argue that it promotes economic growth by providing long-term financing to industrial and commercial companies and that it promotes the efficiency of banks by economies of scale and economies of scope. Opponents of universal banking argue that it distorts credit allocation because of an increase in connected lending; it will lead to a greater concentration of economic and political power. In the universal banks there are conflicts of interests between the lending departments and securities departments. A universal bank can take more risk underwriting or trading securities than the 'classical' commercial bank.

Even the World Bank experts have different opinions concerning universal banking. Finishing this introduction I quote Professor Maxwell Fry (1988, 283): 'There is, therefore no universal case for or against universal banking.' I may add: there is, therefore no universal definition of universal banking.

BANKING REFORMS IN CENTRAL AND EASTERN EUROPE

In Central and Eastern European countries and in the former Soviet Union before the economic reforms there were the so called one-tier banking systems. (I do not like the phrase monobank system because it suggests that there was only one bank). In many countries there was the National Bank or State Bank, which carried out the central bank function and at the same time was the bank of the state-owned enterprises and co-operatives. But we could find other, so called, specialised banks as well. The National Savings Bank was the bank of the households, artisans (and in Hungary the bank of the local councils). The Development Bank allocated credits and non-repayable investment allowances according to the central government decisions. The Foreign Trade Bank served the financial needs of specialised foreign trade companies.

After, and in some countries, before the economic reform the two-tier banking system was introduced. Apart from the former Republic of Yugoslavia, in Central and Eastern Europe Hungary was the first in 1987, Albania the last in 1992. The two-tier banking system means that there is a central bank and some commercial banks, which handle the accounts of enterprises and co-operatives and grant them credits.

The common feature of the establishment of the new commercial banks was that these banks were carved out from the central bank. In some countries some of the commercial banks remained state-owned and carried the former specialisation of the central bank departments. Savings banks and commercial banks were entitled to move into each other's business, but because of the lack of experience and the lack of infrastructure it is a slow process. In every country the main problems were that the commercial banks did not have enough capital and had no loan loss provisions but inherited a lot of bad loans. Because of the deteriorating economic conditions credits granted by the new commercial banks became bad loans as well. For a long time there was no stimulus for the commercial banks to write off bad loans and because of this they rolled over these credits. There were several reasons stemming from corporate problems, such as the collapse of Comecon, reduced subsidies, price liberalisation, the lack of bankruptcy laws and the political pressure to keep alive the big industrial companies which made losses.

Because of the uncertainty and unprofitability of industrial and commercial companies a crowding-out appeared. Commercial banks financed budget deficits and each other on the interbank market. According to the banking laws commercial banks were entitled to carry out several financial activities. In this meaning they could be universal banks.

The other meaning of universal banks, which allowed both classical commercial bank activities and investment bank activities, was followed in most of the Central and Eastern European countries, except Hungary, where commercial banks cannot underwrite or trade securities; they carry out these activities by wholly owned subsidiaries. If the former socialist countries allow the activities of branches or subsidiaries of foreign banks, they usually concentrate on profitable customers, and carry out their activities as niches.

There is a very interesting contradiction in the suggestions of western economists. Some of them argued that state-owned enterprises are loss-making, and because of this they argued that commercial banks should not grant credit to them. Others also argued that newly privatised, established firms are too risky, and because of this they suggested that commercial banks should also not grant credit to them without sufficient collateral. The majority of western advisers suggested that commercial banks must be privatised first. In addition they recommend that the former centrally planned countries must develop securities markets as well.

Non-bank financial intermediaries in the form of pension funds and investment funds, are not developed in these countries and because of this they cannot play such a role as in the western countries. In the field of retail deposits saving banks dominate and commercial banks can hardly compete because of the lack of a widespread branch network.

CORPORATE GOVERNANCE, BANK-BASED SYSTEMS AND UNIVERSAL BANKING

The restructuring and privatising of the former state-owned enterprise system appears as the question of corporate control, corporate governance and the connection with financial institutions. Do banks have a direct role in corporate activities or should the corporates be based on the stock market? The answer is the choice between the German-type universal banking or the US type separation of commercial banks and investment banks. There is a study (Corbett and Mayer 1991), whose title suggests that countries of Central and Eastern Europe have chosen the wrong model. According to the authors the US and UK models are not the most suitable for the transition countries, and share ownership does not solve the problems of corporate governance. In the following pages we shall deal with the types and functions of the banking systems in the Central and Eastern European countries and the roles of the stock exchanges.

It is said that the easiest method of privatisation is using the stock market. The fact is that in the transition countries the stock market does not have a considerable role, either in privatisation or in the economy as a whole. Hostile takeover, which is a frequent phenomenon in the Anglo-Saxon world, does not appear to have been important in Central and Eastern Europe, although there are some examples showing that it occurred by domestic and frequently by foreign investors. The other argument is that share-ownership will not remain dispersed; shares will be accumulated in the hands in institutional investors. My experience is, that in these countries, particularly in Hungary, investment funds and pension funds do not play a considerable role in the corporate securities market. Investment funds, when these investments were tax-deductible, were a very popular form of tax avoidance, but when this possibility was stopped their role diminished.

Some western economists suggest that banks can finance corporates by collecting deposits and granting credits and buying shares of the corporates. If it does not happen, spreading of foreign ownership of enterprises or renationalisation of enterprises through bank recapitalisation (in Hungarian: consolidation) could be the solution. If they choose the banks as the main source of company financing, an elaborate regulatory system, safety nets, capital adequacy standards and balance-matching regulations, is needed.

After analysing the pros and cons of the bank-based and the (stock) market-based system Grosfeld (1994) has a different conclusion from that of the authors cited above. She argues that the banks do not have enough information to control the enterprises because enterprises have an 'inheritance': assets and investment opportunities from the former state-owned era. Even the banks that have had a contact with the enterprise did not have satisfactory information of the prospects of the enterprises because of the changing economic environment, the lack of a modern accounting system, the high leverage ratio and the future performance of the firms' managers. Some opponents of this view argued that the banks have the opportunity to carry out monitoring activity or hiring well-trained, mainly foreign, consultants. Grosfeld states that one of the main problems is that managers and shareholders valued current profit rather than future profit; this contradiction could be solved by venture capital funds, but she states that there were very few venture capital funds in Poland. I can add that the situation is the same in Hungary and, as far as I know, in the other countries of Central and Eastern Europe.

Finally, she concludes that in Central and Eastern Europe the ownership of the industrial sector by banks would lead to maintaining an inefficient industrial and commercial sector, accumulating bad debts for the banks, and sooner or later to government intervention in restructuring the industrial sector. Banks as owners of enterprises become captive creditors and can contribute to slowing down the restructuring and privatisation process. She is not against introducing universal banking in Central and Eastern European countries, but her main argument is that universal banking conforms to the requirements imposed on European financial institutions by the Banking Directives of the EU.

Many economists state that universal banks would be important in corporate governance in transition economies. The relationship between banks and non-financial firms is usually based on the writings of Gerschenkron (1968), who dealt with the situation in Germany in the second half of the nineteenth century (page 137):

> The inadequacy in the number of available entrepreneurs could be remedied or substituted for by increasing the size of plant and enterprise above what otherwise would have been an optimum size. In Germany, the various incompetencies at the individual entrepreneurs were offset by the device of splitting the entrepreneurial function: the German investment banks - a powerful invention, comparable in economic effect to that of the steam engine - were in their capital supplying functions a substitute for the insufficiency of the previously created wealth, willingly placed at the

disposal of the entrepreneurs. But they were also a substitute for entrepreneurial deficiencies. From their central vantage points of controls the banks participated actively in shaping the major - and sometimes even not so major - decisions of individual enterprises.

Other economists stated that Gerschenkron's description is not characteristic of other countries. In Central and Eastern Europe we cannot find German-type universal banks, which own the majority of shares in non-financial enterprises, but to tell the truth the universal banking systems in the other countries in Western Europe differ more or less from the German from-cradle-to-grave model.

In spite of the fact that in Central and Eastern Europe the banks grant mainly short-term credit (the exceptions are Hungary and the former Czechoslovakia), the banks suffer losses in lending. A Polish economist, Professor Rostowski (1995, 30) suggests that before starting medium and long-term financing banks must learn how to grant short-term self-liquidating credit for working capital. He goes further when he states: 'The attempt to introduce German-type universal banking in post-communist economies in the early stages of transition reminds one of other attempts in the region to "speed up history". Like those, it would be a high risk strategy.' I think Professor Rostowski exaggerates a little bit the problem, but the similar situation in transition economies shows that the banks are not on the vantage points and do not have enough capital to own a considerable part of the non-financial companies' shares.

The common problem is that the state-owned or the formerly state-owned enterprises have capital but this capital is not real because of the insufficient auditing methods and the lack of motivation of managers employees, etc. The new private sector enterprises usually have not enough capital and because of this their creditworthiness is questioned by the bank. During the privatisation the leverage of the firms is increasing, which means another risk for the banks either as lenders or as owners. Sometimes the banks became forced owners through a debt-equity swap.

The common characteristic of these countries is that because of the high inflation nominal interest rates are increasing, which cause the decrease in the demand for credit. At the same time the increasing budget deficit financed by the monetary sector is the cause of the crowding-out; the supply of credit for non-industrial enterprises diminishes as well.

A lot of economists are against universal banking but as we can see many authors argued that universal banking is a good model for the Central and Eastern European countries. The main arguments for this model are that there will be more efficient allocations of financial resources and that companies and banks have longer-term objectives when they can co-ordinate the debt and equity owner roles. The banks can send directors to the boards of companies, who can take part in decision-making. The counterarguments are that the banks can concentrate too much power by lending and ownership. Some argued that the banks do not have enough experts to delegate on to the boards of companies. The other question could be the contradiction between the credit and securities departments. Does a bank have to lend to an insolvent company because it is a main shareholder of the company? This contradiction can be limited by establishing 'Chinese walls' and 'fire walls' between the two activities. A further problem is that commercial banking and investment banking require different types of regulation. Neither the rules nor the regulatory authorities are so well established as in the Western countries. Introducing rules and regulatory authorities which can separate commercial banking and investment banking through either subsidiaries or 'fire walls' are preconditions of an effective universal banking system.

The other solution could be market-led corporate governance, but capital markets in the former socialist countries are weak. The turnover on the stock exchanges and on the OTC markets is low and only the best companies can issue commercial paper and bonds. Investment funds do not play a considerable role in the transition economies; the exceptions are in the Czech Republic and Slovakia, where they have an important role in the privatisation programme. As previously mentioned, in Hungary their heyday was when the use of them was a possible form of tax avoidance.

RESTRUCTURING ENTERPRISES

The role of banks in restructuring enterprises is different in the Central and Eastern European countries from elsewhere: in most of the countries banks have no powers to collect bad debts, but in some countries, Poland, for example, banks have become quite aggressive in debt collection and enterprise liquidation, but their role in other aspects of enterprise restructuring remains limited. A World Bank survey of Polish enterprises (Pinto and Wynenbergen 1994) stated that 'banks played a powerful role in disciplining enterprises.'

Banks can discipline firms by withdrawing short-term credit or initiate bankruptcy process. Banks can be owners of corporations if they acquire equities through a debt-equity swap. An interesting example:

Czech banks exercise corporate governance through the investment funds they run.

DEBT-EQUITY SWAPS

In some transitional economies banks become shareowners through debt-equity swaps as a 'solution' to their bad loan problems. World Bank experts summarise the pros and cons of debt-equity swaps as follows:

> Pro: Equity swaps represent nascent venture capital operations. Perhaps only one in ten of these investments may succeed, but this should be sufficient to cover the risk of the other nine losing investments. Given existing low book values and the currently thin market that is likely to improve in the coming years, banks are prudent to allocate a small percentage of assets to enterprises they believe will generate significant profits at a later date. At that point, banks can sell their shares and reap significant profits to bolster capital. All of this makes more sense given the current downside risk, which is limited, as most of these transactions are paper transactions that do not further improve bank liquidity.
> Con: Bank equity swaps are indicative of the failure of governments and banks in transition economies to properly define banks' roles as financial intermediaries streamline their operations, specialise in a few key areas within the limits of their current managerial staffing capabilities, write down their assets to more accurate values, and progress toward a more stable and prudently managed system devoid of excess risk. Investment in losing enterprises raises the risk of future liquidity being drained to prop up these enterprises in the hope of eventual profitability, which puts depositors and shareholders (mainly government, and therefore the budget) at risk. With all the problems banks have had and currently face, there is no reason to believe that bankers as enterprise shareholders will be able to properly manage or supervise these enterprises. Meanwhile, these instruments will consume valuable management time that could otherwise be used to resolve fundamental bank problems.

I think that the cons make more sense than the pros. If banks have bad equities instead of bad loans, they are not in a better position than they were before. In transition countries banks and other owners can hardly sell securities, and they have become 'forced' owners of a weak non-financial company for a long time.

UNIVERSAL BANKING IN HUNGARY

As I mentioned commercial banks are not allowed to carry out security activities in Hungary and some authors argued that this was because, when the present Hungarian Banking Act was drafted, we had Anglo-Saxon experts who preferred the American model. The banks do not play a significant role in insurance activity. The only exception is the National Savings Bank, which owns an insurance subsidiary.

Most of the Hungarian economists suggest that we should introduce the universal banking system. The main arguments are that banks can concentrate funds through lending and equity ownership, and that the participation of banks in security activities could improve the turnover of capital markets, the stock exchange and OTC. I do not know whether it is an argument or a counter argument for universal banks that the credit portfolio of a Hungarian bank is more risky than that of a Western bank, so lending to or owning equities of non-financial enterprises mean equal risk. Another argument could be that banks are the more appropriate actors to lead restructuring and reorganising enterprises which accumulated debts. Universal banks can diversify risk. Introducing universal banking can cause a strengthening of the role and a co-ordination of the activities of the separate bank and securities supervisory authorities. Hungarian banks avoided the prohibition of security activities by establishing subsidiaries specialised in securities. Many economists think that both the banks and the non-financial firms must be privatised. The lack of domestic capital raises the question of allowing foreign investors into the banking and non-financial sector. Finally, a political argument: the increasing German and EU orientation in Central and Eastern Europe demands universal banking as well.

While I am writing this paper many colleagues in different authorities are working on the draft of the new Hungarian Banking Act, coming into force in the near future. As far as I know they will suggest that commercial banks should be allowed to carry out investment banking activities, i.e. universal banking.

CONCLUSIONS

In the Central and Eastern European countries commercial banks can carry out wholesale and retail banking activities. We can consider them as universal banks in the meaning of multiproduct firms. Most Central and Eastern European countries allow commercial banks to carry out traditional commercial bank activities and securities activities as well, except Hungary for the time being. There are different opinions about the advantages and disadvantages of universal banking. These views do not differ considerably from the discussions in the Western countries between the German model and other types of universal banking and the American model.

The main arguments against universal banking are that banks can concentrate too much power and dominate the economy. Some economists think that domestic banks have not enough capital, and because of this foreign banks and international financial organisations will dominate the economies of these countries. The arguments for introducing universal banking are that the banks lending to non-financial enterprises can know them very well and can help corporate control not only as lenders but owners as well. They can delegate members to the boards of corporates, who can take part in decision-making.

The experiences of different Central and Eastern European countries show that there are no great differences between the performance of the banking systems organised as universal banks or as separate investment and commercial banks. There are common problems in different countries: the inefficiencies of accounting systems of both banks and non-financial companies, the lack of domestic capital, the state budget deficit, crowding-out, inflation, balance of payment problems and bad loans in the banks' portfolio.

Because of the above mentioned problems I don't think that the suggestion of introducing universal banking is a panacea. We should improve the economic conditions in Hungary in general, which can improve the performance of the banking system as well. This does not mean that we do not change the structure and functions of the banking system, but that changing the banking system by itself cannot change the Hungarian economy. I think the other Central and Eastern European countries are facing similar problems.

LIST OF REFERENCES AND SELECT BIBLIOGRAPHY

Bloomstein H.J. and M.G. Spencer (1993), 'The role of financial institutions in the transition to a market economy', IMF Working Paper 93/75, Washington DC

Borish, Michael S., Millard F. Long and Michel Noel (1995), 'Restructuring banks and enterprises, recent lessons from transition countries', World Bank Discussion Papers no. 279

Colin, J. (1993), 'Banking and financial sectors in East and Central Europe', Financial Times Ltd, London

Corbett, Jenny and Colin P. Mayer (1991), 'Financial reform in Eastern Europe: progress with the wrong model', CEPR Discussion Paper no. 603 London

Fry, Maxwell J. (1988), *Money, Interest and Banking in Economic Development* (John Hopkins, Baltimore: University Press)

Gerschenkron, A. (1968), *Continuity in History and Other Essays* (Cambridge, MA: Harvard University Press)

Grosfeld, Irene (1994), 'Comparing financial systems', Center for Social and Economic Research, Warsaw

Ligeti, Sándor (1995), 'Kereskedelmi bank - univerzális bank?' (commercial bank - universal bank?), *Gazdaság és Jog*, 5, pp. 10-12

Long, M. and J. Ruthowska (1995), 'The role of commercial banks in enterprise restructuring in Central and Eastern Europe', Policy Research Working Paper no. 1423, World Bank, Washington DC

Luttenberger, Z. (1995), 'Bankbiztosítás (Bankassurance)', Garancia Biztosító Rt., Budapest

New Banking Act in Hungary (1991), Budapest

Pinto, B. and Svan Wijnbergen (1994), 'Ownership and corporate control in Poland: why state firms defied the odds', mimeo, World Bank

Rostowski, Jack (1995), *Banking Reform in Central Europe and the former Soviet Union* (Budapest: CEU Press)

Szalai, Z., 'A fejlett országok pénzintézeti rendszerének fejlődési irányzatai' (Development guidelines of the banking systems in developed countries), *Bankszemle*, 7 and 8, pp. 14-33 and 10-32

Szentiványi, I. (1994), 'Univerzális vagy specializált legyen bankrendszerünk?' (Do we need a universal or a specialised banking system?), *Gazdaság és Jog*, 2, pp. 3-6

Várhegyi, É. (1995), 'Modellválasztás előtt' (Before choosing a model), *Figyelő*, 8, pp. 33-35

CHAPTER 12
TECHNICAL PROGRESS IN SPANISH BANKING: 1985-1994

Joaquín Maudos, José Manuel Pastor and Javier Quesada

1. INTRODUCTION

Over the last decade, the Spanish banking sector has undergone a radical structural change. The old bank *status quo* has broken down because of both the impact of technical change and a strong deregulation process, which has given way to a much freer and competitive economic environment. Actually, the process of integration into a unique European Financial Market increased the role of product and price competition among banks. Such increase in competitiveness, made possible by a more liberalised regulatory framework, reached an intensive level throughout the whole period. Many private commercial and savings banks, without abandoning their own traditional role as financial intermediaries, started to compete among themselves to gain a share in the deposit and loan markets. More specifically, branch expansion was deregulated for private commercial banks in 1985; interest rate ceilings disappeared in 1987; investment coefficients that had frozen a very significant share of total assets in regulated loans and public debt were gradually eliminated; the ban on branch expansion for savings banks beyond their regional markets was lifted in 1989; the limitation that prevented savings banks from performing specialised financial activities disappeared in the late eighties; and the coefficient on demand deposits was dramatically reduced in 1990. As a result, all kinds of banks had to adopt a new strategy to survive under the new environment. To do so, they had additional instruments: branch expansion, pricing strategies, mergers and acquisitions, co-ordination policies, etc.

Similarly, the rapid and intensive diffusion of new technologies of information (computer engineering and telecommunications) has modified the banking industry in an important way. Thus the application of these technologies has allowed banks to widen the range of products and services offered, and it has served them to improve their organisation and to lower some of the production and information costs.

However, the other side of the benefits brought about by the introduction of new technologies is their associated cost. Not all banks have been able to exploit efficiently the capabilities of new technologies in lowering total costs. Actually, it is argued that for some of the new

214

technologies there exists excess capacity, which can explain in part a positive correlation between investment in technology and drops in productivity (the 'productivity paradox'). Thus, at the present time costs related to new technologies are a very important component of operating costs, second only to labour costs. In fact the last available information referring to 1993 indicates that, for the banking sector as a whole, technology costs amount to 33.6 per cent of the total.

The effect of these three phenomena (technical change, deregulation and increased competition) on production costs for the Spanish savings banks is the objective of this study. For that purpose we are using a panel including all savings banks (77 at the beginning and 51 at the end of the period) for the years 1985-94. Following Humphrey (1993), we review three alternative econometric methods of approaching the impact of technical change: first, the standard approach of introducing either a simple time trend or a technical indicator of technical change in the regression; second, the introduction of time dummies; and, finally, the annual shift of the cross-section cost function.

The paper is divided into six sections; section 2 contains some descriptive data on Spanish savings banks for the period under study; section 3 explains the different approaches to measuring the impact of technical change; section 4 contains empirical results; section 5 presents results by firm size; section 6 considers the impact of technical change on operating costs; finally, section 7 presents some concluding remarks.

2.   DESCRIPTIVE STATISTICS

This section summarises available empirical evidence on variables that are related to technical change. More precisely, Figure 12.1 shows the evolution of total average costs throughout the period, which is marked, in particular, by the evolution of interest costs, operating costs having a very stable trajectory. As a share of total assets, total average costs show a slightly decreasing pattern for the first four years of the decade (1985-88), a period of five years of a positive trend (1989-93), and a strong single drop for the final year of 1994. The dependency of average costs on their interest component makes monetary (and fiscal) policy clearly relevant in analysing technical change.

By international standards Spanish savings banks have always had very small branch offices, and they still have as shown in Figure 12.2. The low number of employees per branch has remained fairly stable throughout the period, close to a value of 5.8, approximately one-third of

Figure 12.1   Average costs (% assets)

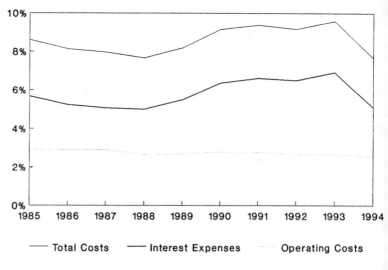

Source: CECA.

Figure 12.2   Employees per branch

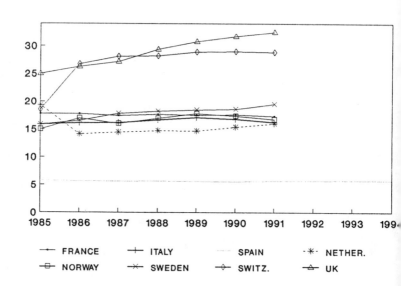

Source: CECA and Bank Profitability.

the average of other European banking systems. An interpretation for the small size of branches is the specialisation of the Spanish savings banks in raising deposits, where they have gained an important fraction of market share in relation to private commercial banks. An indicator of a positive trend in productivity appears in Figure 12.3 where in spite of branch expansion (deflated) assets per branch grow at a steady rate throughout the period. This positive trend implies a more intensive use of fixed capital per unit of intermediated funds and should be reflected in a lower average cost.

Figure 12.3   Assets per branch

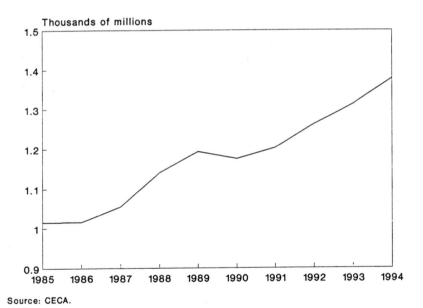

Source: CECA.

To check on the likely effect of firm size on average costs we split the sample by firm size into six different groups. Figure 12.4 shows how large banks have lost the cost advantages they enjoyed at the beginning of the period. We also find a higher cost incurred by small banks, a spread that does not disappear throughout the whole period. For the remaining groups of banks of intermediate size we see a certain degree of convergence. As is seen in Figure 12.5, the behaviour of interest costs can explain that of total costs. Large banks have seen their interest cost increase dramatically after 1989 - when the deposit war started - until 1994, when interest costs fell significantly. Interestingly enough, the fall in interest costs for banks appears a year after market interest rates had experienced a large decrease, following the three devaluations of the national currency in September and November 1992 and May 1993 and the widening of the exchange rate spread to ⁻+15 per cent in the EMS (August 1993). All other types of banks experienced a much less pronounced increase in interest costs, and interestingly enough they converged to an almost identical share of total assets. This evidence can be interpreted as the reflection of an increase in interest rate competition for loanable funds that unified interest costs for banks of different sizes.

Figure 12.4   Average total costs by sizes (% assets)

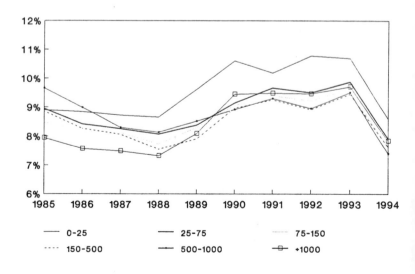

Source: CECA.

Figure 12.5 Average financial costs by sizes (% assets)

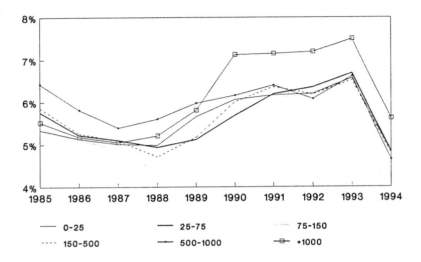

Source: CECA.

The share of financial costs in total costs by bank size appears in Figure 12.6. The larger the bank the higher the share of interest cost. For the largest banks this share amounts to 70 per cent, while for the smallest sized banks this share is close to 55 per cent. By contrast, operating costs as a share of total assets are lower the larger the size of the bank (see Figure 12.7). Furthermore, the size of branches also differs by firm size as shown in Figure 12.8[1]. We find the size of the branch - measured by assets - positively correlated with the size of the firm. More specifically, the average branch of the largest bank is three times as large as that of the smallest bank group. This relative difference is much smaller if we measure the size of branches by their number of employees (see Figure 12.9), where we find much more homogeneous sizes of branches. With the exception of the second smallest group of banks, we find for other sizes a clear reduction in the dispersion of the employment per branch.

Figure 12.6   Financial costs/total costs

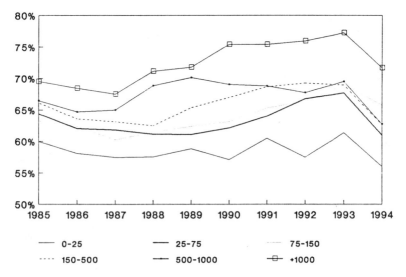

Source: CECA.

Figure 12.7   Average operating costs by sizes (% assets)

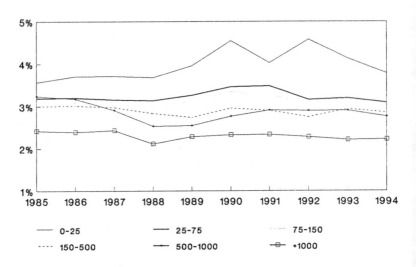

Source: CECA.

Figure 12.8 Assets by branch

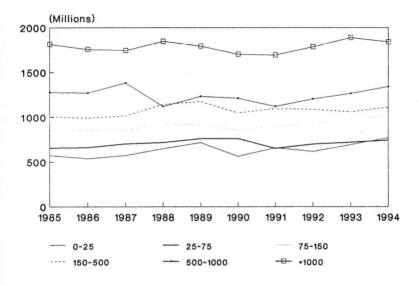

Source: CECA.

Figure 12.9 Number of employees per branch (by size)

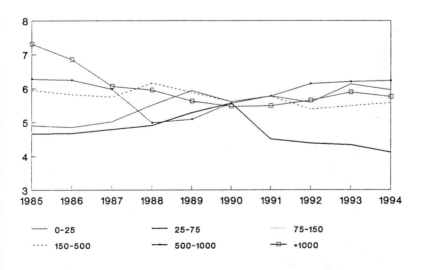

Source: CECA.

3.   MEASURING THE IMPACT OF TECHNICAL CHANGE

In this study we analyse the impact of technical progress using three different approaches. The first approach introduces a given measure of technical change into the cost equation and checks for the estimated parameters. To measure technical change we use, in turn, four different indicators, a time trend that assumes a constant rate of technical progress, and three other technical indicators: namely, an index based on the aggregate number of ATMs; an index based on the number of cash and credit cards issued by all savings banks; and an average combining these last two indexes. As opposed to the simple time trend, technology indicators show a lower and unsteady rate of increase, as shown in Figure 12.10. The time trend is shown by the line labelled (A). Lines (B), (C) and (D) show the indexes corresponding to the diffusion of technical innovations (ATMs, cash and credit cards) and their combined index. These indicators show a slightly increasing rate for the first part of the decade and a slightly decreasing one for the rest of the period. As a result of this, the different intensity at which technical progress takes place is recognised. The different levels of trend (B) and (C) before and after 1989 are the reflection of the distinct behaviour of the rates of growth of ATMs and cash and credit cards after that year. Thus, what is shown in Figure 12.10 for the period after 1989 is a decreasing trend in the number of cards per ATM.

Figure 12.10   'Technological' indicators of technical change

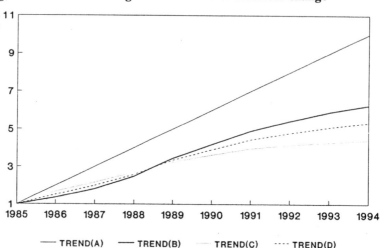

Source: CECA.

The second approach to evaluating the impact of technical change makes use of time dummies. With the estimated parameters an, index of technical change for each year is computed. This approach provides more flexibility than the introduction of a constant time trend because it allows for a non-constant rate of growth of technical progress.

The third and last method used to measure the impact of technical progress consists of the evaluation of yearly shifts in the estimated cross-section cost functions. This approach is quite flexible because the parameters of the translog cost function are re-estimated in every annual regression.

Since we have available an incomplete data panel and with the aim of checking on the possibility that each firm has a particular level of efficiency - captured by the fixed effect - we estimate the function using both techniques, pooling data and panel data.

Equation (1) shows the general form of the second order translog cost function to be estimated[2]. We include two types of outputs, and three input prices.

$$
\begin{aligned}
LnTC = \alpha_0 + \sum_{i=1}^{2} \alpha_i LnQ_i + 1/2 \sum_{i=1}^{2} \sum_{j=1}^{2} \alpha_{ij} LnQ_i Q_j + \sum_{m=1}^{3} \beta_m LnP_m + \\
1/2 \sum_{m=1}^{3} \sum_{n=1}^{3} \beta_{mn} LnP_m LnP_n + \sum_{i=1}^{2} \sum_{m=1}^{3} \lambda_{im} LnP_m LnQ_i + \psi_0 T(.) + \\
1/2 \psi_{00} T(.)^2 + \sum_{i=1}^{2} \psi_i T(.) LnQ_i + \sum_{m=1}^{3} \gamma_m T(.) LnP_m + \epsilon
\end{aligned}
\tag{1}
$$

where TC are total production costs, Q_i are the components of the production vector ($i=1$: borrowed funds, $i=2$: loans), P_m are input prices ($m=1$: labour, $m=2$: borrowed funds, and $m=3$: physical capital), $T(\cdot)$ is an indicator of technical change, where $T(A)$ is a simple time trend dummy variable, $T(B)$ is an index based on the number of ATMs, $T(C)$ is an index based on the number of cards issued, and $T(D)$ is an indicator combining cards and ATMs.

To estimate the impact of technical change we calculate the variation in the average cost due to a given change in technology. This effect can be measured by the partial derivative of the estimated average cost with respect to the used indicator of technical progress. Equation (2) contains this expression.

$$TREND(.) = \frac{\partial LnTC}{\partial T(.)} = \phi_0 + \psi_{00}T(.) + \sum_{i=1}^{2} \psi_i LnQ_i + \sum_{m=1}^{3} \gamma_m LnP_m \quad (2)$$

The first two terms on the right hand side capture the pure effect of technical change, that is the decrease in costs, keeping constant input proportions. The third term measures the technical change associated with changes in output (scale-augmenting technical change). Finally, the fourth term is a measure of the technical change associated with the change in the use of inputs due to changes in input prices.

A more flexible approach is to permit a non-constant rate of technical change - through the introduction of time dummies - in such a way that non-constant annual variations can be computed (see Caves *et al.* 1981 and Baltagi and Griffin 1988). Furthermore, this specification permits us to capture the neutral technical change, the scale-augmentative technical change (through the interaction of temporary and output effects), and the non-neutral technical change (through the interaction of prices). However, after the poor initial empirical estimates obtained for a very broad specification, we chose a functional form that only included neutral technical change. The particular translog function that was estimated was the following:

$$LnTC = \sum_{t}^{10} n_t DT_t + \sum_{i=1}^{2} \alpha_i LnQ_i + 1/2 \sum_{i=1}^{2} \sum_{j=1}^{2} \alpha_{ij} LnQ_i Q_j + \quad (3)$$
$$\sum_{m=1}^{3} \beta_m LnP_m + 1/2 \sum_{m=1}^{3} \sum_{n=1}^{3} \beta_{mn} LnP_m LnP_n +$$
$$\sum_{i=1}^{2} \sum_{m=1}^{3} \lambda_{im} LnP_m LnQ_i + \epsilon$$

According to this approach, the growth rate in technical change was expressed as the difference of two time dummies:

$$INDEX = n_{t+1} - n_t \quad (4)$$

When sufficient observations are available, it is possible to evaluate technical change in a more flexible way than that of temporary effects. The procedure implies the estimation of a different cost function for each period. Thus, whereas in the model of temporary effects technical change affects the cost function through an annual homothetic shift, this alternative approach allows for all parameters to be influenced by technical change. This model is equivalent to the former one after eliminating the temporary effects and estimating the equation for each year in the sample (see Humphrey 1993). In this procedure, the growth rate of technical change is the change in average cost that would be derived if a bank used at time t the technology available one period later.

$$SHIFT = \frac{\left(\hat{AC}^{*}_{t+1} - \hat{AC}_{t}\right)}{\hat{AC}_{t}} \qquad (5)$$

where:

- $\hat{AC}^{*}_{t+1} = \exp\left(\hat{\beta}_{t+1}(X_t)\right)/TA_t$ is the predicted average cost per asset in period t using the technology available in period $t+1$
- $\hat{AC}_t = \exp\left(\hat{\beta}_t(X_t)\right)/TA_t$ is the predicted average cost per asset in period t
- $\hat{\beta}_t$ is the estimated parameter of the cost function for period t
- X_t are data values corresponding to period t
- TA_t are total assets for period t

4.   THE EFFECTS OF TECHNICAL CHANGE: EMPIRICAL RESULTS

Our sample is formed by all Spanish savings banks and extends over the period 1985-94. A merged institution is treated as a different bank from the institutions that existed before the merging process[3]. The number of existing institutions has dropped from an initial value of 77 to 51, and the total number of observations is 659. Data sources are the savings banks association CECA, and the National Bureau of Statistics, INE.

Table 12.1, and Figures 12.11 and 12.12 report the results of computing equation (2) after the estimation of equation (1). Pooling data and panel techniques were used in the regressions. Time trend (labelled A) shows a positive continuous rate of growth of technological change over the whole period which can be interpreted as a continuously decreasing trend on average costs. For pooled regressions (see Figure 12.11), this accumulated reduction in average costs amounts approximately to 10 per cent for the ten-year period at firm level. If we replace the time trend by any of the three alternative indicators of technical change (trends (B), (C)

Table 12.1 Technical change

Year	Pooling Data Estimation				Fixed Effects Model Estimation			
	Trend(A)	Trend(B)	Trend(C)	Trend(D)	Trend(A)	Trend(B)	Trend(C)	Trend(D)
1985	-0.0204***	-0.0204***	-0.0204***	-0.0204***	-0.0093***	-0.0093***	-0.0093***	-0.0093***
1986	-0.0189***	-0.0205***	-0.0197***	-0.0200***	-0.0096***	-0.0103***	-0.0099***	-0.0101***
1987	-0.0179***	-0.0208***	-0.0195***	-0.0204***	-0.0097***	-0.0109***	-0.0106***	-0.0107***
1988	-0.0168***	-0.0205***	-0.0199***	-0.0202***	-0.0091***	-0.0106***	-0.0104***	-0.0105***
1989	-0.0144***	-0.0181***	-0.0186***	-0.0184***	-0.0077***	-0.0093***	-0.0095***	-0.0094***
1990	-0.0129***	-0.0172***	-0.0186***	-0.0179***	-0.0051***	-0.0069***	-0.0075***	-0.0072***
1991	-0.0108***	-0.0158***	-0.0181***	-0.0169***	-0.0032**	-0.0053***	-0.0063***	-0.0058***
1992	-0.0075***	-0.0137***	-0.0167***	-0.0152***	-0.0028*	-0.0054***	-0.0067***	-0.0061***
1993	-0.0050*	-0.0124***	-0.0163***	-0.0143***	-0.0012	-0.0044***	-0.0060***	-0.0052***
1994	-0.0011	-0.0101***	-0.0145***	-0.0123***	-0.0052	-0.0090***	-0.0105***	-0.0100***

(continued)

Year	Pooling Data Estimation				Fixed Effects Model Estimation			
	Trend(A)	Trend(B)	Trend(C)	Trend(D)	Trend(A)	Trend(B)	Trend(C)	Trend(D)
(continued) Average annual rate 1985-1994	-0.0135***	-0.0175***	-0.0185***	-0.0189***	-0.0068***	-0.0085***	-0.0089***	-0.0087***

*** Significant at the 1 per cent level

** Significant at the 5 per cent level

* Significant at the 10 per cent level

Figure 12.11   Time trend and technological indicators of technical change (pooling data estimation)

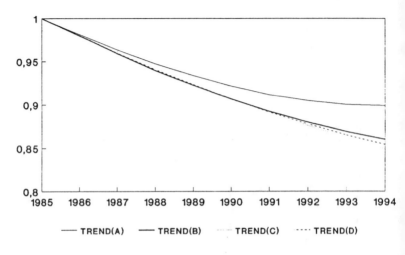

Figure 12.12   Time trend and technological indicators of technical change (panel data estimation)

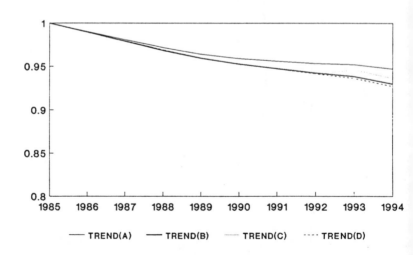

and (D)), we find a larger effect of technical change on average costs - of approximately 15 per cent - that is particularly strong in the case of indicator (C), the plastic cards index.

Figure 12.12 shows the accumulated index of technical change using panel data estimation techniques. As is well known, these techniques introduce in the regression a different constant term for each firm in the sample, which can be interpreted as a measurement of firm efficiency. Two results are worth mentioning. First, the accumulated impact of technical change on total costs is significantly lowered to a level of 5 per cent. Second, the different effects derived from using distinct indicators are much more alike than before.

The difference in the estimated impact of technical progress derived from pooling data or from a model with fixed effects, can be as high as 50 per cent. Such a difference can be interpreted as evidence in favour of introducing individual effects that capture the influence of unobservable characteristics of each firm in the sample that we attribute to differences in their levels of efficiency.

The results of Table 12.1 show that, in general, technical progress is reduced throughout the period with the exception of the last year. Furthermore, in the case of trend (A) the estimated values are not statistically different from zero for the last years of the period.

The results obtained with the fixed effects model with the standard time trend approach are similar to those obtained by Maudos (1994)[4]. More precisely, this author finds for the Spanish savings banks a significant technical progress of -0.5 per year.

A second method of evaluating the impact of technical change implies the use of time dummies - one per year - in our estimating process. With this method we do not impose a constant rate of change in average cost. In fact, the estimated parameter associated to each dummy variable measures the variation in average costs that is not explained by other explanatory variables and that is attributable to the technical change experienced during that period. Table 12.2 contains the results. The outcomes that we get correspond quite closely with the behaviour of average total costs that was shown in Figure 12.1. Thus, we can observe that there exists statistically significant technical progress (fall in average costs) over the periods 1985-88, 1991-92 and 1993-94, whereas there is technical regress (increase in average costs) in the years 1988-90 and 1992-93, although not statistically significant. On the other hand, the average annual rate of technical progress is relatively similar to that obtained with the time trend approach.

Table 12.2   Time dummies approach to technical change

Year	Pooling Data	Fixed Effects
1985-1986	-0.308*	-0.0034
1986-1987	-0.0378*	-0.0125**
1987-1988	-0.0341	-0.0154**
1988-1989	0.0233	0.0049
1989-1990	0.0514**	0.0154**
1990-1991	0.0070	-0.0104
1991-1992	-0.0380	-0.0122*
1992-1993	0.0150	0.0060
1993-1994	-0.1536***	-0.0274***
Average annual rate 1985-1994	**-0.0204***	**-0.0055***

*** Significant at the 1 per cent level
** Significant at the 5 per cent level
* Significant at the 10 per cent level

These results are similar to those obtained by Pastor (1995). This author, using a non-parametric frontier approach with Malmquist indexes, finds technical progress for the periods 1986-88 and 1990-92 and technical regress for the period 1989-90.

The third method of evaluating the impact of technical change is the shift method. This approach constitutes a more flexible way of measuring technical change. It allows for the change of all cost-function parameters and is based on the annual estimation of a cost function. If we compare the results obtained from using this method (Table 12.3) with those obtained in pooling data estimation, the impact of technical change behaves

Table 12.3   **Percentage variation in estimated average costs (Shift Approach)**

Year	Shift
1985-1986	-0.0027
1986-1987	0.0056
1987-1988	-0.0274
1988-1989	-0.0169
1989-1990	0.0288
1990-1991	-0.0211
1991-1992	-0.0135
1992-1993	-0.0148
1993-1994	-0.0284

***   Significant at the 1 per cent level
**   Significant at the 5 per cent level
*   Significant at the 10 per cent level

in a way very similar to that found with the time dummies approach, namely a positive technical progress. However, the accumulated level exceeds that of the time dummies approach and is smaller than the value obtained with the method based on a time trend. By contrast, in panel data estimations the accumulated level of the index of technical change exceeds that of the other two approaches. Furthermore, the annual behaviour is much more irregular than that derived with other methods; this is the natural consequence of the larger degree of flexibility of this last approach. Figures 12.13 and 12.14 present a summary of the accumulated indexes measuring the impact of technical change computed making use of the three different approaches and the two different ways of running the regressions, pooling data or panel techniques.

Figure 12.13   Different approaches to technical change (pooling data estimation)

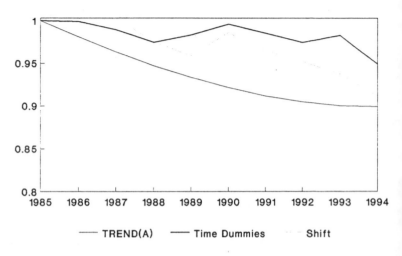

Source: See text.

Our results allow us to conclude that when deregulation takes place (1990) it produces negative effects. Actually, the elimination of both interest rate regulation, and the ban on branching and the reduction in investment and reserve requirement coefficients puts banks into a temporary disequilibrium situation, where some banks, in general the most efficient and most profitable ones, become quite active in raising loanable funds by increasing their interest rates and gaining market share. The evidence for other countries shows similar results. Bauer *et al.* (1991) and Humphrey (1992 and 1993) find negative technical progress at the initial stages of a deregulation process (1980 for the US). On the other hand, Berg *et al.* (1992) find on the contrary that for the Norwegian banking system the situation seems to be the opposite once deregulation starts (1984). However, this evidence does not contradict our previous reasoning since these authors argue that the Norwegian banks seem to have anticipated the deregulatory process, having originated an initial excess capacity that was eliminated once the deregulation process was on its way.

Figure 12.14   Different approaches to technical change (panel data estimation)

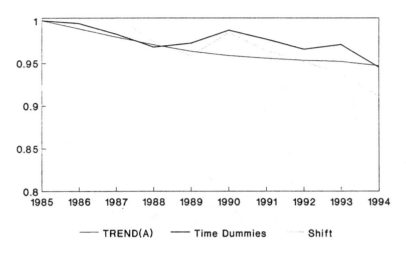

Source: See text.

5.   TECHNICAL CHANGE AND FIRM SIZE

In this section we address the question of whether technical progress affects banks in a different way according to size. Figures 12.4 and 12.9 confirmed the presence of different ratios as a result of a heterogeneous behaviour by firm size. To check on this different pattern we estimate the impact of technical change for different bank sizes. We use the approaches that have been explained in section 3 except for the shift technique which, to estimate the cost function, requires too high a number of annual observations[5].

According to asset size, two different bank groups have been considered, with a dividing line of pta 150,000 million. A higher number of bank sizes could not be considered because of the insufficient degrees of freedom left out in the regressions.

Table 12.4 reports the results on the impact of technical change using the time trend approach (equation (2)) based on the estimation of equation (1) for the two subsamples and the results corresponding to time dummies

Table 12.4 Technical change by sizes: 1985-1994

Thousands mill. pts.	Pooling Data Estimation			
Size	Trend(A)	Trend(B)	Trend(C)	Trend(D)	Time dummies
0-150	-0.0158***	-0.0222***	-0.0348***	-0.0284***	-0.0125***
+150	-0.0109***	-0.0168***	-0.0336***	-0.0219***	-0.0055***
	Fixed Effects Estimation			
Size	Trend(A)	Trend(B)	Trend(C)	Trend(D)	Time dummies
0-150	-0.0014	-0.0011	-0.0019	-0.0006	0.0002
+150	-0.0045**	-0.0061*	-0.0134*	-0.0087*	-0.0085***

*** Significant at the 1 per cent level
** Significant at the 5 per cent level
* Significant at the 10 per cent level

approach (last column). The results show that when data are pooled, 'small' savings banks experience a higher impact of technical progress over the whole period, independently of the indicator used for technical change. By contrast, when we estimate the fixed effects model, the impact of technical change experienced by large savings banks is higher than that experienced by the smaller ones, the latter not being statistically significant. Once more, similarly to the results in Table 12.1, the impact of technical progress for large banks is reduced approximately by half when we consider the existence of individual effects[6].

In the case of pooling data estimation the results are coincident with those of the former approach, showing that small savings banks experience a higher impact from technical progress than the large ones. By contrast, in the case of panel data estimation, large banks are those that experience a higher rate of technical progress[7]. Results appear in Figure 12.15, where average total costs are represented on the right vertical axis and their accumulated variation on the left one. This figure shows that for most of the time, large banks show smaller average costs and also higher cost reduction than small banks.

Figure 12.15   **Accumulated var. technical change and average cost by sizes: levels (AC) and accum. change (TC)**

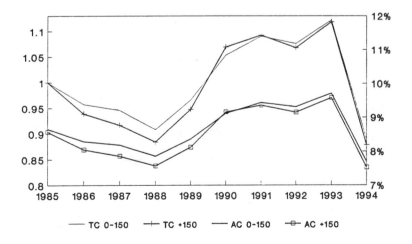

From a theoretical point of view, the concepts of technical change and economies of scale and scope are only applicable to the concept of the efficient frontier (Berger *et al.* 1993 and Charnes *et al.* 1988). However, most of the studies consider an average cost function. This entails a conceptual problem that will be crucial in the interpretation of the results obtained from the regression analysis. Actually, as we have seen above, when we estimate cost functions, data pooling can be mixing technical change with efficiency. However, panel estimation captures the influence of technical change better because it can isolate the efficiency component. In fact, as observed in Figure 12.16, small firms are the most efficient ones[8]. Thus, the superior technical change estimated for small firms using pool data can be contaminated by their higher level of efficiency.

Figure 12.16   Efficiency levels v. size

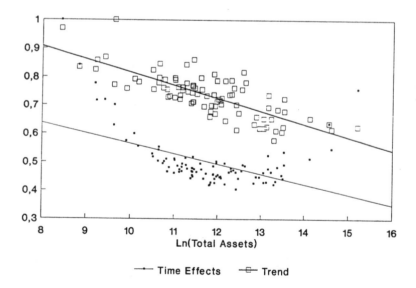

Source: See text.

6.   OPERATING COSTS

As we have seen in section 2 (Figure 12.6), financial costs amount to approximately 60 per cent of total production costs for savings banks. For this reason they dominate the behaviour of total costs, which are in turn determined by the evolution of interest rates. In a similar way, the cost of raising funds was influenced by the increase in competition initiated after the 'deposit war' that started once interest rates had been liberalised and legal coefficients had been substantially reduced. With the purpose of isolating our estimates of technical change from the evolution of financial costs and, therefore, of the role of competition and deregulation, we estimate in this section a cost function using only operating costs. In this way we obtain a stricter measure of the impact of technical change. Our intuition is that savings banks have fought rising financial costs experienced during this period with a reduction in operating costs that should give rise to a higher estimate of the impact of technical change. We estimate the translog cost function using data on operating costs and considering only capital and labour as inputs and excluding loanable funds[9].

Tables 12.5, 12.6 and 12.7 contain the results on technical change using data panel techniques corresponding to the three approaches that were followed. In the time trend case, according to Table 12.5, a statistically significant rate of technical progress of an annual -1.94 per cent is found. If we compare this estimate with that obtained using total costs, we find an impact of technical change three times as high (-0.68 per cent). This result is evidence of the effort made by savings banks in reducing operating cost to compensate for the large increase in financial costs. This higher technical progress estimated using operating costs can also be obtained when we use the alternative indicators of technology (Trends (B), (C) and (D)). Similar results are obtained if we use the time dummies approach (Table 12.6), getting an annual rate of technical progress (-1.93 per cent), much higher then that obtained previously in table 12.2 (-0.55 per cent). Table 12.7 shows the results corresponding to the shift cost approach. With the exception of the period 1989-90, for the rest of the decade we find a much higher impact of technical change on operating costs than that obtained using data on total costs.

Figures 12.17 and 12.18 show the accumulated variation of operating costs due to technical progress corresponding to the three approaches used. Comparing them with Figures 12.12 and 12.14 we can observe how the accumulated technical progress is quantitatively higher for operating costs, although the time pattern is quite similar to that of total costs. The existing differences with the shift cost approach are clearly highlighted.

Table 12.5   Technical change in operating costs

Year	Trend(A)	Trend(B)	Trend(C)	Trend(D)
1985	-0.0231***	-0.0243***	-0.0229****	-0.0231***
1986	-0.0217***	-0.0247***	-0.0217***	-0.0223***
1987	-0.0214***	-0.0260***	-0.0224***	-0.0227***
1988	-0.0203***	-0.0257***	-0.0220***	-0.0221***
1989	-0.0193***	-0.0233***	-0.0211***	-0.0215***
1990	-0.0186***	-0.0223***	-0.0210***	-0.0213***
1991	-0.0179***	-0.0211***	-0.0208***	-0.0212***
1992	-0.0172***	-0.0197***	-0.0207***	-0.0214***
1993	-0.0157***	-0.0181***	-0.0201***	-0.0207***
1994	-0.0146***	-0.0172***	-0.0199***	-0.0206***
Average yearly rate 1985-1994	-0.0194***	-0.0228***	-0.0214***	-0.0218***
Sizes				
0-150	-0.0045	-0.0015	-0.0073	-0.0035
+150	-0.0200***	-0.0205**	-0.0458***	-0.0318***

***   Significant al 1 per cent level
**   Significant al 5 per cent level
*   Significant at 10 level

Table 12.6 Technical change in operating costs

Time Dummies Approach	
1985-86	-0.0126
1986-87	-0.0420***
1987-88	-0.0317***
1988-89	-0.0187
1989-90	0.0268*
1990-91	-0.0308**
1991-92	-0.0355**
1992-93	-0.0047
1993-94	-0.0430***
Average yearly rate 1985-1994	**-0.0193***
Sizes	
0-150	-0.0045***
+150	-0.0200***

*** Significant al 1 per cent level
** Significant al 5 per cent level
* Significant at 10 level

Table 12.7   Technical change in operating costs

Shift Cost Approach	
1985-86	-0.0418
1986-87	-0.0591
1987-88	-0.0633
1988-89	-0.0346
1989-90	0.0351
1990-91	-0.0500
1991-92	-0.0506
1992-93	-0.0306
1993-94	-0.0821

***   Significant al 1 per cent level
**   Significant al 5 per cent level
*   Significant at 10 level

Figure 12.17   Time trend and technological indicators of technical change: operating costs (panel data estimation)

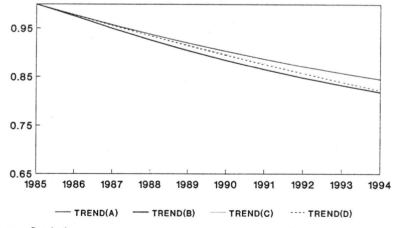

Figure 12.18 **Different approaches to technical change: operating costs (panel data estimation)**

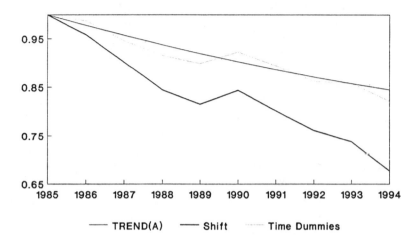

Source: See text.

The results by size confirm our results in section 5, since the largest savings banks are those that experience a higher rate of technical progress (panel data estimation). In contrast to the result shown in Table 12.4 for total costs, operating costs for small savings banks do experience a significant reduction throughout the period. This result implies that small banks have also made an effort to reduce operating costs, although to a lesser extent than the bigger banks, given their lower increase in financial costs (Figure 12.5).

Summing up, the results using this stricter measure of technical progress show how our estimates of the impact of technical progress are higher than when we use a broader definition of technical change that includes the effects of deregulation and of an increase in competition. Likewise, the larger banks that have seen their financial costs increase at a higher pace are those that have experienced the largest reduction in operating costs.

7. CONCLUSIONS

The aim of this paper was the analysis of the influence on average costs
of the Spanish savings banks arising from three main causes: a rapid
deregulation process, the introduction of new technologies and a significant
increase in competition. Likewise, we draw a distinction between the
influence of technical progress on total costs and operating costs. In the
latter case we get a more adequate indicator of technical progress without
taking into consideration the influence of deregulation and the increase in
competition on financial costs. To do so we estimate a translog cost
function for the period 1985-94. Three different approaches are used: the
introduction of an index of technical change in the regression, the use of
annual time dummies and the analysis of annual shifts in the cross-section
cost functions estimated for each of the ten years of the sample. Four
indexes of technical change are used: a time trend and three different
indicators of the diffusion of technology. All the results are derived using
two alternative forms of treating the data: pooling the observations and
using data panel econometric techniques.

We observe important differences in the estimates of the impact of
technical change derived from the way data are considered. This is due to
the fact that pool data estimation may capture as technical change what
actually is a higher level of efficiency. In this respect, the fixed effects
model enables us to isolate the efficiency component of each firm and
generates more adequate estimates.

The results obtained using data panel techniques are the following:

- Over the last decade the impact of technical progress on Spanish
savings banks has been reflected in an accumulated reduction of
average costs of roughly 5 to 10 per cent, independently of the
approach considered in the analysis. The estimated average impact
of technical change on average costs from introducing a particular
index of technical change runs from an annual rate of -0.89 per cent
for the credit and cash card indicator to -0.68 per cent corresponding
to the simple time trend
- Similar results are obtained from the time dummies approach, with
an annual rate of change of average costs of -0.55 per cent
- Likewise, the outcome of the procedure involving the annual shift of
a cross-section estimated cost function gives similar results to those
of the other two approaches. However, the accumulated level of cost
reduction is not exactly the same; it exceeds that of the time
dummies approach and is smaller than that of the method based on

the time trend. Furthermore, the annual behaviour is much more irregular than the outcome shown by the other approaches. This is the consequence of the larger degree of flexibility of this procedure
- The results that are obtained by using a more adequate measure of the effect of technical progress, like operating costs, show a higher rate of technical progress. This finding is evidence of a real effort made by Spanish banks to reduce operating costs to compensate for the significant increase in financial costs, the result of deregulation and increased competition
- Splitting the sample into two different subsamples according to the size of banks shows that large savings banks benefit more from total cost reduction than small banks, and this is true even more in the case of operating costs. However, the levels of efficiency of small banks are higher than those of the large banks. This distinct level of efficiency justifies the different results obtained when using pooling or panel data, since under the former method there is attributed to technical progress what is due to a distinct level of efficiency

NOTES

Acknowledgements

Thanks for financial support are due to Instituto Valenciano de Investigaciones Económicas (IVIE), whose Financial Economics research area is sponsored by Caja de Ahorros del Mediterráneo and CICYT PB90-0579. The authors also give thanks for the comments received at the Workshop 'Productivity, Efficiency and Profitability in Banking' organised by the IVIE, and specially comments by David B. Humphrey and Francisco Pérez, and also for the comments received at the 12th International Conference in Finance, Association Française de Finance (Burdeos, France). We thank V. Cuñat for his help with the data. Remaining errors are ours.

1. In Figure 12.1 we observe a steady increase of the asset per branch ratio. However, Figure 12.8 shows that for all bank groups such a relation is relatively stable. Both figures show that there has been a relative increase in the number of banks in the largest groups.
2. We estimate (equation 1) imposing the usual restrictions of symmetry and homogeneity of degree one in prices.
3. In this study we do not consolidate backwards merged institutions

creating fictitious banks. If two institutions merge into a new one, they disappear from then on and a new bank is born.

4.   In this paper, using the same technique, a third order translog cost function is estimated for the period 1988-1991.

5.   Alternatively for the time trend approach we could estimate the impact of technical progress for groups of banks of different sizes substituting in equation (2) the mean values of the variables for such groups. However, the drawback of this strategy is that one implicitly assumes that the estimated parameters of the cost function are the same for the whole sample, an assumption that may not be the correct one.

6.   When we estimate the impact of technical change using a unique cost function for the whole sample the results are different. Large banks are those that experience a higher impact from technical change, independently of the econometric technique used. This different result is nothing but additional evidence of the argument raised by McAllister and McManus (1993) in the sense that the translog is a local approximation to the underlying cost function used to extrapolate and that, consequently, it can be subject to potential errors of specification.

7.   In this approach, the absence of crossed products with time dummies makes the comparison of the results with those of the global sample impossible.

8.   Following Kumbhakar (1987) and Gong and Sickles (1992) we compute efficiency measures (E_i) dividing the lowest fixed effect coefficient by the corresponding one of each bank in the sample $E_i = R_{min}/R_i$.

9.   This implies the disappearance of the price equation associated with loanable funds (P_2).

LIST OF REFERENCES

Baltagi, B.H. and T.H. Griffin (1988), 'A general index of technical change', *Journal of Political Economy*, **96**, pp. 20-41

Bauer, P.W., A.N. Berger and D.B. Humphrey (1991), 'Efficiency and productivity growth in U.S. banking', Chapter 16 in H.O. Fried, F. Selsmidt and C.A.K. Lovell (eds), *The Measurement of Productive Efficiency* (New York, NY: Oxford University Press)

Berg, S., F.R. Førsund and E.S. Jansen (1992), 'Malmquist indices of productivity growth during the deregulation of Norwegian banking

1980-89', *Scandinavian Journal of Economics,* **94**

Berger, A.N., W.C. Hunter and S.G. Timme (1993), 'The efficiency of financial institutions', *Journal of Banking and Finance*, **17**, pp. 219-49

Caves, D.W., L.R. Christensen and J.A. Swanson (1981), 'Productivity growth, scale economies, and capacity utilisation in US railroads, 1955-74', *American Economic Review,* **71**, pp. 994-1002

Charnes A., W.W. Cooper and T. Suesyoshi (1988), 'A goal programming/constrained regression review of the Bell System Breakup', *Management Science* **34**, 1, 1-26

Gong, B.H. and R.C. Sickles (1992), 'Finite sample evidence on the performance of stochastic frontiers and data envelopment analysis using panel data', *Journal of Econometrics,* **51**, pp. 259-84

Humphrey, David B. (1992), 'Flow versus stock indicators and scale economy measurement', Working Paper, Federal Reserve Bank of Richmond

Humphrey, David B. (1993), 'Cost and technical change: effects from bank deregulation', *The Journal of Productivity Analysis*, **4**, pp. 9-34

Kumbhakar, S.C. (1987), 'Production frontiers and panel data: an application to US Class 1 railroads', *Journal of Business & Economics Statistics*, **5**, 2, 249-55

Maudos, J. (1994), 'Cambio tecnológico, costes y economías de escala en las cajas de ahorros', *Papeles de Economía Española,* **58**, pp. 126-40

McAllister, H. and D. McManus (1993), 'Resolving the scale efficiency puzzle in banking', *Journal of Banking and Finance,* **17**, pp. 389-405

Pastor, J.M. (1995), 'Eficiencia, cambio productivo y cambio técnico en los bancos y cajas de ahorros españolas: un análisis frontera no paramétrico', *Revista de Economía Española*, forthcoming

CHAPTER 13

THE INTERNATIONALISATION OF DUTCH BANKS: NEW BEGINNING AND FUTURE DEVELOPMENTS

Simon Sijbrands

INTRODUCTION

As the borders between European nations are fading, the largest Dutch banks are internationalising their business at a steady pace. Revenues coming from outside the Netherlands are increasingly becoming a major financial resource. At first sight their strategy and international scope appear similar, but major differences come to light when taking a closer look.

This chapter deals again with the internationalisation of Dutch banks - again because an earlier version was published in *Long Range Planning* (1994). Because much has happened since, we have updated the information for this chapter. First, we will explain why the three major Dutch universal banks ABN AMRO, RABO Bank and ING Bank (the former NMB Bank) internationalised their businesses in the period 1983-92. Second, we will give an overview of their internationalisation before 1983 and their reasons for adopting it. And we will show how they have implemented it. Third, we will discuss major managerial implications of this strategy and discuss strategic issues with which the financial services sector will be confronted with respect to internationalisation. Finally we will look into the internationalisation activities after 1992 and we will discuss the predictions we made in 1994. Again we will not look at other Dutch banks because their role in the international markets is still relatively small.

Data were collected by means of semi-structured interviews with members of the executive board and other line and staff members of ABN AMRO, RABO Bank and ING Bank. Extensive desk research of internal and external publications was also carried out.

INTERNATIONALISATION BEFORE 1983

The year 1983 was not the first time that the banks went across borders. Therefore it is necessary to focus briefly on their individual histories and explain their starting positions.

ABN

In 1964 De Twentsche Bank merged with Nederlandsche Handels-Maatschappi and created ABN. The purpose of the Nederlandsche Handels-Maatschappi was to strengthen the trade relations between the Netherlands and its colonies. This made ABN the Dutch bank which had, historically, an international background. ABN built up a strong branch network in South-East Asia and in the Middle East. In 1968 ABN took over Hollandsche Bank-Unie, which had a relatively strong position and a large network of branches in South America. This explains the relatively high degree of internationalisation of ABN in 1982. In North America and Asia it mainly performed banking business at that time within the framework of international funds flow. In Central America it was also retail-orientated. It participated in a number of consortium banks, of which ABECOR is perhaps the most best known. In 1982 the policy of ABN was to expand its international network of branches by acquisitions (for example, Taiwanese business of Continental Bank or LaSalle Bank in the USA) or mergers[1] (Banque de Neuflize, Schlumberger, Mallet) with foreign banks.

AMRO

AMRO arose from a merger between the Amsterdamsche Bank and the Rotterdamsche Bank. Historically, these banks were strong in the Dutch wholesale market. Internationally their position developed rather slowly because of a focus on building a home market branch network; the development of an international network only began in the mid-seventies. At that time it also acquired the Dutch merchant bank Pierson Heldring & Pierson (PHP). In 1992 PHP merged with ABN's merchant bank, Bank Mees & Hope, in the new Mees Pierson company.

In 1982 AMRO had nineteen points of sale abroad and a number of participations in foreign banks. The latter were mainly created within the framework of the EBIC organisation. In this consortium seven banks created a number of joint ventures in the main financial centres in the world. In 1982 AMRO's international goal was to have its own branch in those centres.

ABN AMRO was created in 1990 through a merger between ABN and AMRO. Today ABN AMRO is market leader in the Netherlands in the wholesale market; in 1989, 70 per cent of the largest Dutch corporations did business with ABN AMRO.

RABO Bank

RABO Bank is a co-operative bank whose member banks are in principle autonomous within their regional business areas. Its members are usually small- and middle-sized businesses that work mainly in the agricultural sector. The mission of RABO Bank is to lend money to its members at the lowest possible interest rate. It is market leader in the savings market (in 1989 around 40 per cent). Since 1982 RABO Bank has been focusing more seriously across borders. In 1982 it had branches in New York (opened only in 1981), Frankfurt and Curaçao. It also participated in a consortium, the UNICO banking group. For RABO Bank its international activities are a logical extension of its national activities.

NMB Bank

NMB Bank arose from a merger between NMB and Postbank in 1989. The NMB had a strong position in the small- and middle-sized segment of the wholesale market, and Postbank, which was largely owned by the Dutch government, dominated the retail market. In 1989 - at which time they were still named NMB Postbank Group - their market share in the number of payment accounts was over 40 per cent. In 1992 the name was changed to ING Bank. Today, they constitute ING Group together with Nationale Nederlanden[2].

The international activities of ING Bank were originally developed by NMB. In 1982 it had 14 branches abroad. At that time its aim was to expand its banking services abroad and to focus more actively on the growth regions in the world. It is also participating in the activities of a consortium bank (the INTERALPHA Group), in affiliates and joint ventures.

WHY INTERNATIONALISATION?

In the seventies and the early eighties the financial services sector was confronted with some important developments which explain its internationalisation strategy. Among them are:

- spreading risk
- follow your customer
- deregulation and harmonisation

- economies of scale

Spreading risk

After a period of slower economic growth in the seventies, the small and overbanked home market had become less attractive. Banks recognised that their dependence on this market had to be reduced. In an attempt to spread their risks they internationalised their business. If banks conduct business in markets which are in different stages of their life cycle and/or in countries with different economic situations (surplus and deficit countries), they can spread their risk by offering their services to these different markets.

In the beginning of 1983 we saw an economic revival, which lasted until 1989. As was shown in two earlier issues of *Long Range Planning*[3], in the case of insurance services, growth numbers in GNP determine revenues, and this is also true of banking services. Table 13.1 shows that the net value added (NVA) of all three banks increased in this period.

Table 13.1:   Net value added (NVA) for 1987 and 1990 (1984 = 100)

Year	ABN	AMRO	ING Bank	RABO Bank
1987	109	128	102	117
1990		162	124	151

Nevertheless, there were clear signs that the industry was entering its maturity; competition was enormous; market shares were stabilising; customers became better informed; and the interest margin, nowadays still the main resource for revenues, was shrinking. So the increase in

NVA enabled banks to invest abroad and, by doing this, also to spread their risk.

Follow your customer

In addition, the client base of banks expanded internationally. As there is a strong relationship between the manufacturing and services industry, there is also a strong relationship between the international expansion of industries and the foreign diffusion of banks. When customers try to sell their products outside their home market they develop a need for financial services. Therefore banks followed their customers across borders. Comparative advantages, like existing relationships and the availability of specific client information, can be exploited. Entrepreneurial bankers always try to find ways to exploit their core competences.

Deregulation and harmonisation

In April 1982 the European Community presented its policy White Paper on financial integration. Together with a proposal for full liberalisation of capital flows and a harmonisation process on banking deregulation, this was to be the beginning of the establishment of a European financial market. The 1988 proposal for a Second Banking Directive gave way to the possibility for universal banks to establish branches or supply financial services without further authorisation.

The Netherlands was already a relatively highly deregulated country; barriers of entry for foreign banks were therefore low. It meant increased competition, but Dutch banks also recognised their opportunities to move across borders.

Economies of scale

There are several factors concerning the question of economies of scale. Primarily, the apparently never-ending advancement of information technology (IT) in the financial services industry enables banks to deliver services that require a low degree of consultancy through large automation centres. The investments in IT will be huge in the forthcoming years. A bank which has internationalised its business can spread these investments over a larger client base. ABN AMRO especially is emphasising this point by underlining the necessity to create a certain critical mass. Secondly, potential economies of scale also exist in the procurement of financial resources. Funding costs can be lowered because of the strong bargaining position an international bank has. Its larger capital base and (possibly) better credit rating enable it to do this. Thirdly, the fixed costs of expensive employees, like regional managers who work in a number of different countries, or global relationship managers, can be allocated over more than one market. Finally, a potential advantage is created through the international image; having an international network of branches and being able to participate in large syndicated loans can mean that multinational corporations favour your bank instead of a bank which does not have this image.

INTERNATIONALISATION: HOW MUCH AND HOW?

After having discussed the international starting positions of the three banks and the reasons why they went across borders we will now look at the implementation of their international strategy.

Implementation will be discussed with respect to five issues:

1. The degree of internationalisation
2. The modes of entry
3. The organisational structures
4. Management control
5. The current internationalisation strategy

1. The degree of internationalisation

The degree of internationalisation will be discussed in terms of the number of foreign branches and foreign personnel and gross profit per region.

Figure 13.1 shows the development in foreign points of sale over the years 1983-91. The diagram shows that in 1987 ABN had the largest international network with 250 branches. Until then it had developed gradually but in 1988, after a rationalisation, the number decreased to 232 and then rose again in 1989 to 249. After the merger in 1990 ABN and AMRO together had 458 branches. This number increased to 466 in 1991. The foreign points of sale of ING Bank also show a gradual increase. Figure 13.1 shows the clear differences in numbers between the banks. RABO Bank has the fewest points of sale, but the numbers show that in the late eighties it began to build its

network.   From 1983 to 1991 it opened 33 points of sale.   ING Bank
opened 29 points of sale in the same period, whereas AMRO opened 42
(1983-89).   The fact that the number of foreign points of sale increased
and that the domestic points of sale decreased shows that the
international activities of the four banks were becoming more important
(see Table 13.2).

Figure 13.1:   Development of foreign points of sale 1983-91

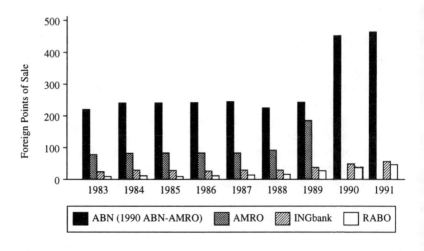

**Table 13.2   National points of sale in 1983 and 1989 of ABN,
AMRO, ING Bank and RABO Bank**

Year	ABN	AMRO	ING Bank	RABO Bank
1983	961	873	483	2,400
1989	960	796	400	2,192

Figure 13.2 shows another indicator of the degree of international-isation, namely the development in numbers of employees working at points of sale outside the Netherlands.

Figure 13.2   Development in numbers of personnel working outside the Netherlands 1983-90

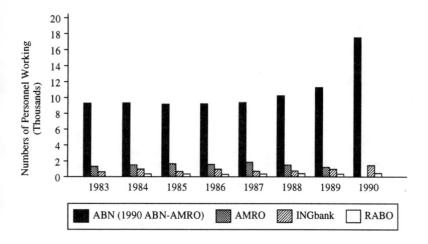

Note: It was not possible to deduce from the ING annual report how many employees were working abroad in 1991, because this number was given as a pro forma total of the ING Group (including ING insurance). From the interviews we learned that there were no substantial trend differences with the previous years for all three banks

The diagram shows a development to the degree of inter-nationalisation. ABN has by far the largest work force abroad. A gradual build-up resulted in 11,554 people working in foreign points of sale in 1989. In the same year AMRO had 1,592 foreign employees, ING Bank 1,533 and RABO Bank 730.

Table 13.3 shows the total foreign gross results as a percentage of total gross results. Where ABN AMRO was confronted with a decrease (caused by losses in North America), ING Bank experienced a major increase. They both, however, had their own problems, ABN AMRO in South America and ING Bank in Europe.

Table 13.3: **Total foreign gross results as a percentage of total gross results**

Year	ABN AMRO	ING Bank
1989	30.0	16.7
1990	37.3	20.3
1991	29.1	31.7

2.   Modes of entry

There are a number of ways in which a bank can enter a foreign market. Among them are:

■   a representative office
■   a full banking branch
■   a strategic alliance

A representative office cannot give loans or attract funds; communication with customers and referring them to affiliates, banking branches or subsidiaries are its main activities. It is usually the first step a bank takes when it is becoming international. After a while the representative offices are transformed into a banking branch or subsidiary.

A banking branch can carry out all banking activities in the name of the bank and therefore it is under home country control. A subsidiary is a legal autonomous entity and has to comply with host country law. For convenience we will call them both full banking branches.

Going international in banking means not only answering 'the make or buy' decision, but also 'the co-operation decision'. A strategic alliance is, in its ultimate form, a merger. A joint venture can also be labelled a strategic alliance. In this kind of agreement a new legal entity is established in which the parties co-operate, but outside these activities they remain autonomous. An affiliated bank, also a form of strategic alliance, is a local bank which is operating under its own name. The foreign bank usually has a minority share in this bank. This is not always the case when strategic partners agree to co-operate in specific fields of their value chain (for example on selling or development) and establish no new legal entity. It enables a firm to enter a market very quickly at relatively low cost, but it also means sharing control and effective management of inter-company relationships. The goal is to help your home country customers who are internationalising to conduct their banking affairs with a local bank. Usually these banks have the same history and perception of service level. RABO Bank especially has opted for this mode recently. It has strategic alliances with Crédit Agricole in France, with Banco Popular in Spain, with RZB in Austria, with Cariplo in Italy, with Lloyds Bank in the UK and with CERA in Belgium.

Table 13.4 shows the modes of entry which are used by the three banks. All banks have opened representative offices in new international markets. As we have stated before, these offices have a 'first step' function. Getting information about the host country's financial system, economic risks, local customs, and commercial possibilities has to lead to the assessment whether it is profitable to open a full branch.

In the first years the profitability of a full branch is low: most of the time it means accepting high losses. Banks expect losses from branches for up to five years. They do not easily give information on this matter, but we have found that the five-year time span is used as a rule of thumb. We have found circumstances in which a foreign branch was already highly profitable in its first year, but also examples where profit never materialised, or only after nearly ten years, mainly because of government regulations. For example, until December 1980 the Japanese government allowed only foreign banks to issue so-called 'impact loans'; this resulted in a 1.5 per cent spread. At the beginning of 1981 this was also allowed to Japanese banks which resulted in more competition and a decreased 0.25 per cent spread.

Table 13.4:   Modes of entry used by ABN, AMRO, RABO Bank and ING Bank

	Representative office	Full branch	Strategic alliance
ABN	+	+++	++
AMRO	+	+++	++
RABO	+	++	+++
ING	+	+++	++

Key
+++   = most used relative to other modes
++   = used a lot
+   = least used relative to other modes

Sometimes a representative office is opened with the agreement of the consortium in which a bank participates. A consortium bank is also a strategic alliance, usually in the form of a joint venture bank. Such a bank is owned by two or usually more banks of different nationalities.

All Dutch banks are or were participating in a consortium for example:

ABN in ABECOR
AMRO in EBIC
RABO Bank in UNICO Banking Group
ING Bank in INTERAPLHA

This consortium construction is also a way to enter a foreign market at relatively low risk as several banks make a financial contribution. The disadvantage of this mode is that decision-making is complicated and therefore usually very slow. In addition banks realise that not sharing control and benefits means having your own network of branches. One can say that the consortium has to cope with a decreasing popularity. ABN AMRO have even opted out of the consortia. On the other hand in 1991 ING Bank opened a representative office of ING Bank together with its INTERALPHA partners in Moscow.

We will delay our discussion of a new type of strategic alliance and analyse it at the end of this chapter.

3.   International banking structures

The structuring of international banking activities seems to develop in three phases. Phase one is characterised by the presence of a regionally-orientated sector or directorate for *foreign affairs* which manages the international network of branches. When it is recognised that corporate clients/multinational corporations demand a tailor-made service, phase two begins and often a division, *foreign affairs* and *global clients*, or a separate business unit, *corporate clients/directorate business relations*, is installed. In phase three a matrix-organisation is formed in which there are three divisions: *domestic affairs, foreign affairs* and *global clients* (including investment banking).   This is the ABN AMRO situation.   To deal with aspects of co-ordination, ABN AMRO recently (1990) started to work with so-called global relationship managers (GRMs).   These GRMs handle no more than twenty global clients.   For efficient relationship management they have been divided regionally (into four regions) and by industry (telecommunications and oil).   They also have their own front and back office support.   The GRM is the pivot between product departments and bodies which grant credits.   He has the final responsibility for his global client and can communicate with a specially appointed member of the board.

RABO Bank and ING Bank have developed other organisational structures.   ING Bank can be categorised as being in phase two.   It is obvious that ING Bank, because of its more developed and mature (for example in size and specific activities) international activities has made some suitable adjustments (for example a special department which is responsible for their debt conversion and asset trading activities). RABO Bank is at the beginning of phase two.

Figure 13.3 shows the scheme of the organisational structure of the international activities of RABO Bank.

Figure 13.3   RABO Bank structure of international activities

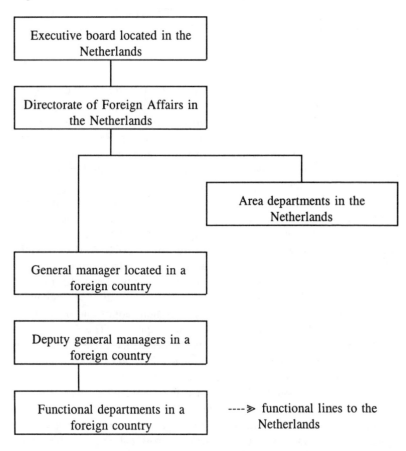

At its head office RABO Bank has installed a 'Euro desk' to assist firms that are internationalising their business. It also agreed with its strategic alliance partners to install Dutch desks in the main offices. When a Dutch client enters a Spanish office he can be sent to the Dutch desk of, for example, Banco Popular. In the Netherlands, RABO Bank has a Spanish desk at its head office. RABO Bank has no offices in Spain and because of this agreement no expatriates are involved; the customer has to speak Spanish. The desk employees visit each other once a year. In France RABO Bank has a full branch and a representative office in Paris. When financial services are needed within the region, a Crédit Agricole office can provide them.

The other banks also have Dutch desks in their main branches abroad, but they also work with product-orientated units/desks. ING Bank, for example, has Trade and Commodity Finance Desks in the main financial regions, which are co-ordinated from Amsterdam. International Private Banking Desks are co-ordinated from Zürich. ABN AMRO has developed corporate finance units and private banking units in some foreign offices

4. Management control

Looking at the procedures and methods which the management uses to ensure compliance of international branches with strategy and policy it can be stated that with respect to operational management a high degree of decentralisation is pursued; nevertheless a high degree of centralisation exist with respect to risk management. All banks have their own standards (based on volume of the transaction, importance of clients and required service time) for control procedures. A number of formal written reports have to be sent to the head offices and to the regulatory bodies of the host country and the home country. Regular visits from top managers of the head office and the regulatory bodies are made, and several times a week telephone contact takes place between the home and foreign countries. This high degree of centralisation is necessary in banking (and also in treasury management) because huge losses can be made when control is less strict.

In the case of a large credit transaction a special credit committee with a member of the executive board is usually formed. At ABN AMRO there is a *Credit Division* where a so-called 'director-general' is appointed to deal with international credits. To a certain degree the regional manager or country manager is entitled to conduct financial transactions. The amounts differ from country to country.

5.   Current international strategies

ABN AMRO

Internationally ABN AMRO is trying to expand its business mainly in Europe and the US by means of selective takeovers as LaSalle National Corporation (Chicago) did when it took over Exchange Bancorp Inc. and European American Bancorp (New York and Long Island). In these regions it is trying to be a large player in the retail as well as the wholesale market. With regard to specific financial services one can follow the same strategy to become a large niche player in, for example, corporate finance, private banking, trade and asset financing or treasury and leasing.

Recently ABN AMRO stated that it wanted to be one of the ten (as estimated by an ABN AMRO top executive in an article) global players. But today they prefer not to talk about this (in public) any more and talk about worldwide banking, because of the accompanying high expectations of this strategy and the complex managerial implications.

It continues to strengthen its position in North America; recently (1995) it bought Chicago Corp., but it is also very active in the field of investment banking. The acquisition of Alfred Berg (a Swedish-based investment bank) and Hoare Govett (a UK-based investment bank) illustrates this strategy.

RABO Bank

RABO Bank's strategy is to be a global niche player in the 'agribusiness market'. It wants to be able to deliver all financial services to these customers. It is also focusing on Dutch-related customers. These are Dutch wholesale clients internationalising their businesses or foreign companies that are internationalising in the Netherlands.

This strategy is developed mainly by strategic alliances, but it also makes acquisitions. But, according to RABO Bank, the strategic alliance concept is, 'as time will show', a link to Europe. Its alliances with, for example, Crédit Agricole (France) and Banco Popular (Spain) illustrate this strategy. Specialising in the securities industry is made possible by its alliance with the Dutch ROBECO group, a large securities firm. International leasing is conducted by 'De Lage Landen', a Dutch leasing firm which is fully owned by RABO Bank.

ING Bank

ING Bank, as a part of the ING Group, has a large capital base with which it is trying first and foremost to establish a second home market in Europe in which it will operate as a universal bank. An attempt to gain control over Banque Bruxelles Lambert in Belgium failed, but recently it has made some noticeable acquisitions.

Its strategy, as it is reported in formal publications, is to focus on profitable niche markets. This broad statement leaves a lot of space for the entrepreneurial and - sometimes - opportunistic state of mind of especially the NMB bloodgroup. Historically it has to be said that it was the first to enter the debt conversion and asset trading market. Today it is, as other banks, focusing on the so-called 'emerging markets' in Eastern Europe and on special services like investment banking, private banking and trusts, export financing, credit facilities, project financing (for example films and aircraft), factoring and leasing.

ING Group has recently been characterised by the *Wall Street Journal Europe* (December 1995) as the most 'adventurous' in international banking because it is very active in acquiring other financial institutions.

One has to bear in mind that ING Insurance (the former Nationale Nederlanden) also has an extensive network of foreign points of sale, so it can be expected that integration of banking and insurance services will result in a multinational financial institution in which - from an operational point of view - banking and insurance services are partially integrated but - from a legal point of view, because of Dutch law - still separately supervised by the regulatory bodies. Possible synergy is created when acquisitions offer opportunities for banking and also for insurance. The participation in the Italian financial group Sviluppo is given as an example to illustrate this. However, US legislation prohibits commercial and investment banking being conducted within the same financial institution. After some years in which ING Group received dispensation from the US government it will now start to 'de-bank' (giving back its banking licence) its business in the US. This means that it can no longer fund its business through deposits but has to rely on commercial paper instead. This is a sign that it is focusing more and more on investment banking, which is of course a very logical choice because life insurance and investment banking have major natural synergies. It is also an explanation why they acted so quickly and decisively when Barings Brothers (the UK-based investment bank) went bankrupt.

MANAGERIAL IMPLICATIONS AND STRATEGIC ISSUES

Banks are confronted with two major developments that raise several strategic issues which could affect their future international position. Bankers will perhaps have to adjust their perspective on how the industry will develop and on how to initiate organisational changes. Firstly, the industry structure - nationally and internationally - is changing and, secondly, financial services can be divided in a new way.

Recently the structure of the Dutch home market has been experiencing a dramatic change. The positions on the home market of the three banks are still very strong but all parties, incumbents and new entrants, are fighting for the same savings. As the CEO of RABO Bank stated recently, 'Parasites are entering the battle for the savings guilder'. Competition in the retail market is very intense. In the wholesale market ING Bank, and especially RABO Bank, have profited from the merger of ABN and AMRO. Many companies that were previously banking at ABN or AMRO have chosen either RABO Bank or ING Bank as their second home bank. The securitisation process (businesses trading debt instruments directly, without the use of the specific knowledge of banks, on the capital market) results in lower revenues. International competitors have more advanced international cash management systems which can attract traditional customers. Internationally, concentration tendencies are creating large and powerful financial institutions that are diversifying into banking *and* insurance.

Financial services can be divided into two new major categories, which we name information technology-driven (IT-driven) and human resource-driven (HR-driven). There are services which can be developed and distributed with the use of information technology (IT-driven financial services, for example developing a payment mechanism system for a certain client), while there are also services that have to be tailor-made and delivered direct to the client (HR-driven financial services, for example introduction of companies to the Stock Exchange).

IT and future internationalisation

We expect that banks will internationalise their businesses by the use of information technology. In the US we saw the same development. The McFadden Act prohibited interstate banking, but 'telecommunications and electronics began to replace bricks and mortar as a delivery system of retail products'[4]. This new mode of entry requires the use of computer centres and training of new personnel. Investments will be huge, but cost advantages will be enormous and will certainly lead to a competitive advantage as banks that cannot follow this development have to deal with these services manually and therefore at higher cost. Banks which are too small cannot attain the necessary critical mass to make these huge investments. However, banks have to make a strategic decision on the question of the marginal costs which occur when IT-driven financial services are standardised in compliance with the demands of local, culturally different, markets as opposed to standardisation that is not culturally based.

Certainly, this means that concentration and co-operation within the financial services industry will not be at an end. In trying to attain a larger capital base by creating a second or third home market, spreading risk, financing huge IT investments, being able to service your client through a larger network of points of sale or acquiring knowledge of doing business outside your home market, cross-border takeovers and/or more strategic alliances will take place. This will result in increasing dynamics within the industry.

Another consequence can be that routine paperwork (financial data entry) in which IT plays an important part will be done by people working in countries in which wages are relatively lower than in the home country; this already occurs in the services industry in the US where data transmission is done by satellite. Certainly it will lead to enormous cost advantages, but the dependence on the satellite and the internal situation within a certain country will be large. The interruption of payments caused by a systems breakdown can result in high claims.

Strategy and services

Customers will buy these IT-driven financial services as if they were commodities, therefore price will be important. Consequently, given the fact that the ambition of top management is to be competitive in this area of banking and insurance (for example in a second and third home market), a low-cost strategy has to be followed. Banks that are effectively competing in more than one home market can profit from economies of scale. The fixed cost of a computer centre which is covering a market four times the size of the Netherlands can be recovered sooner than if it were covering the Netherlands only.

For other financial services, like corporate finance, private banking and complex finance projects, a differentiation strategy (quality and strong customer relationships) has to be followed. The better informed and more demanding (corporate) customer will ask for a high degree of service in terms of tailor-made products, appropriate distribution channels and so on. Choices have to be made. There is no doubt that financial consultancy will become more important. It also means that banks will have to manage their international networks more effectively.

Multinational clients demand uniformity when they are approached by banks. This means that foreign branches have to co-operate more in serving these customers. When opportunities occur for a foreign branch which will benefit another foreign branch, direct contact should be possible, or to put it even stronger, required. Of course this means that an effective cost and revenue allocation system has to be developed. It is obvious that a foreign branch which has been incurring costs to acquire business on behalf of another foreign branch wants to share in possible profits. International bank managers should therefore be motivated to pass business to each other. These principles should be followed in banks when their international strategy and structure are further developed.

Institutional integration of banking and insurance

Today we are experiencing the development of bancassurance/Allfinanz. We define bancassurance as the ability of a financial services institute *to develop and distribute* a broad assortment of banking and insurance services according to its clients' wishes. Before January 1990[5] financial services with a banking and insurance character were already on the market. Institutional integration on a national, European and global scale, however, means initiating a process of organisational change of great magnitude. Different distribution channels, different organisational and national cultures, different information technologies and different structures have to be fully integrated. Horizontal strategies, which deal with issues of synergy and flexibility within the banks' value chain, have to be developed and implemented.

Today bancassurance activities are mainly undertaken in the retail market. Some executives see the future of bancassurance only in segments where there are large numbers of customers. Nevertheless a lot of opportunities exist. How should 'high net worth individuals (HNWIs)' respond, for example, to the integration of risk management services and private banking? Is it possible that a private banker posesses not only the technical knowledge and skills concerning his own traditional discipline, but also knows something about insurance services? If the HNWI is looking for a 'business partner' he may demand this. Within companies it is perhaps more likely that organisational specialists will prefer to talk with the specialist from the banks or insurance companies.

The high cost of *de novo* development of banking and/or insurance activities leaves only space for joint exploitation of the current infrastructure. This is certainly the case if this question is considered from an international point of view. Co-operation problems occur mainly in the exploitation of each other's distribution channels. Joint development of new financial services is an important question in some Allfinanz institutions, but it is not really dealt with in an innovative way and therefore it is a question that can be answered only when formal power over each other's distribution channels is settled. That is why the development of really new bancassurance services is relatively infrequent and cannot live up to the high expectations which occurred after January 1990 and the spectacular mergers which followed.

Competitive battle field

Not surprisingly we think that with respect to banking and insurance, the competitive battle will in fact be on distribution channels. Customer preference decides whether a certain distribution channel or combination of distribution channels will result in a competitive advantage. Following the concentration within the Dutch financial services industry, management programmes have to be started up to exploit their joint channels. Having distribution channels does not necessarily imply having a competitive advantage. The internal capabilities, like the development of general management know-how on Allfinanz and the development of personal motivation and skills, are major points of attention. The structure has to develop in line with a distribution-orientation criterion (D-criterion). This means structuring into electronic channels, direct mail, personal sales staff, branches, agents and, if this is not enough, crossing traditional national and international barriers. This will create new borders and probably new conflicts at these borders for which new co-ordination mechanisms have to be developed. As mentioned previously, traditional structures of banks are divided into three business units: *domestic affairs, foreign affairs* and *global clients*.

In international wholesale banking global relationship managers (GRMs) will prove to be useful. However, this will only be true when a financial institution deals effectively with the traditional problems which occur within a matrix organisation. It will perhaps be necessary to give the GRM decision-making power with respect to other (functional) line officers who are involved.

Strategic alliances

As co-operation between financial institutions will not end, strategic alliances will become a more important mode to organise it. We showed that there are a number of forms in which strategic alliances can be recognised. Strategic alliances have proved to be a way of creating value for the firm and its customers. Examples usually concern the manufacturing business (ICL and Fujitsu in developing mainframes or Motorola and Toshiba in distribution). These new modes of strategic alliances clearly differ from the traditional modes of merger and joint venture, namely co-operation agreements on certain company activities of the firms' value chain through which no new legal entity is established. With respect to the strategic issues we discussed before it can be an effective mode of co-operation.

There are, however, a number of pitfalls with regard to this concept. Consider, for example, why RABO Bank expanded its participation in Interpolis (a Dutch insurance company) from 10 per cent to 95 per cent within a short time in 1990? According to the theory on alliances one should not be impatient, not think in terms of equity, learn from each other and trust one another. The answer is easy. When two partners are fighting for the same funding, and one partner gets the upper hand, the concept does not work. One profits from the other, and it shows. Learning from each other is less apparent and will only show in the long run. Loss of money shows immediately and will affect the balance sheet.

Internationally this means that a strategic alliance can be an effective tool if the partners are not competing for the same funds and commercial target groups. When the only objective is to serve your customers without the worry of earning money from your alliances, as a RABO Bank executive stated in an interview, it is an effective mode. Using knowledge of local markets, using the same service levels (as has become apparent from a partner review analysis) and using a broad network of local branches illustrates this statement. But one should not think in terms of disadvantages arising from the inability to achieve financial consolidation or to make huge profits in the short run.

A strategic alliance is, however, like a modern love story: the couple decide to live together first before getting married. Both learn intensively from each other in this pre-marital phase. When translating this to the financial services industry, it will not amaze us if after a while two strategic alliance partners decide to merge. But what one has to realise at a strategic and operational level is the pre-marital phase. Personnel have to be interchanged at the operational level, only in this way can one company can learn from the other intensively. Otherwise, after a while hidden shortcomings lead to a costly divorce.

A new beginning?

In the 1994 article in *Long Range Planning* Professor Eppink and I asked ourselves whether the Dutch banking industry was standing at a new beginning with respect to the internationalisation of its business: the answer was 'yes'. We predicted more cross-border co-operation by acquisitions and competition on distribution channels. Much has happened since. ING Group took over Barings Brothers. ABN AMRO bought the UK investment bank Hoare Govett, the Swedish investment bank Alfred Berg and - to strengthen their position in the Chicago area - Chicago Corp. Also RABO Bank had some take-overs, mainly in the agribusiness industry.

We also predicted internationalisation by the use of information technology and we indeed saw that the possibilities for Dutch retail customers to take out money in foreign countries through automated teller machines were enlarged. On the wholesale side, more particularly in the field of international cash management (ICM), the developments were much slower. It seems that Dutch banks are always one step behind the market leaders. A major threat for all banks with respect to ICM, but also on international payment systems, is coming from new entrants in these markets. Software houses are offering network services, which is leading to disintermediation of banks.

If companies are able to pay their bills through a network with which they can easily reach all the necessary banks, this will probably be the end of the concept, 'international payments'. It simply does not exist any more.

Recently (November 1995) Intuit (a US-based software company) announced that it is introducing a facility for clients which enables them to do their financial business with banks over the Internet. To do so these clients can download freely accessible software from the Internet.

The banks are paying Intuit a fee for providing this service. So customers do not need software which is exclusively attached to a company (for example, the Microsoft software) or to a bank. In the US the launch of the Security First Network, which exists only on the Internet, marks a turning point for banks and banking.

Banking in E-space (*The Banker*, December 1995) or banking in a market space will be the talk of the town when the future of banking and international business is discussed. Dutch banks see these as threats (in some cases also as opportunities), and they are conducting a lot of experiments to stay in business. It is worth mentioning an experiment of Interpay, a company which is providing services in the field of payment mechanisms and which is owned by the Dutch banks and KPN Multimedia, a subsidiary of the Dutch Telecom giant, which is looking into the question of paying over the Internet. Internationally, they are working on their positions with respect to payment services and clearing in a Single European Market. It is still unclear in which direction(s) these dynamics will take banking.

Concluding, international banking is in transition. Dutch banks are anticipating these changes and they are doing their utmost to keep up with developments, but it may be a slow process. They have to speed up the process after they have made clear strategic decisions. We saw, for example, with respect to ATMs and electronic debit cards that customers can and will adopt new financial innovations very rapidly. Especially large corporations and their network of suppliers are adopting the new technologies very rapidly.

In this turbulent field banks have to combine their huge knowledge and skills on IT-driven financial services. Walls which divide automation and commercial product development and client-based departments have to be broken down. These developments will enforce the need for making strategic decisions now and business transformation.

NOTES

Acknowledgements

The author gratefully acknowledges the valuable information given by Mr H. Visser, Mr G.J. Tammes and Jonkheer Mr W.F. van Tets, corporate executives of respectively RABO Bank, ING Bank and ABN AMRO. The author also wishes to thank Prof. Dr D.J. Eppink for his valuable contribution to an earlier version of the article. Prof. Dr Eppink is a part-time extraordinary Professor of Strategy and Environment and part-time ordinary Professor of Management and Organisation at the Faculty of Economic Sciences and Econometrics of the Free University in Amsterdam. He is also a partner of Felex & Co., Strategic Management Consultants, with offices in Amsterdam and Budapest.

1. Formally this is reported as a merger, but in fact it was a takeover.
2. Nationale Nederlanden is a large Dutch (internationalised) insurance company.
3. D. Jan Eppink and Bas M. van Rhijn (1988), 'The internationalisation of Dutch insurance companies', *Long Range Planning,* **21,** 5, 54-60.
   D. Jan Eppink (1987), 'Competitive strategies in the Dutch insurance industry', *Long Range Planning,* **20**, 4, 30-37
4. Anthony M. Santomero (1990), 'European banking post-1992: lessons from the United States' in *European Banking in the 1990s* (Oxford: Basil Blackwell)
5. At that time financial institutions were allowed to take financial participation within each other's companies without any further limitations.

INDEX

270